CW01467076

Toubab Tales

Toubab Tales

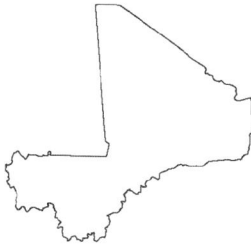

Rob Baker

Toubab Tales by Rob Baker

Published by Rob Baker & Kindle Direct Publishing

© 2020 Rob Baker

All rights reserved.

Cover by Tun I Yen

Cover photo of Rob taken by Mike Webb. Many thanks.

Dogon Cliffs photo (p.84) taken by Dr Clive Rahn, used with his kind permission.

Mali map used according to the terms of d-maps.com

The principal characters in this book, besides the author's immediate family, are the product of the author's imagination, and any resemblance to actual persons, living or dead is entirely coincidental. Historical, political and famous characters referred to are thoroughly researched and, to the best of my knowledge, accurately portrayed.

ISBN: 9798641687186

For Lois, Madelaine, Ruth and Micah

The family I'm incredibly blessed to have shared this adventure with

Contents

Acknowledgments

Many thanks to Rosie Archdale, Lois Baker, Andy Connolly, Chris Gassler Kimberly Henson, Sue Jarrett, Jonathan Johnston, Dawn Michelson, Laurel Miller, Janet Parker, Oli Rayner, Richard Sedding and Bethany Waugh for their invaluable assistance in proof-reading the book; and special thanks to Peter Chiverton, Simon Michael, Andy Rayner, Glenna Sollenberger, Tim Tillinghast and Mike Webb for their in-depth contributions. I couldn't have done it without you all!

Thank you to Tun I Yen for his amazing cover design. I had a decidedly dull cover in mind; he saw it and said: "I think I can do something better." He most certainly excelled himself in this.

Thanks too to Chris Jagusz and Steve Neal for allowing me to house-sit their homes in order to hide away and write. I completed roughly 40% of the book during these two retreats (and consumed way too many microwave meals).

Thank you Olivia Nelson for coming up with the book's title. It started life as Saharan Shadows, then became Notes from Mali. Desert Diaries was also considered, but none of these quite seemed to fit the bill. Then Olivia suggested 'Tales of a Toubab' and this led to the final title, which I love.

And finally, a big thanks to everyone who supported the Baker family during our time in Mali; for your thoughts, prayers, parcels, financial contributions and visits. It was a genuine honour to have you share in our work in these ways.

Mali,
West Africa

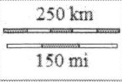

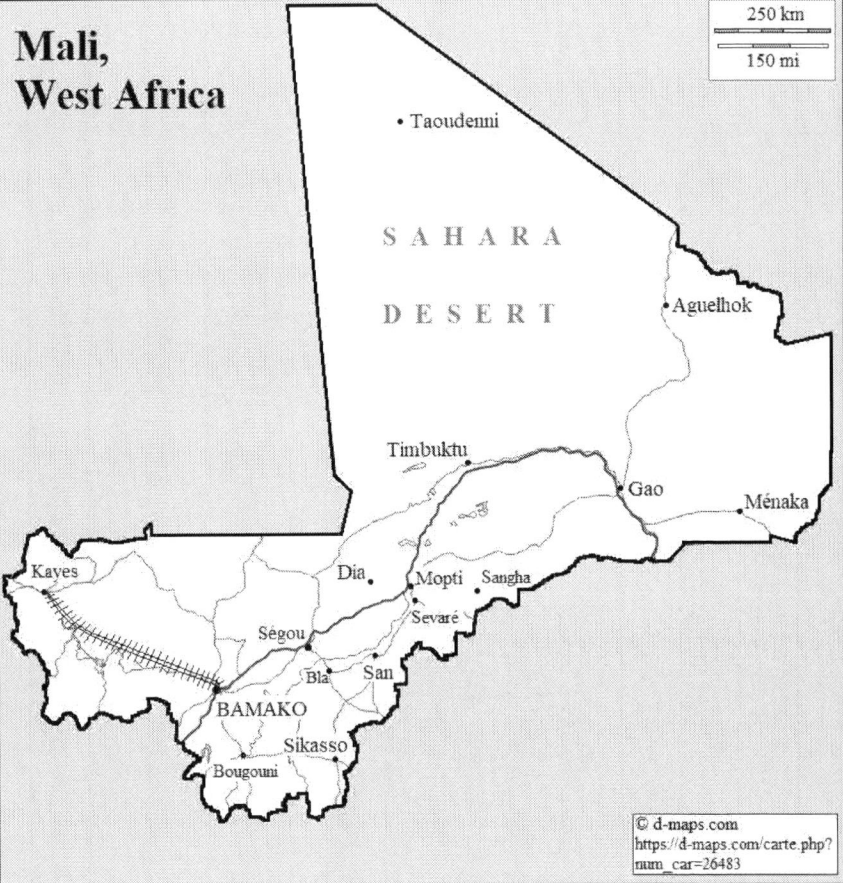

250 km

150 mi

• Taoudenni

S A H A R A

D E S E R T

• Aguelhok

Timbuktu

Gao

Ménaka

Kayes

Dia

Mopti   Sangha

Ségou

Sevaré

Bla   San

BAMAKO

Sikasso

Bougouni

© d-maps.com
https://d-maps.com/carte.php?
num_car=26483

Foreword

Toubab Tales is based on personal experience, and the events described herein are mostly true and in the order they occurred. However, some poetic licence has been used to enhance the flow and richness of the narrative.

The main characters are all fictitious, having been created out of a broad knowledge of Africa's indigenous and expatriate population. The historical, political and well-known characters were thoroughly researched, and information about them is, to the best of my knowledge, accurate. Similarly, the political events which occur throughout the book actually happened, and at the times/dates stated.

The purpose of this book is to take you on a journey to an entirely different world; one of great richness, variety and fascination, but also one where danger, difficulty and frustration lurk round every corner. You will live through three key years in Mali's recent history, experiencing all it has to offer; the good and the bad.

I hope you enjoy the read and come away entertained, informed and enriched.

Rob Baker
May 2020

Chapter One – Bumpy Landings

"It's good to be back!"

"LADIES AND GENTLEMEN, please return your seats to the upright position and fasten your belts for landing. The weather in Bamako is 27 degrees Celsius and *very* stormy."

Thousands of feet above the vast beige carpet of the Sahara, our Airbus 310 hurtles south towards the city we'll be calling home for the next three years. It's taken just six hours from London via Casablanca – a remarkably short journey given how far away West Africa feels in every other sense. Lois and I are not new to francophone Africa, having lived several years in Benin as well as Côte d'Ivoire, where we met. But Mali offers a new and exciting challenge, as we trade in the balmy humidity of coastal areas for the harsh, arid climes of a country which is fifty per cent sand.

Africa's eighth largest nation, landlocked Mali is said to resemble an enormous butterfly with a broken wing. Its population is the third youngest in the world, with a median age of only 16. The northern half of the country contains little else but dunes, camels and Tuaregs, whilst the relatively populous south is fertile and somewhat more humid. Although 90% Muslim, other religions including Christianity are tolerated here, along with a good smattering of African traditional religion, found in a variety of forms across this vast continent.

Lois will be teaching international kids in a tiny mission school in Bamako, while I continue my work as an *ethnomusicologist*, studying Mali's musical traditions and harnessing these to aid development and promote local artforms.

Our children, Madelaine (11), Ruth (10) and Micah (8) are all huddled asleep in their seats beside us; not surprising at 3am. Bizarrely, breakfast was served a few minutes ago: crispy French pastries and strong, dark coffee – very pleasant, despite the ludicrous hour. I've just downed my last mouthful of caffeine-infused beverage when the plane begins to shudder.

BOOM!

What was that? My bottom just left the seat as we dropped several metres in half a second. Cups of coffee are flying across the cabin, spewing out their warm, brown contents in every direction, as loud screams emanate from the wide-open mouths of petrified faces.

BOOM!

And again. The plane is now shaking and bouncing non-stop, babies are crying, and across the aisle a young African girl is throwing up violently onto the patterned red carpet. Out of my small oval window, heavy rain – almost horizontal – is battering the sides of our hapless jet, bright flashes of lightning illuminating its quivering wings. In terror and panic, I grasp Lois's hands and she mine, as though holding onto each other will somehow save us. The aircraft continues to pitch, judder and drop, as a cold sweat – like an unwelcome visitor – bursts out through every pore in my body, my heart pounding fiercely in my head.

BOOM!

Our children are starting to wake, but are too dozy to show much concern. I peer through my steamy oval window: below the dim lights of Bamako's sprawling suburbs are already visible, and we're *still* falling. I've never liked bumpy flights and, as turbulence goes, this is the worst I've known. I clench my wife's hands even harder, fervently praying for safety, yet still convinced I'm about to die.

The plane veers to one side and begins climbing again: clearly an aborted landing. The lack of any communication from the cabin of this budget airline only makes matters worse, as my imagination runs all the wilder: *Are the pilots clinging on for dear life in there, unable to even make an announcement? Maybe they're unconscious…*

BOOM!

This time, the plane went *upwards* – is that even possible? A few rows in front, an overhead locker flies open and a large grey suitcase plummets to the ground, narrowly missing a wrinkly African nun, who lurches awkwardly to one side. It bursts open on landing, ejecting a mass of brightly coloured clothes and multiple boxes of Moroccan tea.

The bumps, flashes and tremors continue, as plastic coffee cups roll across the aisles and concerned mothers attempt – in vain – to appease their wailing offspring. The only two visible members of the cabin crew are strapped tightly into their fold-down seats on either side of the aircraft, eyes firmly shut.

Having turned an entire 360 degrees, we descend again – this time through somewhat calmer skies – exiting the clouds to reveal a thin strip of tarmac before us, rain still pummelling the fuselage. The aircraft bounces twice before settling onto Malian soil, as the roar of forward-thrusting engines finally brings us to a halt. Our arrival is greeted with tumultuous applause; some passengers are cheering, some giving standing ovations, while others exchange long, warm hugs of relief. The aged nun crosses herself in gratitude, and the vomit-splattered face of the girl opposite is now adorned with a huge smile. A large Nigerian lady near the front rises to her feet, waving her arms victoriously in the air and boldly proclaiming: "Praise the Loooord!"

Although turbulence almost never causes a plane to crash, I still believed with every inch of my being that my life was about to end. Hugely relieved and grateful, Lois and I look at each other, our hearts still pounding furiously with adrenaline.

"We made it!"

"Ko ko ko!"
Ugh! What was that? Where am I?

I turn over and attempt to open my eyes, dazzled by the bright sunshine streaming through my thin, multicoloured curtains. It's almost 11am on 1st August, 2009. I attempt to rouse myself from an unusually deep sleep; the kind which inevitably follows a late night. My mouth and throat are sandpaper-dry, my head feels like it's stuffed with marshmallows and, even though I know I'm awake, my body is refusing to move.

"Ko ko ko!"
The familiarity of this phrase finally dawns on my semi-dormant brain: AFRICA! I'm back in Africa! It's all coming back now…the flight, the bumpy descent, the Nigerian lady. I'm not in rural Bedfordshire any more but in a hot, sunny, exciting place. I tentatively open my eyes and glance through the mosquito net. Hanging from the stained, cracked ceiling above, a wobbly metal fan is groaning incessantly. It was a relatively cool night after the storm, but the mid-morning heat is making me sweat buckets into my mattress and pillow.

"Ko ko ko! Monsieur Robert! Vous êtes là?"

In West Africa, people say *'ko ko ko'* instead of knocking, even when there *is* a door available.

"*Oui, oui. J'arrive,*" I mumble, dragging myself out of bed. I enjoy, for a moment, the pleasant coolness of the tiled floor on the soles of my feet, as I sling on a T-shirt and make my way, bleary-eyed, to the solid wooden apartment door. It creaks open to reveal the broad smile of a tall African man in a brightly coloured cotton shirt and matching trousers. His head is shaved and his eyes are warm and friendly. He reaches out his huge right hand to me.

"*Bienvenue au Mali! Je m'appelle Modibo.*" I've never come across this name before but rather like the sound of it.

"*Bonjour Modibo*, my name is Robert," I respond, my hand withering beneath his titan grip.

"Yes, I know," he says, laughing. "Come! Your landlord is here."

Although we're currently staying in a charity guest house, our home should be ready in a few days' time. We were expecting to see it soon but perhaps not quite *this* soon after arriving.

"Can you give me a few minutes please, Modibo? There's a seat here for you."

"Of course, *monsieur*. But I will wait on the veranda."

For the first time in months I enjoy the feeling of a cool shower in a hot climate (so much more refreshing than the reverse back home). We join Modibo on the veranda half an hour later; a completely normal amount of time to wait for almost anything in Africa.

"It was a big big storm last night, Monsieur Robert," he says, raising his massive hands energetically into the air.

"Yes, it was," I reply, shuddering.

Lazing in the shade of neem trees in the damp courtyard below, our new landlord is a surprisingly young chap sporting pristine black jeans, a plain, long-sleeved shirt, and a brand new pair of Nike trainers. Seeing us, he rises nonchalantly to his feet and shakes my hand, saying nothing and certainly not smiling. His air of austerity is far from uncommon amongst African landlords I've known; neither is his abnormally smart dress code.

"*Viens!*" he says, impolitely using the familiar 'tu' form in French, seconds after meeting. We follow him through the large rusty-red compound gate onto the dirt road outside, passing concrete shacks with tin roofs: some are houses, others shops. Straight ahead, a flash of vivid turquoise catches my eye: the Niger River glistening in the distance.

The adrenaline rush of being back in my favourite continent heightens my senses, making every detail around me ultra-vivid: old men drinking tea beneath damp mango trees, animated conversations in strange and incomprehensible languages, the smell of sizzling Nile perch on roadside grills, the piercing buzz of welders in their makeshift shack on the corner, semi-clad children rolling old bicycle tyres along the uneven road, the rancid stench of open drains, shabby goats in small herds braying as they forage the neighbourhood for scraps, and the red dust invading my pristine sandals with every step, tarnishing my hitherto spotless toes. Chickens clucking, teapots slowly boiling on tiny trivets, leaves rustling in the breeze, lazy dogs snoring, and the hot African sun beating down incessantly on my pale, sweat-covered forehead. It's good to be back!

Buzzing, rusty motorbikes slalom past at close proximity, as large women in colourful, loose-fitting *boubous* skilfully balance wicker baskets on their heads. At random intervals, heaps of rubbish several feet high litter the roadside, bilgy and fly infested. At the next dusty crossroads, effluent is oozing out of a cracked pipe, forming a pungent grey pool covering half the road. We carefully step over this stream of filth and turn the corner, where a huge pile of bricks is sitting slap-bang in the middle of the street for no apparent reason. None of the houses here are more than a storey high, though most have a small gated courtyard at the front. The road here opens out onto a large dusty square surrounded by neem trees, with a sandy sports pitch in the centre and a small mosque at the far end, its green dome and semi-lunar pinnacle glinting in the sunlight. A handful of young boys are playing soccer (in this heat!), kicking an underinflated ball around their beige arena with great vigour and joy.

"*Là-bas, c'est le marché,*" says our landlord, pointing apathetically ahead.

I love an African market, so make a mental note to visit one day soon. Our district is called *Badalabougou*, which aptly translates as 'village beside the river'. Many of Bamako's districts have similarly 'catchy' names: there's Lafiabougou across the river (village of peace), Daoudabougou (David's village) on the hill behind us, and Magnambougou downstream from here, named after a colonial Frenchman called Magna. And if you enjoy a challenge, try asking your taxi driver for Torokorobougou, Bakojikoroni or Boulkassambougou.

As we wander through Badalabougou, children periodically call out: *"Toubab! Toubab!"* which means 'Westerner' or 'white person' in the local language, Bambara. The term originates from the Arabic word *tabīb*, meaning 'physician' and found its way to Mali via the French language (where *toubib* is still a slang word for doctor). Often, the plural form *toubabou* is used, and this phenomenon is by no means limited to Mali: every part of Africa has its own word for Westerners. In Kenya, I'm a *mzungu*, in Benin it's *yovo*, and in parts of Nigeria I'm called *batouré*. There are dozens more, and local folk do not see such terms as impolite or derogatory; Africans call a spade a spade, so addressing me as 'white man' is acknowledging who I am but without stigma or negativity. On a similar note, it's also acceptable – common in fact – to say: 'Good morning, fat man!' This takes some getting used to, but being portly is considered a *good* thing here; most Malians cannot afford an excess of food, so anyone overweight *must* be rich. Many times, I've been congratulated for becoming overweight, when I'm anything but pleased by my excess pounds.

Just beyond the market, a thin man is sitting at a simple wooden loom weaving long strips of brightly coloured, stripy fabric. His bare feet operate the loom's crude wooden mechanism, as he throws the shuttle between the parallel woollen strands at great speed. A heavy rock three metres away keeps his cords taut and is gradually pulled towards him through the sand as he weaves. The size of his machine means he cannot make strips any wider than eight inches, so he creates a dozen identical bands and sews these together to make blankets or wall hangings.

We turn a final corner into a 'white' neighbourhood and the difference is striking: litter-free, paved streets with neatly covered drains and sparkling four-by-fours. The whitewashed houses are two – sometimes three – stories high, surrounded by large shrub-filled gardens, many with swimming pools. Tall boundary walls are adorned with vibrant pink and white bougainvillea, but also barbed wire, spiralling menacingly across the top. Official-looking security guards stand in front of many of these castles of affluence, proudly wearing freshly ironed, chocolate-brown uniforms. Some are armed, many are not.

Our landlord stops in front of a large white garage door, upon which he heavily bangs with one hand, causing its sheet metal to resonate loudly. Within a second, the door opens ajar and a round, jolly-looking face wearing a *Chicago Bulls* baseball cap peers curiously out. The landlord mutters to him in Bambara and he listens intently, punctuating what he hears with: "Aha…aha…mmm…aha." He then turns his chubby face towards us, shaking our hands vigorously and loudly exclaiming: "Welcome to Bamako! Welcome to your new home! My name is Bourama Kouyaté, your night guard."

"Night guard?" I turn to Modibo.

"Yes, you must have a guard, Robert."

"Okay…Pleased to meet you, Monsieur Kouyaté. Thank you for your work."

"Where is your vehicle, *monsieur?*"

"My car? It's still on the boat," I reply, making wave-like gestures with my hands.

"On a boat? How is this possible? Is it a very small vehicle?"

In landlocked Mali, Mr Kouyaté has never encountered a container ship. I explain how we took our Mistubishi Montero to Tilbury docks a few weeks before leaving, and had hoped it would be here in time for our arrival. The ship (apparently called 'Samantha') is due to dock in Dakar, Senegal in a few days' time. I explain to Kouyaté that the vehicle is inside a large metal container on a huge boat, as he listens, wide-eyed.

"In a metal box, on a boat?"

"Yes! And from Dakar it will travel over 1000 kilometres eastwards to Bamako on the back of a long train."

After a moment of astonished pondering, he responds: *"Je vais laver!* I will wash!"

"Did you not have a shower this morning?"

"No, the vehicle," clarifies Modibo. "He will wash your car."

"Not necessary. I can wash my own car, but thank you all the same."

"No, I wash," Kouyaté insists. "Every morning I *will* wash your car, monsieur."

Apparently, an extra perk of having a night guard is getting your car washed every morning and your garden watered. I suppose they've got to do something to avoid nodding off in the wee hours.

We made the decision to buy our car in the UK as they're actually cheaper back home than in Africa. With a plethora of Western charities, embassies and missions all vying for reliable vehicles here, low supply and high demand inflates prices. And when it comes to distance covered, one African mile equates to two or three British ones: bumpy roads, heat, dust, floods and rocks all take their toll on vehicles here, wearing them out much more quickly. Add to this some pretty dodgy mechanics with little access to quality tools, training or parts (out of no fault of their own), and buying back home starts to make a lot more sense. The shipping is costing us a couple of grand, but the car is also filled with our belongings, thereby serving as a mini-container.

"Viens!" Our monosyllabic landlord orders us into the house. We pass through a decent-sized front garden with paved footpaths, pale-green box hedging, a large mango tree, and a small swimming pool to one side.

"C'est la piscine!" says Mr Landlord, rather stating the obvious.

"Can we swim, daddy?" asks Ruth, eagerly. She's always loved water. Approaching the pool, the answer is instantly clear: two feet of grimy, dark-green water lines the bottom. No swimming today then.

Our single-storey house is painted white but stained brown with dust, and has a flat concrete roof which extends over a sizeable veranda at the front. The windows, all closed to keep the heat out, have sturdy metal bars across them, giving the house a disconcertingly prison-like feel. The metal front door creaks noisily open to reveal a dingy, windowless L-shaped corridor leading to all rooms. A surprisingly long lounge-diner and slightly pokey kitchen make up the entire width of the house to the front, with three bedrooms at the back. The floor of the entire house (and veranda) is covered with tiny mosaic tiles, mostly off-white and mustard yellow. No carpets, and you wouldn't want them here. The bathroom has a basic shower: a plughole in one corner surrounded by a curtain, with a simple metal pipe and showerhead fixed to the concrete wall. In mine and Lois' room there's also an en-suite with a bathtub; quite a rarity in these parts.

The house is already partly furnished, having been previously occupied by a Dutch Embassy family. We agreed to buy most of the Van Pijkeren's furniture and other household goods, which has done both parties a big favour. So we already have a wicker sofa with matching armchairs, a TV cabinet (but no TV), a chunky wooden dresser and a long dining table.

The kitchen, which smells of rotting onions, boiled rice and weevils, has a small, rusty Calor Gas cooker in one corner, and on a hefty dark sideboard sits a tall, cylindrical water filter: vital if we are to safely drink the tap water here.

My first impression is how stark everything looks compared with my cosy, wall-papered home in England: plain white walls, metal doors, hard floors, light-fittings with bare wires, and an overall atmosphere of echoey emptiness. It's also a very dark house, which is astonishing given Mali's penetratingly bright sunshine. Stepping outside the back door, I quickly realize why: a thick trellis of pink bougainvillea runs around three sides of the building at roof height, bridging the eight-foot gap between the house and the tall compound walls. This will certainly keep our home cooler but lets virtually no daylight through.

"Regarde!" says Mr Landlord, opening a concrete shed in the garden to reveal two things: the pump system for the swimming pool and what looks like a huge pile of straw matting.

"What's that for?" I ask, perplexed.

"It's for the roof, *monsieur,*" interjects Mr Kouyaté, incredulous at my ignorance.

"But the roof is made of concrete, not straw…"

"Non, non, monsieur. In hot season, we put straw on the roof to keep your house cool. Come and see!" And with that, he ascends a rickety ladder leant precariously against the house, beckoning me to follow. Its rungs, made of rough planks, are almost two feet apart, some severely cracked. I glance at the Landlord, who is only too happy to acquiesce.

Peering over the rim of the flat concrete roof, I see rows of evenly spaced pillars, three breeze blocks high. Resting on these, roughly 18 inches above the surface, is a grid framework of straight branches, tied together at their intersections with twine.

"We put the straw mats on here, *monsieur,* to stop the sun shining onto the roof."

"But why aren't they up there now?"

"Because it's *rainy season,*" interjects Mr Landlord, almost audibly tutting at my ignorance. "After rainy season, it's cold season, then hot season."

It turns out that 'cold season' means 25 Celsius in the day, occasionally dropping as low as 12 degrees at night; a pleasant summer's day where I come from.

"The rains make the straw rot," Kouyaté explains, "so I only put it up in hot season. Then I take it down again afterwards." Seems like an effective if somewhat labour-intensive system.

"But it must rain *sometimes* during hot season too, doesn't it?" I ask, dumbfounded.

"No, never!" he responds, waving his chubby finger at me with pride. "From November to March, no drop of rain. Just dry, dry, dry. Every day."

"Ko ko ko!" Someone's at the door and their voice sounds strangely familiar.

"Monsieur Pierre is here," says Modibo. "He is waiting to take you to eat."

Monsieur Pierre, or Canadian Pete, is the charitable soul who got up at three this morning to meet us at the airport. He works for a small charity and is normally based in the parched Saharan north. He also has an office in Bamako and spends two or three months a year here, stocking up, planning, and enjoying the luxury of air-conditioning.

I shake my mysterious landlord's hand and thank him for his time.

"See you tomorrow!" he says, in English.

"You speak my language?" I ask, astonished.

"See you tomorrow!" he reiterates.

"What's happening tomorrow?" I enquire, still in English.

"See you tomorrow!" he repeats firmly, leaving me wondering whether these are the *only* three Anglo Saxon words he actually knows.

Back at the guesthouse, Pete is waiting with his white seven-seater Land Cruiser 'ambulance' – a long white vehicle with just two doors at the front and double doors to the rear. Pete bought his in Côte d'Ivoire, where it had *actually* been used as an ambulance during the civil war in 2002. On either side of the vehicle, the letters 'UN' have been painted over, though are still just about visible.

"Did you sleep well, buddy?" Pete asks. "Thought I'd take you oot for a wee bite to eat. A place called Broadway Café – I think you'll like it!"

Canadian Pete is one of those seasoned expatriates who's been on the African continent for decades and really knows the ropes. Though born in

New Glasgow, Nova Scotia, he grew up as a missionary kid in the Congo, then studied soil science and water management in Quebec, so is also fluent in French. A hefty chap with thinning mousy-brown locks and a huge greying beard, he speaks with a most curious accent, even for a Canadian. Pete never married and spends most of his time working on irrigation projects with the *Songhai* people of Gao, a desert town beyond Timbuktu, 20 hours' drive north-east of Bamako.

"Hop on board, folks!" says Pete, his ruddy *Captain Birdseye* face beaming warmly at us. He turns the key, and the three litre turbo-diesel beast roars into action.

"You guys ready to see Bamako then? Brace yourselves, eh?"

The Tour de l'Afrique, Bamako

Chapter Two – Crocodile City

"We enjoy a rather unconventional route home."

OF ALL THE African cities I've visited, there's one which, for me, stands head and shoulders above the rest. An immediately agreeable place with a decidedly civilised ambiance: vibrant yet laid-back, urbanized yet picturesque, sprawling yet incredibly personal, bustling yet somehow ordered, impoverished yet unbelievably optimistic. Although not the most salubrious of places – and by no means the richest city on the continent – Mali's capital, Bamako, has warmed me to the core in more ways than one.

What makes it so likeable? It's certainly not the open sewers, whose streams of acrid filth ooze alongside the streets with a putrescent stench of dead goat. Neither is it the almost unbearable heat, which soars to a sizzling 45 Celsius during hot season, transforming the Niger valley into a dust bowl and which, combined with almost zero humidity, turns your hair to straw and blights the feet and lips with more crevasses than the Grand Canyon. And it's definitely not the seemingly endless traffic jams which scourge the city's streets for hours every morning and evening. With a population of two million and only two bridges over the river, a 'rush hour' of this kind is an inevitable consequence, which Bamako's inhabitants have learned to tolerate but certainly not relish.

Despite all of the above, I love Bamako because it is dynamic and exciting, but without the aggression of, say, Lagos or Cotonou. I love Bamako because, in spite of its palpable poverty, there is an underlying vibe of warmth and positivity, largely down to its resilient and good-natured people. Take the city's iconic taxi drivers: rarely will you find one bemoaning his 16-hour, monoxide-infused day on busy, potholed streets. Rather, he will laugh, joke and chat with you in a warm, friendly way. He may also discuss politics with you on a complex level, as these chaps are by no means ignorant or uneducated. Moreover, they are polite, charming and unbelievably honest: a friend of mine left her laptop in the back of a Bamako taxi. The following morning, the driver turned up at her house, saying: "You left this in my car," and without even a hint of expecting a reward.

Another reason I love Bamako is for its amazing musicians: Mali has an impressive musical tradition going back centuries – if not millennia – and many of its artists are known throughout the world today: Toumani Diabaté, Salif Keita, Oumou Sangaré, Bassekou Kouyaté and the late, great Ali Farka Touré. These talented *griots* skilfully blend traditional Mandé music with Western elements to create a fresh and inspiring sound revered by Malians, fellow Africans and the rest of the planet. Across the vast city of Bamako (and on either bank of the Niger River), you will find bars, clubs and restaurants pounding into the wee hours with these infectious Mandé melodies, as players of the *kora, ngoni, tama* and *balafon* wow audiences with their inspirational talent.

I also love Bamako because it is an altogether aesthetically pleasing place; from a distance, at least. Surrounded by picturesque hills on either side of its valley, the broad, majestic Niger River meanders through Bamako before heading north towards the mystical desert city of Timbuktu. Its banks are adorned with groves of lush mango trees, sinuous city date palms and, further north, majestic baobabs. Look a little closer and you'll see industrious market gardeners growing lettuces, carrots – even potatoes – on the exposed flood plains beside the river. With a rusty watering can in one hand, they painstakingly irrigate every square inch of their neatly arranged rectangular plots, to ensure the best yield possible in this sandy earth. If you're lucky (or perhaps very *unlucky*) you might see a crocodile or two lurking by the banks, or even a hippo basking in muddy pools at the river's edge. It's not altogether surprising, therefore, that the word *Bamako* means 'Crocodile River' or that *Mali* translates as 'Hippopotamus'.

There are two major hills in Bamako, one on either side of the Niger, and these can be seen from almost anywhere in the city. To the south is *La Colline du Savoir* - The Hill of Knowledge, home to Mali's only university, and to the north, a huge white house adorns the summit of *La Colline du Pouvoir* - The Hill of Power, which is home to Mali's president: Amadou Toumani Touré (affectionately abbreviated to ATT).[1]

And so, between the hills of knowledge and power, lies bustling Bamako with its crowded streets, towering minarets, busy markets and

---

[1] Pronounced [ah-tay-tay]

swanky hotels. The main roads are surprisingly wide and straight, many with two lanes *and* a separate motorcycle lane. These intersect at roundabouts, many of which contain elaborate monuments. There's the imposing dome-shaped *Monument de l'Indépendance* in the centre (built to commemorate Mali's breakaway from France in 1961), the seven-storey *Tour de l'Afrique* (Africa Tower) at the city limits, and the beautiful, thirty-foot *Monument de La Paix* (Peace Monument) by the river, which depicts an enormous globe held up by two arms, a dove perched on its summit. Smaller monuments scattered around the city include an elephant, a hippo, an obelisk reminiscent of *Cleopatra's Needle,* and a green and yellow crocodile kicking a football. It often surprises – even shocks – Western visitors to see such opulent edifices in the midst of poverty. Yet, these are commonplace in cities throughout the continent and are a way of celebrating culture and identity, as well as fostering national pride.

Most of all, I love Bamako because of its wonderfully welcoming people, their warm smiles and friendly handshakes a treat any time of day. Their sense of humour is refreshingly original too, with playful taunts a part of everyday life. They always have time for others, and within five minutes of chatting, it feels as though you've already made a lifelong friend.

"Hold tight in the back there, guys! Things might get a little bumpy!"
Pete's Toyota copes admirably with the uneven roads of our neighbourhood, and my head only hits the ceiling a couple of times. We bounce up onto a tarmac road, ascending a small hill with a nice-looking French bakery at the top. At the T-junction, we're bombarded by half a dozen guys selling mobile phone recharge cards, each chanting:
"Orange! Orange! Orange!"
One of them puts his chain of cards through my open window, holding them inches from my nose while continuing his mantra:
"Orange! Orange! Orange!"
Mobile phones here work on a pay-as-you-go basis: as many Malians don't have bank accounts, these scratch cards are used instead.
"Toubab! Il faut acheter crédit!"[2] says nose-dangler man, as his partners in crime persist with their nauseating carillon.

---

[2] White man! Buy some credit.

This kind of blatant invasion of privacy and personal space is far from uncommon in Africa, but is one of the hardest things for the Western psyche to understand or adapt to. The African mindset says: 'the more we insist, the more likely we are to make a sale', whereas in the West it's: 'don't bother your customer; they'll make a decision when they're comfortable and ready'. It's a clash of cultures you just have to get used to.

"Ach, we'll sort your phones oot tomorrow, eh?" says Pete, sensing my rising stress levels. He zooms off, winding up the window and whacking on the air-con.

As we round a corner, two men in neatly ironed blue shirts, smart black trousers and black berets are sitting under a small shelter looking mildly menacing.

"Hey, watch oot for them police when ya start drivin'! They'll pull you over just as soon as look at ya!"

"How do they stop you?" I ask, noticing they have no vehicle.

"If they blow their whistle you have to stop – it's the law here. If you don't, they could impound your vehicle. But it's for money-making more than safety, ya understand?"

"I understand. Are they armed too?"

"With a small revolver, but I've never seen one used. In town you'll see the military guards with semi-automatic weapons. Now, you don't wanna mess with *them!*"

The King Fahd Bridge spans the vast Niger River, linking both sides of Bamako. Named after the former Arabian ruler, it was built with Saudi funds and opened in 1992. The slip road to the bridge is instantly busier than dreamy Badalabougou; rather than one or two vehicles, there are now dozens: cars, lorries and vans, all vying for a place on this lifeline to the capital. Wider and newer-looking than I'd expected, there are two lanes in each direction and, in spite of the chaos, traffic is moving pretty smoothly and is by no means as insane as many other African capitals I know: Cairo, Cotonou, Dakar, or Ouagadougou. On either side of the main carriageway is the motorbike lane: a great system for prolonging the lives of two-wheelers.

The preponderance of taxis in this maelstrom is immediately obvious; all painted yellow, though in the very broadest definition of the colour: some are pale orange, others almost green. I notice that most are Mercedes

Benz 190Ds, which seems strange in such a poor country.

"Cast offs from their rich Arab brothers," Pete explains, tossing one hand nonchalantly into the air. "Most are at least 20 years old, some more than 30. But they sure do keep on runnin', eh?"

Looking more closely, it's clear that many of them have seen better days: ill-fitting doors, cracked rear lights and the occasional missing bumper. One particularly ancient specimen, with the words 'Air Mali' emblazoned across the side, has splayed rear wheels and is carrying three rather large African ladies and a live goat. Its front dash is covered in gaudy yellow fake fur and on the rear shelf there's an ornate golden tissue box.

"I'll tell you a funny story aboot a taxi," says Pete, taking his eyes off the road for a disconcerting amount of time. "It's absolutely true, I promise! My neighbour's son, Harouna, came to Bamako last year and took up taxi driving. He could only afford the cheapest of cars."

"Not a Mercedes then?"

"No, a Peugeot, I think. Well…ya see that hill over there?"

"The Hill of Power?"

"Ah, Mr Rob has done his homework! Yes, the Hill of Power. Well, can you see how the road zigzags sharply all the way to Koulouba at the top?"

I nod, squinting through the midday haze.

"Well, young Harouna was driving down that hill one day, and as he went round a sharp bend, he actually fell oot of his own taxi!"

"What?! Didn't he have a seatbelt?"

"Seatbelt? Take a look in these taxis – most don't have any, and the rest don't want to use them."

It's true: try pulling out the seatbelt in a Bamako taxi and you'll probably get showered with dust, if it even moves (or still exists).

"And because his car was cheap and cheerful, the catch on the driver's door didn't work properly, so oot he fell."

"Was he hurt?"

"Only a few cuts and bruises. Thankfully, he'd just dropped his last passenger off in Koulouba, so was on his own. He rolled down the grassy slope and landed up in some bushes a few feet from the edge there," he adds, pointing excitedly at the sheer craggy rock face in the distance. "His taxi carried on for 50 yards, then hit a tree – otherwise he may have lost it over the cliff!"

Halfway across the bridge is a glut of twenty or so motorbikes, their drivers leaning over the barrier looking down into the river.

"That'll be hippos, or maybe a crocodile or two," explains my ever-informative guide. "Either that or some poor soul has fallen in."

Perish the thought.

"This is the new bridge and over there's the old bridge," he continues, pointing to the right, where a smaller, lower bridge is visible. "Besides that, there are no other bridges apart from the submersible bridge."

"The submersible bridge? What's one of those?"

"Well, at the end of hot season, the river's low, see. Then ya can drive over the submersible bridge – it's just a solid raised track from one side to the other. When the rains come, it gets submerged again, but it helps ease traffic for a few months of the year. The Chinese are planning to build a decent third bridge oot by the submersible one in the next year or two."

"The CHINESE?!"

"Sure, they're investing all over Africa these days."

As we near the opposite bank of the river – almost a kilometre later – I can't help but notice an imposing sand-coloured building on the riverbank. It has large mirrored windows, pointy towers and roughly eighty air-conditioning units, all mounted in neat rows on its lofty walls. Its most striking feature is the enormous green Hollywoodesque lettering across the top, which reads: 'MALIBYA'.

"Ah…that's the government administration," Pete tells me.

"Why does it say MALIBYA?"

"Because Colonel Gaddafi built it."

"Gaddafi, here in Mali? But why?"

"Well, Libya's not a million miles away, and Gaddafi's been forging links with lots of African countries in recent times. They say it's his dream to become president of a United States of Africa."

Pete takes a right turn off the bridge, narrowly avoiding another policeman about to blow his whistle.

"But that's not likely to happen, is it?"

"No, but Gaddafi is popular here. Many Malians see him as a benevolent patron, helping the country develop. He's built several mosques and schools here."

"So, does 'MALIBYA' mean he sees the two countries as one?"

"Kind of. Ya see that there big hotel?" He points at a pale-brown sixteen-storey building up ahead. "That's the *Hôtel de l'Amitié*, Bamako's largest and poshest hotel, built by the Colonel himself."

"Really?"

"And ya know what *Amitié* means?"

"Friendship."

"Right! So, he's befriending Mali and other countries to try and bring a united Africa with a single currency."

"Wouldn't that be a good thing, though? I mean, West Africa already has a common currency and that seems to work well. So does most of Europe."

"Maybe, but not everyone would want this guy as their leader."

He certainly seems to polarize people, and has seldom been portrayed favourably by the Western World. Pete continues:

"Libya has leased 100,000 acres of Malian land for agriculture up near Ségou – they call it the *Office du Niger*. Fertile land on the Niger Inland Delta, and they say Libya is growing hybrid rice there. They paid peanuts for it[3] and have employed the Chinese to build irrigation canals up there. Mali's Minister of Agriculture thinks it's a win-win arrangement, but not all local folk are keen. They say the rice will benefit China or Libya more than Mali."[4]

Amidst the plethora of yellow taxis, I'm noticing lots of green minibuses too, full to the gills with passengers.

"Is that public transport?"

"Yep! Instead of buses, we have these *sotramas*," he explains, as one whizzes past at great speed, almost taking off our wing mirror. "They call 'em sotramas because they're 'so traumatic' to travel in."

"Really?" I respond in complete credulity.

"No, I'm joking man! Sotrama stands for *Société de Transports Malienne* – the Malian Transport Company." I'm impressed with Pete's French pronunciation, though his accent is a bizarre blend of Africanized Québécois.

---

[3] https://en.wikipedia.org/wiki/Office_du_Niger
[4] Radio Canada - https://www.youtube.com/watch?v=U7yebsqQq7Q

To 'make' a sotrama, simply take a van (preferably an old, battered up one) and remove the sliding side door completely, replacing it with a single chain (for safety!). Next, cut windows into the sides (no glass required) and add a chip board partition between the driver's seats and the rear, not forgetting a six-inch square opening for communication purposes. Then, put foot-deep wooden benches all the way round the inside of the van and, for good measure, a huge spare tyre right in the centre for folk to trip over as they board. To finish, hand-paint the entire vehicle bottle green. Now all you need is roughly 20 passengers to cram into this tiny space. It's hardly travelling in style, but at 100 CFA francs[5] for the two-mile journey into town, it's certainly the cheapest.

From the outside, sotramas are a lot more exciting to look at than the taxis. Not one of them is merely plain green – they've all been pimped up in some way or other, giving each its own funky individuality. Most have pictures painted on them: maps of Mali, crocodiles, African village scenes, or cartoon characters (Mickey Mouse being a popular choice). There are also various attempts at the American flag, none with quite the right number of stars or stripes, or even the correct shades – or combinations – of red and blue. Others are emblazoned with thought-provoking slogans like: *'Dieu Merci'* (thank you God) or *'La Souffrance est un Conseil'* (suffering is a counsellor). Another simply asks: *'Pourquoi divorcer?'* (why divorce?). Many sotramas have names of famous people scrawled across the side, Barack Obama being the most popular by far. One has the words: 'Bill Gate' on the front in huge yellow letters, which sounds more like a scandal in a restaurant than the founder of Microsoft. Then there are the paintings or stickers of famous people:

"Look Daddy. Madonna!" says Mads, excitedly.

The eight inch sticker, depicting the American pop idol blowing a kiss, has somehow found its way to Mali. And it's almost as popular as the Obama one of a similar size. Bizarrely, the most common face of all is that of Argentine revolutionary Che Guevara. Although Che comes in sticker form too, his angry, bearded, beret-clad head is more often painted on. You'll see his steely glare on hairdressing salons, bridges, market stalls and monuments. I guess he represents the fight against injustice for many

---

[5] At this time, 100 CFA is worth roughly 20 US cents, or 15 pence

Africans. Very occasionally, you'll see a sticker of Muammar Gaddafi, and I've even seen Osama Bin Laden once or twice.

Another green beast roars past, and we all laugh; this one has two stickers on its rear doors: Madonna blowing a kiss in the direction of Obama!

We arrive at the space-like Independence Monument, where the traffic lights are equipped with a display which counts down the seconds until green. I've never seen this before, not even in the UK.

"Chinese lights," says Pete, noticing my fascination.

"There seem to be more Chinese working on projects here than Malians."

"There are!" Pete adds with a smile.

As is the case in much of urban Africa, the lights are swarming with salesmen. No phonecards here, but instead baseball caps, watches, sunglasses ('genuine Raybans, monsieur!'), maps of Africa – even a parrot in a cage. Meanwhile, Pete is having his windscreen washed (whether he wants it or not), but doesn't seem to mind. Two young sisters, one of them blind, approach our vehicle singing undulating Malian melodies in two-part harmony; a truly beautiful sound. Always keen to reward good artists, I wind my window down ever so slightly and hand the sighted sister a 1000 franc note. She smiles and bobs down in gratitude.

Pete interjects: "Don't do tha…"

But it's too late; within half a second, we're mobbed by every salesperson present: *the toubab is handing out banknotes!* There must be 20 people vying for our custom, banging on the windows and roof, and loudly shouting the name of their product. It's practically dark inside the car now, they're all so close. Through a small gap I watch the red numbers on the lights go: 03…02…01, and we're free!

We take a left onto the straight, broad and somewhat majestic *Boulevard de l'Indépendance,* built to celebrate Mali's autonomy from France in 1961. Malian music fans will also recognize this as the title of an album by world-famous kora player Toumani Diabaté, who lives just a stone's throw from here. On either side of the avenue are lush green gardens, tennis courts and some rather weathered colonial buildings. Beyond these is Bamako's only cinema: the huge air-conditioned *Babemba,* which seats 400 people but has an average nightly clientele of around 30. The films (all in French) are relatively recent, and entry costs a mere 2000 CFA – how they even afford to run the air-con at that rate is beyond me.[6]

We turn right into a district known as Medina Koura. Just north of here, at the base of the Hill of Power, is Bamako Zoo (not far from where Harouna had his taxi mishap). It's a pretty decent place: well-stocked and with proper footpaths around the various enclosures. For a miniscule entrance fee you can see hyenas, lions, storks and antelope; you might even get to pet their solitary baby elephant. There's a large outdoor aviary, an air-conditioned reptile house full of scary-looking snakes, and even a number of pristine aquariums filled with tropical fish. Apparently, they used to have a couple of manatees in a large pool; until they died, that is.

We turn onto a quieter cobbled street with very little traffic, passing single-storey concrete shops in neat rows, typical of many 'middle class' Malian outlets. Poorer shopkeepers have tin shacks or a market stall, and the poorest of all walk around selling goods on their head. Pete pulls into a small but tidy parking lot beside the *Broadway Café*, which comes complete with its own parking attendant. This tall uniformed Malian not only guards the parked vehicles, but also 'helps' you manoeuvre into your space, energetically gesticulating in every direction and blowing his whistle roughly every second in a vain attempt to communicate.

The single-storey building is painted chocolate brown, with its logo – a four-foot-wide coffee mug with steam rising from the top – proudly positioned above the double-glazed doorway between the words 'Broadway' and 'Café'. Car park man leads the way, holding the door open for us as though we're royalty and warmly announcing:

"Bienvenue messieurs-dames!"

From a hot, dusty African street, we step into air-conditioned paradise, infused with aromas of fresh filter coffee, grilled beef and French fries. The walls, painted in deep pastel shades of burgundy and jade green, are decorated with framed black and white photos of jazz greats: Louis Armstrong, Nina Simone and Miles Davis who, incidentally, is also playing through the restaurant's sound system right now: his timeless classic *All Blues*. Stylish up-lighters illuminate the walls and dim spotlights glow from the ceiling, while plush, upholstered sofas surround sturdy oblong tables of

---

[6] 2000 CFA is roughly equal to US$4 or £3

varnished wood. This could hardly be further removed from the Bamako I've just travelled through, but I feel strangely at home here.

The menu is varied and reasonably priced: a hamburger is just 2000 CFA, cheeseburgers are 2400, and something the menu calls a 'chiken burger' is 3000 francs. And it's not just American fare: there's also lasagne, chilli con carne, burritos and several different salads. We sit down and order a range of high-carb delights from our friendly waiter. Considering the obvious quality of this place, it's relatively empty, with only half a dozen other guests: three *Peace Corps* volunteers sharing a burrito in one corner, a pair of young Lebanese chaps drinking tall cool beers in the other, and a stocky French businessman, optimistically hoping to pick up a Wi-Fi signal on his iPhone.

"They need to order Coke floats too!" Pete adds, repeatedly stabbing the menu with his chubby finger. "Guys," he says, turning to my kids, his eyes aflame with anticipation, "this is the best thing *ever*. Ya get to drink soda with ice cream in it!" With a huge range of ice cream flavours and a choice of Coke or Sprite, my kids take about two seconds' persuading.

"I'll have Coke with a scoop of mango and one of erm...pistachio!" says Madelaine.

"I'll have sprite with mint choc chip and double choc please," adds Ruth, ever the chocolate fiend.

Micah's turn: "Okay, I'll have....erm...a Coke with coconut and bubblegum!"

Unfazed by my kids' random choices, he heads off with our order, and we're soon tucking into tasty burgers and slurping luridly coloured beverages.

"Ya see the lady behind the bar?" says Pete, nodding towards a grey-haired black woman in her late 50s. "That's *boss lady*. She lived in New York for a decade before coming back to Mali and opening this place; hence the name."

"Thanks for bringing us here, Pete. It feels like we're back home, but more interesting, much cheaper, and definitely less busy."

"You're welcome pal!"

Pete takes the same route home, but after half a mile the road is blocked by three large oil drums painted red and white (and filled with concrete). Beside these stand three soldiers, armed to the eyeballs and staring menacingly at us. One of them steps up to the driver's window, which Pete obligingly winds down (though not *too* far, I notice).

"*Monsieur,* you cannot come this way. There is a *manifestation* on the *Boulevard de L'Indépendance.* Turn around at once!"

Thanking him politely, Pete makes a U-turn.

"What are they protesting about, Pete?"

"I dunno. It's usually dissatisfaction with the government for one reason or another."

We enjoy a rather unconventional route home, which involves crossing a football field, navigating narrow, muddy dirt tracks, edging our way past overhanging market stalls, and briefly driving *along* the city's only railway line. *Ge-dung, ge-dung, ge-dung.*

We eventually arrive at the Old Bridge, narrower and less pristine than the one we took into town. At this time in the afternoon ('rush' hour), the bridge is one-way out of town; a clever system, which helps us somewhat. I dread to think how bad the traffic here would be without this rule in place, as it takes us roughly 25 minutes to even get onto the bridge, via a circular slip road. On the plus side, we get plenty of time to admire this part of town, and the river. Beside us is another huge hotel, still concrete-grey due to its half-built state.

"That'll be a lovely place to stay when it's finished," I comment.

Pete turns to me: "That's Gaddafi's too!"

Chapter Three – Tea Time

"The second cup is always the best."

"NOT *AGAIN!*"

THAT'S the third tin-opener I've bought this week and, like its two predecessors, it has just fallen apart. I'm going to have to get one sent from the UK at this rate…

We moved into our new home last week and are slowly finding our feet. As many Western household items are not easily (or cheaply) available in Mali, we've had to keep our ears to the ground to glean the rest of our furniture (including waterbeds), mostly from a couple of British linguists returning home and an Austrian professor, leaving due to long-term illness.

For those unacquainted with the waterbed, it's a curious but highly effective way to sleep in a hot climate. As water is denser than air, it stays cool longer, drawing heat from your body as you sleep. Sharing a waterbed is always interesting, my dear wife having to endure a mini tsunami every time I get in or out. Even turning in your sleep is a tricky technique, achieved only with practice. Getting waterbed frames made in urban Africa is easy enough: there's always a local chippy willing to create a made-to-measure masterpiece. But the water bladders themselves are generally only available via the second-hand expat market.

I'm about to assemble waterbed number two in Micah's room. Its frame of thick, sturdy wood runs all the way to the ground, and heavy interlocking planks inside provide the necessary extra support. A horizontal sheet of MDF then slots inside, leaving a 12-inch deep rectangle where the rubber mattress sits.

Out in the garden, Mr Kouyaté has just arrived for his night guard duties. Every evening, after asking how our family is, he moves on to his favourite topic:

"Et le véhicule? C'est pas venu d'abord?" He asks, in good African French, clearly missing the joys of car washing. In the meantime he's lent me his redundant hosepipe – a length of grubby yellow tubing – to fill the mattresses. He suggests I use some rubber strips (originally from an inner tube) to lash the pipe to our bathroom tap and, remarkably, it works.

There's a satisfying swoosh as I turn the tap on, but this will now take a good hour to fill, so I get on with hanging some of the Austrian prof's curtains (depicting zebras and giraffes) in our lounge. The children, meanwhile, are sticking posters on their walls. It's impossible to find Blutak anywhere in Mali, so I've asked my mum to post some out. Until then, sticky tape will have to suffice.

I called in a local electrician to mend our non-working lights, many of which merely needed new lightbulbs. But electricity can be a dangerous and unpredictable thing in Africa, so I preferred not to attempt the job myself. Just last week, an expat friend was literally thrown across the room by her own washing machine.

The final stage of filling the waterbed is by far the most exciting, but definitely a two-person job.

"Lois! Can you come and help me get the air out?"

She's just back from Azar's, our local Lebanese-run supermarket, with plenty of groceries to keep us going: powdered milk, tinned tomatoes, a sack of white rice (ironically imported from Thailand), hot dog sausages, eggs, apricot jam, *Laughing Cow* soft cheese, herbs and spices…she's even found Cornflakes, though at £5 a box, we may not be eating these too often.

In the bedroom, we carefully remove the hosepipe from the mattress, holding the opening as high as possible to avoid water flooding out, then screw in the stopper. Now comes the fun part: lying on the waterbed, I roll over from one end to the other, forcing the air bubbles towards the stopper in the corner. Lois then slightly unscrews it to let the air hiss out, screwing it back in as soon as the splutter of water comes, rather like bleeding a radiator. We'll now leave it a few hours, then repeat the process again. If you don't bleed your waterbed, it's less effective and will slosh around all night, every time you move.

Our househelp arrived yesterday: Abdoulaye Poudiougou worked for the Van Pijkerens who lived here before us, and for a Swedish family who were here before them. So you could say he came with the house. Abdoulaye is *Dogon,*[7] a fascinating ethnic group who live on cliffs in eastern Mali, grow onions, know a lot about astronomy and occasionally walk on

---

[7] Pronounced [Doh-gon]

stilts.[8] They're also renowned for being resilient and hard-working, which bodes well.

Originally from a small village at the foot of the Dogon Escarpment, Abdoulaye came south for work and actually got as far as Abidjan on the Ivory Coast, where he ended up cooking and cleaning for some American missionaries for a couple of years. Then, when civil war kicked off in *Côte d'Ivoire*, he was forced to leave, dodging bullets all the way and almost being taken hostage by rebels at one point. In Bamako, he found accommodation with his 'brother' downriver from here in Magnambougou. With a contact his Ivorian employees gave him, he began working for the Swedes, then stayed on for the Dutch folk. And so Abdoulaye is able to cook a range of international dishes including meatballs, lasagne, pancakes and omelettes, as well as the famous local dish of *sauce arachide* – beef stewed in a tasty peanut sauce.

Like most Dogons, Abdoulaye is not tall in stature, standing at roughly five feet nothing, and is of slender build. A fastidious worker and excellent cook, he has never learned to read or write but speaks fluent Bambara and decent French, as well as Dogon. At the moment, he's cleaning the floors, windows and sills as well as helping Lois sort the kitchen. He's looking quite worn out, though, as Ramadan began a couple of days ago. Like most Malians, Abdoulaye is Muslim, and his name means 'Servant of God'. For 28 days he will eat or drink nothing during daylight hours. A good Muslim, they say, will not even swallow his own saliva during the month of Ramadan.

RIIING RIIING!

No, it's not the phone – we don't even have a landline. It's the door – the garden door out on the street. Mr Kouyaté dutifully answers it for us and, seconds later, taps on the house door.

"C'est Monsieur Coulibaly!"

Coulibaly is a terribly common name here in Mali, a bit like Smith or Jones in the UK. This Mr Coulibaly has come to sort out the swimming pool. For a few pounds, he's going to pump out the filthy green sludge and fill it up with clean water and chlorine.

"I dan se!" I say, welcoming our aging, bespectacled visitor in his native

---

[8] See chapters 7-9

Bambara.

"*I ni ce!*" he responds, thanking me.

"*I ni bara!*" I wish him success in his work.

"*M'ba!*" he replies: the positive response to just about anything round here.

As I watch him work, I'm being feasted on by dozens of mosquitoes, and my ankles and elbows – two of their favourite parts to nibble – are itching terribly.

At least it's daytime; the malarial mozzies only bite after dark. Seeing me scratching, pool man says:

"You have a mosquito problem here. Monsieur Coulibaly can kill them all for you!"

"Really? That would be good. How will you do that?"

"*Non, non, Monsieur.* Not me - Coulibaly the mosquito exterminator. He will come with his tank of special liquid and spray your whole garden."

I take down the chap's number and give him a call. Like most appointments in Africa, he says he can come right away.

"No, not today, the pool man is here. How about tomorrow?"

"*Pas de problème. Demain!*" he says, hanging up without so much as a 'goodbye'. He'll be here in the morning and will charge a mere 10,000 CFA to rid my world of insect bites. Sounds like a good deal to me. Meanwhile, swimming pool Coulibaly has finished his work and warns us: "Don't swim in it for a week – the chemicals have to do their work first."

Tonight we're invited to dinner with Doctor Dave and his wife Bertha. An expert on tropical medicine, slender, bald-headed Dave is in his mid 40s and wears plastic-rimmed glasses, giving him a look of musician Moby. He also plays a spot of saxophone, so I'm hoping for a jam session later. Bertha is short and plump with ginger hair, and seems to sweat continuously, in spite of having lived here for several years. Their twin sons, 16, are both at boarding school in Dakar, Senegal, a thousand miles west of here.

Still without our own vehicle, we pile into a taxi to get to Dave's house. Now, there's a strict *five people per taxi* rule here in Bamako (another reason for the police to blow their whistle and fine you), and there are six of us including the driver. But we're okay: I just discovered that children only count as *half a person* in vehicles here, so by that reckoning our total is only 4.5! The taxi, another Mercedes-Benz, has foam spilling out of the entire back seat, no upholstery on the passenger door, and the words 'God is One' written across its rear. To avoid an awkward silence, I ask the driver his name.

"Coulibaly," he responds. Just for a change…

Nobody much uses street names or house numbers here (even though they exist), so Dave has texted me details as follows:

> *Ask driver for Radisson Bleu hotel in Lafiabougou. Then 2 blocks west, left by tailor's shack. 200 yds down hill. We're on RHS. Big garden. Look for palm trees.*

On the way, we pass one of Bamako's best medical surgeries: *Clinique Pasteur*. Doctor Dave doesn't work there though; he's the doctor for the US Embassy, just down the road from here.

Dave's house is massive compared to ours, so I'm feeling less guilty about our pool. Two storeys with a large roof terrace and a *real* grass lawn outside; quite a luxury in this dry climate. Of course, it's the thick-bladed African grass, which grows in tufts, not the fine 'bowling green' kind we have back home. In one corner of the garden, a tall, skinny African man is tending the flowerbeds. He rises enthusiastically to his feet on seeing us:

"*Bienvenue messieurs-dames!* Welcome!"

As Doctor Dave works for the US Embassy, I already know exactly what the interior of his house will look like: beige wall-to-wall carpets, a green and golden four-piece suite (with matching footstool) and 'Stag' mahogany furniture. It's the same in US Embassy houses worldwide and, of course, there's 24-7 air-conditioning in every room too.

As we're touring the 'mansion', I tell Dave about my mosquito infestation.

"Oh yeah, that's a big problem here, especially where you are, by the river. They die off a bit in dry season, but at this time of year, they breed in every conceivable pool or swamp."

"When's dry season again?"

"November. Your guy's spray gun ought to do the trick, for a while at least. It kills the mosquitoes which are there but doesn't stop others from coming in."

Dave's medical brain kicks in, and he asks: "What anti-malarial pills are you taking, Rob?"

"Lois and I are on doxycycline. I tried Lariam when we were in Benin, but it didn't agree with me." That's an understatement – my heart beat so fast it would regularly stop for a second or two, returning with a giant, finger-tingling BOOM! Add to this a constant state of panic, frequent insomnia, vivid dreams (when I *could* sleep!) and dramatic mood swings, then Lariam really isn't my drug of choice. Our kids take it, though, as doxycycline would cause their adult teeth to emerge a permanently grey colour – a curious side-effect indeed.

"Bertha took Lariam when the boys were babies," Dave tells me. "If you're breastfeeding, the kids get the Lariam through the milk too, so don't need their own anti-malarials. But we both take Malarone now." The best choice in many ways, but pricey at one pound per daily tablet.

I ask Dave about the malaria risks here.

"In Bamako, you're likely to get around 20 infectious bites per year, but if you go down to the coast, to Abidjan, Lomé or Accra, then you can expect at least 200 a year."

So, although I'm being constantly devoured by mozzies here, I'm ten times less likely to get malaria than in Benin; a small but significant consolation.

"You could get dengue fever, though, but that's fairly rare and seldom fatal."

Nice to know. Sensing my slight unease, Dave changes the subject:

"Do you have a Malian surname yet, Rob?"

"No. Why would I want one of those?"

"Oh, you MUST have a Malian name. Without one, you won't be fully accepted by the locals."

"But…it won't be my *real* name, just a made up one. Won't they see through it?"

"That doesn't matter. What's important is being willing to adopt a Malian identity so that you can take part in all the greetings and banter."

"Sounds fun. What's yours?"

"Coulibaly."

As Dave is the *fourth* Coulibaly I've met today, I resolve to choose any name but this. I think of other surnames I already know: I met a Keita –

sounds a bit boring though.   There's Koné, Diarra, Diabaté, Kouyaté...then there's Konaré, Kamara...

"Dave, there was a bloke singing at the church in town last week. He was very good. His name was Trowley, or something."

"That would be *Traoré*. It's a good choice if you like it. There was even a Malian president with that name a few years ago."

That's that then. From now on – to Malians at least – I shall no longer be Baker, but Traoré.[9]

Our kids are eager to go back outside, where there's also a pool – twice as big as ours – complete with a small slide.   They excitedly ascend its concrete steps and whizz down one by one, splashing contentedly into the cool blue water.   Growing up in Benin, they've always loved pools and can happily spend hours in the water, making up their own games, or playing ones they've picked up.

"Marco...Polo...Marco...Polo!"

As the four adults look on from the veranda, each with an ice cold 'Flag' beer, I begin to relax and feel I could get used to Malian life. After tucking into a dinner of *sloppy Joes* with corn on the cob and fried plantain, Dave gets out his alto sax and I join him at their Roland electric piano. He's familiar with some of my favourite jazz tunes: Georgia on My Mind...Satin Doll...Autumn Leaves. We jam the night away in air-conditioned bliss, each song followed by applause from the others.   Mali is not an easy country to live in, with an oppressive climate, dangerous traffic, confrontational police and mosquitoes galore, but times like this make life here just that bit more bearable.

Next morning, I continue my seemingly interminable quest for a reliable tin-opener. Five minutes away, surrounded by muddy roads littered with black bags, lies the chaotic mass of wood, tarpaulin and sheet metal known as Badala Market. I stoop through a tiny opening into a labyrinth of dingy corridors, uneven floors and corrugated stalls. Everything is arranged by theme, rather like in a department store, though that's where the similarity ends. The first stalls all sell African fabric: multi-coloured and stacked in neatly folded rolls from floor to ceiling.   Every conceivable colour

---

[9] Pronounced [*tra-oh-ray*]

combination seems to exist: purple and yellow; brown, red and pink; orange, lime green and royal blue – you name it. There's seldom anything black, grey or too white, and I notice that red is less common than other colours. These *pagnes* are hugely popular, brightening streets and markets across the Dark Continent, and include some rather culturally incongruous designs: parrots in cages, knives and forks, toasters, beer bottles, hairdryers. I once bought one covered in iPods, and another featuring the face of Barack Obama.

The tradition of wearing these colourful fabrics doesn't even originate in Africa, but rather in Indonesia. In the late nineteenth century, passing ships would stop off in West Africa and sell their Javan batiks to make a spot of cash. The locals got the taste for these vibrant designs, and the rest is history.

Mali has its own traditional brown, white and black fabric, known as *bogolan,*[10] which has a genuine rustic beauty of its own. But the lightweight, lurid, imported fabrics are favoured by the majority of Malians, even though they are produced in Europe these days.

"*Monsieur*, you want to buy?"

I've made the mistake of momentarily touching one of the *pagnes* – a clear non-verbal sign I'm interested in making a purchase (which I'm not).

"How much?" I ask, out of politeness and convention.

"7000."

"Ah! Surely not!" You have to be shocked by the first price they give, as it's bound to be inflated at least twofold, especially if you're a toubab.

"But this is Wax, *Monsieur*. Best quality."

Fabric impregnated with wax is common these days and gives your costume shiny and vaguely waterproof properties. With 'Wax' fabric, you can see the design clearly on both sides, though I've never understood why this is important.

Further down this dingy corridor is the *Dead Toubab Market*, selling second-hand clothes from Europe and the States. T-shirts and jeans are the most popular items, along with footwear, baseball caps – even sweatshirts, coats and hoodies ('for the cold season'). It's called the Dead Toubab Market as it is assumed the only reason a white man would part

---

[10] Meaning 'mud cloth'

with his clothes is if he were already dead.

Clothing moves to shoes, bicycle repairs, mobile phones, and finally hardware and kitchenware. Here I somewhat optimistically buy yet another tin opener; a different model from the first three.

Next comes my least favourite section: huge slabs of raw beef, goat and lamb sitting on rickety, blood-soaked wooden tables, plagued with swarms of flies. No pork in Muslim Mali, of course. I hold my breath and move fast, although the next section is little better: live chickens, turkeys and guinea fowl, all clucking away in tiny cages, waiting to be bought and slaughtered. Finally, there's fruit and veg: tomatoes in neat parallel rows, oranges in pyramids, bunches of bananas cut straight from the plant, juicy ripe mangos, lush green papayas, and even a few punnets of strawberries (imported, I'm told, from Burkina Faso next door). There are spices too: cinnamon, ginger, chilli peppers and sackfuls of *dah:* dried purple hibiscus flowers, which are boiled up to create a tasty drink.

In one corner of the market is an unusual tent-like structure, where a man in a pale-blue turban is sitting on a large mat adorned with pretty silver bracelets, earrings and necklaces. He's pouring what looks like treacle into a small glass. I poke my head inside the tarpaulin and am greeted with a welcoming smile from his wrinkly dark face:

"*Mon ami, asseyez-vous!*"

I perch on a carved wooden stool little higher than the ground itself, facing a tiny metal stove, whose white coals are slowly heating a slender silver teapot. Unlike a British teapot, this one has a hinged pointy lid, a thin curved spout and an ornately embossed handle, giving it a much more Turkish look.

"*Vous aimez le thé?*"

"I do like tea, but I've never tried *this* tea before."

"Ah, you must try *les trois tasses,* my friend."

"Three cups? Isn't one enough?"

"Ah, my friend," he laughs, "you don't know the three cups! How long have you been in Mali?"

"Just a few days, actually."

In front of him is a round silver platter containing what look like half a dozen shot glasses. He pours tea into one of them from a height of around two feet, then empties the glass back into the top of the teapot, repeating the process several times to aid the brewing process. Finally, he pours my cup, but before serving it, empties it into another glass and back again several times – all from a great height.

"To add more oxygen to the tea, my friend," he explains.

He hands me my first 'cup': dark, rich and frothy on top, looking more like a miniature pint of Guinness than a cup of tea.

"*Lentement,*" he advises.

I slowly sip the tea. Arrggghhh! It tastes horribly bitter and unbelievably strong. No milk either. I attempt to suppress my facial expressions, but fail abysmally.

"This is a normal reaction, my friend. The first cup is *amer comme la mort* – as bitter as death."

Why drink it then? I can't help but wonder…

"My name is Youssouf Ag Alwali," he continues. "I am Tamasheq, from Timbuktu."

The Tamasheq are also known as Tuaregs (but prefer being called the former), and can often be seen riding camels or fine horses in the north of the country. They number over half a million in Mali and are even more numerous in Niger next door. The Tamasheq lay claim to the northern half of Mali, which they call Azawad, and have fought for its independence many times.

"Pleased to meet you, Youssouf. My name is Robert…Robert Traoré."

"*Enchanté!* But you should have chosen a Tamasheq name."

He adds more water and sugar to the teapot and gives it a stir, repeating his 'pour and return' routine several times as it heats up. He serves my second cup and I take a tentative sip: this one is not bad at all.

"*Doux comme la vie.*"

"Sorry?"

"The second cup. We say it is as pleasant as life."

"It's definitely an improvement on the first!"

"Monsieur Traoré, are you a Christian?"

I hesitate. Although he seems delightful, this guy is a Muslim from an ethnic group renowned for violence.

"Yes." I respond, "I am a follower of Isa."[11]

---

[11] Jesus

"I don't like Christians!"

"But you like me…don't you?" I ask, nervously.

"You are okay, but Christians are not truly submitted to Allah. Not like Muslims," he says, adding yet more water and sugar to his pot. "Islam means submission; you claim to follow the ways of Allah, but you are gluttonous, you love money and you get drunk."

"I try not to love money or food too much, and I don't get drunk."

"But do you drink alcohol?"

"In moderation, yes."

"Why? Why do you need this drug?"

"Well…I suppose I like the taste. It's also a cultural thing. You drink three cups of tea; we drink beer…and tea."

"Why not just tea?"

"I don't know. I admit my country has an alcohol problem; getting regularly drunk is a major pastime there. But most Christians do not buy into this; like you, we believe it's not good to get drunk."

"You do?" he responds, raising his eyebrows so high they disappear beneath his turban.

"Yes."

"So, why does England call itself a Christian country?"

"I suppose it was once, but it is becoming less so. But the followers of *Isa al Masih* do their best to submit to God and follow His ways."

He ponders momentarily, then pours my third cup. "This one, we say, is *sucré comme l'amour* – as sweet as love."

It barely even tastes like tea, more like sugary water.

"I like it, but the second cup was best."

"You are right, Monsieur Traoré, the second cup is always the best."

On a day-to-day basis, thousands of Malians will gather for this simple, three-cup ritual. Chatting under neem trees, joking together in courtyards or simply relaxing at the market. And so these three cups: bitter as death, pleasant as life and sweet as love (always in that order), form a delightful and unmistakable part of Malian culture.

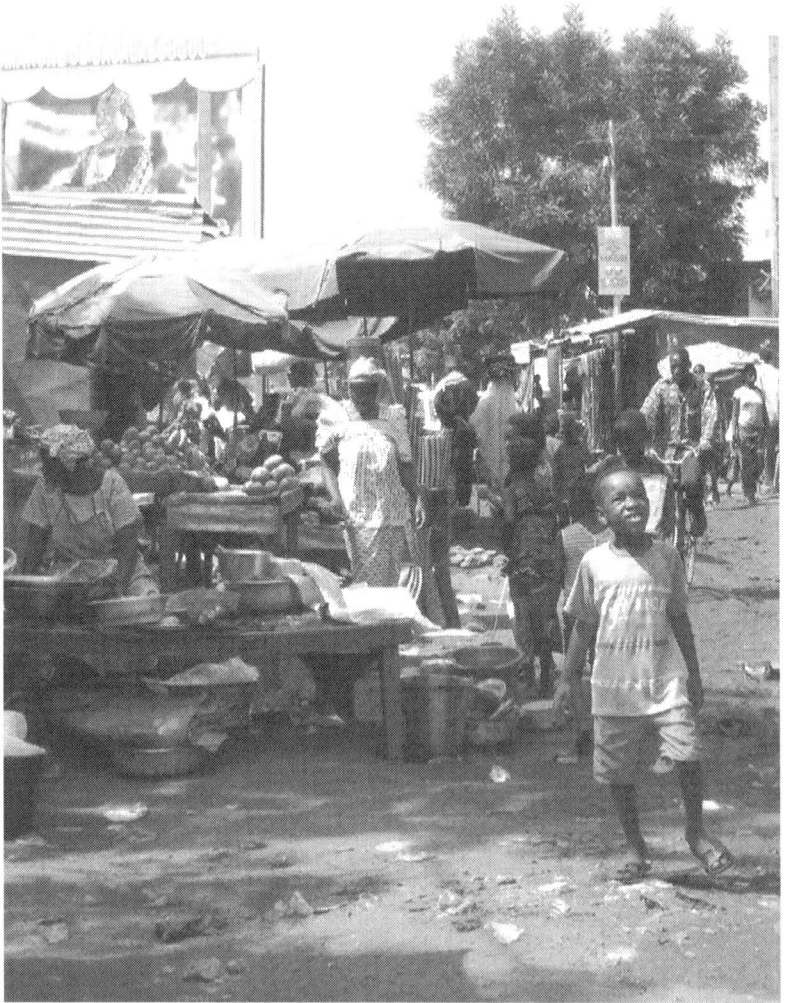

Badalabougou Market, Bamako

Chapter Four – Sickening!

"Always find a reputable dentist in Africa, even if it's expensive."

"GIVE ME YOUR thumb, *monsieur*. Have you had this done before?"

"At least a dozen times."

I'm at the *Clinique Pasteur* for a malaria test, known locally as the *goutte épaisse,* or thick smear. If positive, this will be my seventh ever bout of malaria, the first being almost 20 years ago in *Côte d'Ivoire*. Back then, I had the recurrent variety, which returned every few weeks and was finally cured by a brutal regime of quinine and tetracycline. By the end of this, I weighed a shocking 130 pounds and looked like an extra from a zombie apocalypse movie. It's no fun waking up with buzzing ears, blue lips and a head that feels like it has a spear through it.

This morning I could barely get out of bed, stricken with fever and non-stop shivers; both early signs of malaria. So Lois drove me straight here for *the test*. It only takes a few seconds – a prick on the thumb and a drop of blood squeezed onto a glass slide. Always make sure it's a freshly opened needle, though.

"Call at noon, sir."

Three hours later, I rouse from a deep slumber, head pounding, mouth dry as a bone, and wearily fumble for my Nokia 3010.

"Monsieur Baker. C'est positive! Quatre cents."

My fears are confirmed. A parasite density of 400 per microlitre of blood is pretty mild but still potentially fatal. I've had counts of over 1000 in the past, and have heard of people surviving 5000 or more.

To imagine what Malaria is like, think of your worst case of the 'flu, then double it. No, treble it. The first symptom for me is waking up feeling like I've had a lousy night's sleep, even though I didn't. By the second day, I notice I'm sweating more than normal, and by day three, I struggle to stand up and am wrought with nasty shivers. This is today – the point at which it's always wise to go for a blood test. The malaria parasite has already begun to destroy my red blood cells, and this destruction will increase exponentially. Untreated, I'd be dead in less than a fortnight.

No need for a doctor's prescription here in Africa; I simply write down the medication on a piece of paper and send Abdoulaye to the local chemist's, where they will read it (as he can't) and hand over the medicine, always in a neat brown paper bag. In recent years, a Chinese herb called *artesunate* has revolutionized malaria treatment, as it's fast-acting and has virtually no side-effects. Within a couple of days, you're already feeling better, but a second malaria treatment is taken alongside it, to be sure the parasite is killed off for good. I'm taking *Co-Arinate* which, the box says, is artesunate combined with pyrimethamine and sulfamethoxypyrazine, whatever those are. Let's hope it works.

I cancel everything planned and spend the rest of the day in bed, doing virtually nothing. I feel like an 80-year-old and am too tired to watch TV or use the computer; even reading is a strain on my poor deoxygenated brain. They say that when you first come down with malaria you worry you'll die, but then after a few days of the illness, you're more concerned that you're *not* going to die…

Two further days of headaches, lethargy and shivers, and the medication finally begins to work: I wake up and feel *good* for the first time. And I actually have some energy too, as my red blood cells begin to replenish, providing my body with the vital oxygen it has been lacking. This doesn't last long, though, and I'm back in bed by mid-morning, with the side effects of the other drugs now making me feel lousy. I also have a stiff neck and non-stop headache, so am alternating paracetamol and ibuprofen every few hours. The inside of my mouth tastes metallic and feels red raw, and to top it all, there's a power cut today, so the house is boiling and almost pitch black. Around 6pm, just before nightfall, I take a short stroll down our undulating street. The exercise and relative coolness of the evening do me good, but I collapse into bed upon return, only minutes after setting out.

I wish I could say malaria was the only trauma of the past few weeks but, alas, there have been many others. So much so, that I've considered jacking it all in and going home; were it not for our clear sense of calling to this country, we might easily have done so.

The arrival of our much-awaited Mitsubishi Montero has not been straightforward either. Back in the UK, I bought it on eBay from a Hungarian minicab driver in Slough named Zoltan. The vehicle sat on our driveway for several weeks before being shipped. It was due to arrive in Mali around the time we did but got held up in Dakar – some mix up at customs. Then in late August our clearing agent, Mr Cissé, called.

"Monsieur, votre véhicule est arrivé!"

In the middle of nowhere, on the edge of Bamako, lies a huge muddy yard surrounded by high concrete walls. Inside is nothing but a small building and several sidings. In one of these sat a rickety railway transporter carrying seven cars, including ours. Unbelievably (by British standards), I was allowed to climb up on top via a severely deformed ladder and physically touch the car.

"Can I drive it home today?" I asked excitedly.

"No, my friend!" smiled Cissé. "There's lots of paperwork first, and customs checks. Maybe before the end of the week."

Eight days later, the car was finally freed. I pulled up outside our house and honked proudly. Within seconds, Mr Kouyaté's joyous face appeared at the garage door.

"Ah, le véhicule! Jolie voiture! C'est venu enfin! Bravo, bravo!"

Once we've unloaded our stuff (including Micah's drum kit, an electric piano, a TV and, of course, a didgeridoo), we decide to take it out for a spin. The children climb up excitedly into their new car, vying for who gets to sit in the third row of seats, right at the back. The rear windows are all tinted, which will be good for keeping out the sun; it also means our kids won't be pestered by beggars and salesmen at every junction.

As we trundle off down our bumpy dirt road I turn on the radio and discover a CD still inside: 'Ocean Drive' by The Lighthouse Family. It must've belonged to Zoltan – I hope he's not missing it too much! As it's the only CD in the car at present, I press play and the joyous tones of *Lifted* ring out.

Alas, our joy is short lived: round the next corner, an angry-faced policeman blows his whistle and pulls us over.

"What is this?" he bellows.

"It's The Lighthouse Family," I say with a smile. He's not impressed.

"Your number plate, monsieur. Where is it from?"

"England."

"It is not legal here. I will have to impound this vehicle. Step out at once!"

"But…but…I've just picked it up," I blurt back in panic, "and my children are in the back."

He glances at the rear of the car. "And that's another offence: tinted glass is illegal in Mali. This is a republic."

I'm not sure what that's got to do with it. "Look, I'll remove the tinted layer from the glass, but please let me take my car home. I'll go right away and not drive it again. I live very close…"

"No! I have to enforce the law, *monsieur*, and your car is not legal."

Just then, I have an idea: "Let me call my clearing agent!"

Without even waiting for his approval, I pull out the Nokia and call Cissé's number as the officer looks on menacingly.

BRING BRING…BRING BRING…BRING BRING...

Come on…pick up!

BRING BRING…BRING BRING…

"This is the voicemail of Malik Cissé…"

"Let me try one more time," I beg, desperately trying to buy myself more time. To my great relief, Cissé picks up this time and I explain our predicament.

"Hand your phone to the *policier*." he says. I do so reluctantly, fearing I'll lose that too. The policeman listens, saying 'Mmm' and 'Aha' every now and then. After a rather lengthy chat, he hands me back my phone.

"*Allô?*"

"Yes, Cissé, what did he say?"

"You can take the car home. And you're fine to drive it any time. I explained that the paperwork is done and the new plates are being made." With that, I give a cursory nod to the policeman and drive slowly away, straight home.

"Mummy, my tooth hurts!"

Madelaine, our eldest, has just come into our room at 5am. Lois grabs a torch and shines it into her mouth: the gum around one of her lower molars is very red and she's in a lot of pain. Back home, toothache would be easy enough to solve, but here decent dentists are few and far between. Someone at work mentioned *Monsieur André*, a French dentist, which sounds promising. As soon as it's light, we hop into a half green, half yellow taxi with the words 'OBAMA' emblazoned across the side and no knob on its gearstick. Although it's still Ramadan, I notice the driver is eating a piece of bread.

"Are you not a Muslim?"

"I am, but I have a fever. If you are sick, you do not have to observe the Ramadan fast."

"But you're well enough to drive this taxi."

"Yes. I'm sick, but I still need to feed my family."

The dental surgery is accessed via a creaky door in a small courtyard behind a two-storey, grey building. At the top of a narrow, uneven staircase is a small, dark landing with a warped metal door in one corner. A dog-eared piece of A4 paper pinned to the door reads:

Monsieur André, Dentiste

I give a hollow knock on the rickety door. No reply. I try again, this time adding the customary '*Ko ko ko!*' for effect. A skinny young man, no older than 19, opens the door and beckons me into a tiny waiting room, then promptly disappears. The floor is patchily tiled and the walls are painted the ubiquitous matt mint green, tarnished with multiple brown stains. There are three cracked plastic chairs down one side of the room and a slatted glass window opposite, looking down to the tiny courtyard below; several of the glass slats are dislodged or missing. On the ceiling hangs a wobbly fan and beside it a single, dim lightbulb suspended from curled red and black wires barely illuminates the top half of this tiny room. On a small dark table sit a handful of magazines, most of which, bizarrely, are in Portuguese. After roughly half an hour, the young man reappears.

"*Entrez!*"

In the centre of his dimly lit surgery is a huge mustard yellow, vinyl-coated chair with beige foam protruding at various points. An antiquated angle-poise lamp hangs from a rusty metal stand and, beside it, a heavy wooden table is home to a disturbing range of Victorian implements which wouldn't pass an audition for *Little Shop of Horrors.*

"What can I do for you?" the young boy asks.

"Erm…where is *Monsieur André?*" I ask, perplexed.

"*Monsieur André?*" he responds, shocked at my even mentioning the name. "He's in France. He retired years ago. I work for *Monsieur Koné.*"

"And where is he?"

"It's his day off today."

Monsieur André, it turns out, came to Mali in the Eighties, having managed a successful dental surgery in the Dordogne. After a few years, he took on a young apprentice by the name of Koné. A quick learner, Koné was soon working full-time as his assistant, and as the years went by he picked up Monsieur André's dentistry techniques – or most of them at least. André gave him formal training in fillings, tooth extraction and even root canals (a procedure he never quite mastered). Nevertheless, Koné began practising dentistry under the close supervision of his tutor. Then, roughly a decade ago, Monsieur André retired back to France and Koné continued the practice, recently taking on his own apprentice – the young chap we're seeing today.

"I'd rather see Monsieur Koné – is he back tomorrow?"

"Yes, but we're fully booked tomorrow…and the day after that." I can't help noticing the waiting room is completely empty today, though.

"Tell me the problem and I'll see if I can help – today," he adds, tapping the arm of his dodgy yellow chair. He may have learned dentistry by Chinese whisper, but that doesn't necessarily make him incompetent, does it?

Madelaine takes a seat, looking slightly terrified. His dim search light creaks in protest as he carefully manoeuvres it into position.

"*Ouvre la bouche!*"

He pulls Madelaine's right cheek out with his gloveless forefinger and peers inside, inserting his little round mirror for a clearer view. He spends what feels like an age staring, pulling, changing angle and scratching his head, then finally turns to me:

"She has an abscess. Look!" he proudly announces, grabbing a spiky tool and poking violently at Mads' gum, as she winces with pain. Yellow pus oozes out.

"Ewww, yes, I see. What's the solution?"

"I will remove the filling to open up the nerve, then give her antibiotics."

"No need, *monsieur,* just the antibiotics will be fine. Which ones?" I ask, keen to make a swift exit.

We pass by the pharmacy on the way home and pick up her antibiotics. The treatment has limited success, and we're back a week later; this time I make sure Mr Koné is in. He removes the filling, puts wadding in the gap and prescribes the same antibiotics again, along with pain-killers. A further week of these and we return to have the tooth filled, and all is well. For about ten days, that is. Then the pain returned, twice as bad. Giving up Koné and his mate as a bad job, I call Doctor Dave to enquire about other dentists in Bamako:

"You didn't go to Koné, The Bamako Butcher, did you?!" he exclaims, reassuringly. "Try Barouche, the Lebanese guy, over the river in the *Cité du Niger.*"

There are plenty of Lebanese folk in West Africa, but Barouche is the only one in dentistry; most of his compatriots run restaurants, own supermarkets or import vehicles. He's an excellent dentist but doesn't come cheap. His state of the art clinic makes many British ones look antiquated, though. After a couple of X-rays, he confirms that Mads needs her root canal removing and offers me a cup of coffee while I wait – strong, black and gritty, just how the Lebanese like it. It'll take three further visits to rectify the problem and will cost a total of £300 – almost half a year's wages for many Malians.

"She's lucky not to have lost that tooth, *monsieur,*" he tells me. "She'll need a crown on it when she's eighteen, but until then she mustn't bite down hard on the tooth, as it could split in two."

She's only twelve now, so that's six years of 'no toffees on the right side'. We live and learn: always find a reputable dentist in Africa, even if it's expensive. Or, better still, get your teeth done when you're back home.

One piece of good news (or so we thought) was finding a violin teacher for Madelaine – a young chap called Leonard from the American school up the road; a highly accomplished musician who used to play with the New York Philharmonic. Extremely thorough, he gave Madelaine her first lesson at his apartment, correcting her hand position and giving her some first-rate advice. The second lesson was the same: spot on, and Mads was learning fast. We were so grateful for this chap, as skilled Western musicians out here are like gold dust. Third week, we turned up and his Dutch flatmate opened the door, glancing at us in confusion.

"What do *you* want?" he asked, with typical Netherlandic directness.

"It's her violin lesson, is Leonard here?"

"No, he's left."

"When is he back?"

"He's left Mali."

"For a vacation?"

"No. He flew out of Mali two days ago. Forever. He's not coming back. He hated it here, and the violin was his only consolation. It got too much for him, so he left."

Just like that, and without a word to any of his other pupils. This is sadly not the first time I've come across this kind of thing. Some expats become so overwhelmed by the cultural differences, the harsh climate and the constant barrage of things going wrong that they just up and leave. Many don't even have the heart to let people know; they just leave a note on the dining table – almost like a suicide – saying they've gone and won't be back. I do sympathize with Leonard, especially right now, as to be honest I wouldn't mind following suit.

Even my first Malian haircut was a somewhat traumatic experience. Many African hairdressers have little or no experience of cutting straight, Western hair, and some attempt to apply the same rules they use for Afro hair. This was the case in the nice-looking salon I went to, just up the road. After an entire hour in the *chair of doom*, I emerged looking like a cross between Milton Jones and Sonic Hedgehog – and five pounds poorer for the privilege.

The Mitsubishi is now officially on the road, even if the number plates are made of cardboard and held in place with garden twine (a temporary but legal measure, until the proper ones arrive). Having regained most of my energy after malaria, I take it for a drive into town. I'm halfway down the *Boulevard de l'Indépendance*, when I notice the temperature gauge rising. And as I edge my way past a broken down sotrama, the needle goes up rapidly, and I feel the car losing power. I know there's a Total station and workshop about 100 yards ahead, but the engine is smoking now, and I can barely see where I'm going. 50 yards to go…30…10. The car judders forwards and I make a sharp left, free-wheeling down onto the forecourt.

"*Monsieur! Vous-avez un problème!*"

You don't say!

"I can help!" says the young mechanic, nodding convincingly. And with that he grabs an old rag and opens the cap on the water tank, almost scalding his hand in the process. He disappears into the workshop, returning with a large watering can of cold water, which he proceeds to pour straight into the engine.

"I don't think you should do…"

Too late.

"Start the engine, *monsieur!*" he says confidently, as though this will solve everything. For now, the gauge is back to normal. I head straight back home, making it to the top of our street before the temperature rises again. From here, I free-wheel the rest of the way down the hill to our house.

Pete has recommended a good Chinese mechanic in our neighbourhood, so half an hour later my steaming Mitsubishi and I pull up in front of his rust-red metal gates.

A small Chinese lady opens the gates.

"*Zăo shang hăo!*" she proudly proclaims, with a big smile. I assume this to be some kind of greeting. She's in her mid 50s with long greying hair tied in a traditional bun on top of her head, held in place with what look like a pair of chopsticks. Wearing a long multicoloured African dress and a pair of flimsy grey flip-flops, she motions me to drive the car down a sloping concrete driveway alongside their humble, single-storey home, which is adorned with hanging red lanterns. At the bottom I drive onto a makeshift inspection pit, dug out by hand.

"*Bonjour Madame!*" I offer her my hand, which she shakes limply.

"*Bojou. Mari vien. Mari vien!*" Her husband is on his way, she tells me in broken French. A short, scrawny man appears at the door of his sheet metal workshop, wearing faded blue overalls and worn out Nike trainers. *Chao Cheng* has a friendly but heavily wrinkled face and a balding head of hair with a mind of its own. Roughly translated, his name means 'excellent journey', and I'd certainly like to have one of those soon. Popular among rich Malians and expats alike, he's not the world's fastest mechanic, but he is thorough, knowledgeable and – most importantly – cheap.

Chao Cheng, his wife and their one child came over from China twenty years ago when he got a job with a construction company here. With his earnings, he eventually bought this house which, over time, has morphed into his workshop. Their lounge is littered with car parts and the dining room has become the office, so I'm not really sure where they relax. After a good half an hour with his head under the bonnet, he rises and looks at me, shaking his head sadly:

"*Kilasse. Kilasse sepabon!*"

He clearly speaks very little French either – let alone English.

"*Sepabon, sepabon!*"

Ah! He's trying to say: '*Ce n'est pas bon*' – it's not good. But *what* is not good?

Just then, his wife appears with a Chinese-French dictionary, pointing excitedly at the one word: '*Culasse*'. Oh dear…that would be the cylinder head. We attempt to discuss the issue further, but he only speaks Chinese, very basic Bambara and virtually no French. And so, through a series of mimes, drawings in the sand, pointing at the engine and repeating words loudly, I gather that our cylinder head needs repairing or replacing. I spin my finger round in front of my watch, to ask how long the job might take. He pulls a doubtful face and draws five straight lines in the sand. I'm hoping that's days, not weeks.

Zigzagging through Badala Market on my walk back home, I pop in to greet my new Tamasheq friend, Youssouf. He greets me warmly, shaking my hand firmly.

"You want tea?"

"Just the second and third cups, please." The first is far too bitter and left me wired for hours last time.

"I hear there are more troubles in your country," he says, referring to recent riots and a bombing in Northern Ireland. "They need to trust in Allah."

"I agree people need to follow God. But there's violence in Muslim countries too, right?"

"Yes, but your Western countries are depraved. Nothing is sacred anymore. Your children are addicted to drugs, you love money, and you no longer recognize marriage. Allah does not want this!"

"Christians do not want this either."

"And we Africans don't like your Western democracy," he adds, pouring my first-but-second cup from a great height.

"You don't?"

"No! And the only reason Africans accept elections is because your countries give money to democratic nations. Africa doesn't *want* democracy; we try to *look* democratic for you toubabs. But everyone knows who's going to win."

"They do?"

"Of course. That's how it works here. Third cup?"

"Yes Please!"

Thinking of the three cups of tea: bitter as death, pleasant as life and sweet as love, makes me realize that all cultures have a bit of all three in them. There are some sweet and pleasant parts to life in Africa – mangos, sunshine, friendly smiles and wildlife. But there are also some nasty bitter ones, like corruption, malaria and violent elections. Britain too, has its good and bad sides. No one culture is perfect.

I return to the Chao Cheng's workshop a week later. His young Malian assistant is with him today, which helps communication somewhat.

"He says he has replaced the head gasket, but that didn't work. Then he skimmed the cylinder head and that didn't work either."

So now it needs a new cylinder head, which is going to cost almost £1000, way more than we can afford.

"He could try and find a second hand cylinder head…"

"How much?" I interrupt, eagerly.

He mutters to Chao Cheng again, who writes '300,000' in the sand. That's about £400. Below it, he then writes: +/- 100,000. Got it!

He finds one a couple of days later for exactly three hundred thousand, and I agree for the work to be done. But this means that my first big trip – to Dogon Country – won't be in my own vehicle. I'll need to ask around for an alternative, as I really don't want to cancel my first proper trip.

Chapter Five – On Eating Beans

"The Tamasheq people get a bad press."

DARKNESS CLOAKS THE silent marketplace of *Daoudabougou* as the almost full moon casts eerie shadows of empty stalls across the litter-ridden ground. It's 5.30am and I shiver at 21 Celsius; something I never thought possible back home. I tentatively tap on Monsieur Keita's small metal gate, almost whispering: *"Ko ko ko!"* then step into the courtyard. A single storey concrete building sits in one corner, with a ragged curtain hanging across its timber-framed doorway. Tiny square windows are the only other source of light or ventilation, each equipped with a corrugated metal shutter, hinged at the top and propped open with a short branch; a simple but effective system. A pair of *papaya* trees stand proudly in the opposite corner, both fifteen feet tall with half a dozen green, rugby-ball-shaped fruits hanging from the top. A dozen chickens cluck and peck their way around my feet as I wait for my friend to rise. A couple of grubby goats bleat to greet the new day and a sole rooster crows intermittently, lit only by the waning moon.

"*Ko ko ko!*" I repeat, with slightly more force, though not wanting to wake everyone else. Keita's house consists of two interconnecting rooms: one where he and his wife sleep, the other for the children.

"Traoré, i ni sogoma!" [12]

Wrapped in a typically colourful African cloth, Madame Keita emerges from behind the curtain and greets me warmly.

"Keita tara sisan!"

She tells me her husband will be right out. Within seconds, the curtain swings open to reveal a tall, skinny man wearing nothing but a towel round his waist and holding a stripy plastic bucket in one hand. His face is warm and full of energy, and between his somewhat prominent ears, his eyes sparkle with joy at seeing me. He bares his crooked, discoloured teeth in a warm smile.

---

[12] Good morning, Traoré

"*I Traoré!*" he exclaims (You Traoré!), shaking my hand warmly, as I hope to goodness his towel is well-attached.

"*I Keita!*" I reply in the customary fashion.

"I'm going to take a shower," he announces. I'd surmised as much.

Madame Keita offers me a seat outside while I wait. With a single match, she lights the logs in the firepit, as she does every morning, then rests a heavy iron cooking pot on three large stones over the roaring flames. The smell of smoke fills the air, masking the stench of the open sewer just outside the gate.

Two cheeky faces appear from inside the house: Prosper and Dieu-donné, the Keitas' two boys. Aged six and four, these young chaps have typical African Christian names (meaning 'prosper' and 'God-given'). Other classic examples include *Patience*, *Fidèle*, *Divine*, *Abondance* and the somewhat curious *Conception*. The Nigerians are the masters of such names, where even their current president is called Good Luck!

The two boys catch sight of me and almost instantly launch into their customary greeting:

"*Toubab! Toubab! Toubab!*"

Their 'white man greeting' continues for some time, until mum intervenes: "*Les enfants! Ça suffit!*"

My second colleague, Monsieur Coulibaly, should be here by now. We agreed on a 6am departure, but punctuality is not a particularly important part of most African cultures.

"*Coulibaly be min?*" I ask Mrs Keita, wondering where he has got to.

"*A tara sisan.*" She says he's coming right away. We'll see...

Our plan today is to reach the edge of *Dogon Country* by nightfall – a mere 400 miles northeast of here. As my car is still with the Chinese mechanic, we'll be travelling in a borrowed Toyota Hilux today. The Dogon have a rich and fascinating culture, quite different from others in Africa. Because of this, they have been the subject of much research over the years, and many books, documentaries and papers have been devoted to their study. So much so that there is a well-known saying in these parts:

> *How many members are there in a Dogon family?*
> *Seven: Mum, Dad, four children and one French anthropologist.*

The main purpose of my visit is to find out how the Dogon make music and what they use it for. I've learned a bit about the Dogon from Abdoulaye, our house help, but am looking forward to experiencing their lifestyle first hand.

It's 7.30am, and the rising sun is shining obliquely across the courtyard. Keita is now showered, dressed and ready to go. Moments later, we hear the distant buzzing of a moped engine as it turns the corner of the sandy road. The engine cuts out and the courtyard gate swings open to reveal a short, portly chap in his forties, beaming all over his face. More jovial than his colleague (though, interestingly, less talkative), he carefully lifts his pale-blue Chinese-built 'Power-K' moped over the concrete threshold. No crash helmet, of course, or rear view mirrors, and I can't help noticing that the seat of his moped is covered in pink plastic depicting *Barbie*. I doubt he has any idea who she is.

"*Aw ni sɔgɔma!*" he joyously announces, wishing us all a good morning.

Warmly shaking each other's hands, Messrs Coulibaly and Keita launch into the lengthy Bambara greetings, which they reel off every time they meet:

"You Keita!"

"Ah! You Coulibaly!"

"Good morning!"

"Good morning!"

"Was your sleep peaceful?"

"There is peace."

"How are the folks at home?"

"They're well."

"And your wife?"

"She's well."

"And your children?"

"Fine."

"And your father?"

"He's well."

"And your mother?"

"Fine."

"How's your work?"

"Work is good!"

"And the animals?"

"They're fine."

"God bless your morning!"

"Amen!"

"God bless your family!"

"Amen!"

"God bless your journey!"

"Amen!"

If we ever get started on our journey, that is. These greetings are then repeated in the opposite direction, the whole tirade lasting no more than a few seconds, as rapid questions and responses bounce back and forth like a ping-pong ball. Of course, it sounds much nicer in Bambara, where the word 'amen' (*'amiina'*) is said with oozing enthusiasm and positivity. Greetings move straight into humorous insults – a curious but important part of this culture. Coulibalys and Keitas are 'joking cousins' and will never miss a good opportunity for this kind of light-hearted mockery. Coulibaly starts the ball rolling:

"Keitas are bad!"

"Ah, no! Keitas are very good. Coulibalys are bad!"

"Ah, my friend! You are making a mistake. Coulibalys are the best; Keitas are the worst!"

Then comes my favourite bit:

"Coulibalys eat beans!" accuses Keita.

"No! Coulibalys *never* eat beans; it's the Keitas who eat all the beans!"

"Coulibalys are the biggest bean-eaters; they even grow beans!"

"Then we grow them to sell to *you* Keitas!"

"Never! Keitas would never eat beans; Coulibalys are thieves!"

"No, Keitas are thieves!"

"It's not true! Keitas are the kings of Mali."

"No, Coulibaly is king and the Keitas are our slaves!"

"Ah! You are mistaken, my friend. Coulibaly is the slave of Keita!"

This last insult shocked me greatly the first time I heard it; can you imagine calling anyone a *slave* in this day and age? And yet, these joking relationships are centuries old and are never seen as offensive within Malian culture. Their exchanges were carried out amidst much smiling and laughter, and many local folk attribute the peaceful, tolerant nature of

Malians to this kind of lively banter, which acts as an effective ice-breaker whilst reinforcing cultural identity. The bean-eating jokes are terribly common; the president himself has even been known to make such jibes in his speeches. But why choose bean eating as an insult? A student in Minnesota wrote a whole paper on the subject, stating:

> "*Beans* have the annoying property of causing one to bloat and break wind when one abuses them [...] Thus, beans whose consumption can lead to being discourteous (in breaking wind) are not sensibly consumed by any person of quality."[13]

Joking over, we climb on board and roar off, rising out of Bamako away from the Niger River on straight dual carriageways punctuated by traffic lights and crossroads. The city is already quite busy, with every other vehicle a yellow taxi or green sotrama. On either side of the road are rows of concrete shops selling clothes, second hand furniture, car parts and fast food. The ubiquitous hair salons display colourful hand-painted images of outlandish hairstyles on their walls. One such establishment, *Obama Coiffure*, portrays the US president brandishing an enormous pair of scissors. We're almost out of town now and turn left at the *Tour de l'Afrique*, whose gargantuan cooking pot rests upon three giant hands at its pinnacle.

The checkpoint at the city limits is surrounded by swarms of people selling sweetcorn, clothing, plastic bags of water, manioc, biscuits – even hair extensions. And, of course, more phonecard salesmen, chanting their favourite song: "*Orange! Orange! Orange!*" In addition to this pestilent maelstrom, there are some permanent stalls selling vegetables, water melons and large sacks of charcoal.

"*Ah, Monsieur Robert! On va acheter du charbon! Du charbon!*"

Mr Keita thinks we should buy some charcoal; I've no idea why we would want to do that.

"You see, Monsieur Robert, it's for the Hilux. The Hilux needs *le charbon!*"

"The Toyota needs coal? Doesn't it run on diesel?" I reply, tongue in

---

13 "You Eat Beans!" © Rachel Jones, Anthropology Department, Macalester College, April 30, 2007

cheek.

"*Ah, non monsieur!*" he laughs, "Not for fuel! It's to help with traction on the road."

"Traction?" I ask, with a frown.

"Yes, traction. Every time we travel in the Hilux, we have to buy four sacks of coal to put in the back of the vehicle. The extra weight helps the vehicle stay on the road; Madame Helga told us this."

Madame Helga is a former Austrian colleague who retired a year or two ago. She spent several decades doing charity work in Mali, so I guess she knew what she was doing. We purchase four sacks, which the burly salesman slings effortlessly onto the open cargo bed.

"When we get to Sevaré, we can give the charcoal to my brother," adds Keita, almost under his breath. "He will be very grateful."

"What about the return journey?" I ask.

"We will buy sacks of Dogon onions to bring home."

They've got it all planned out – and guess who's going to foot the bill in both cases. Mustn't complain though; Messrs Coulibaly and Keita are intelligent, hard-working, adaptable colleagues, whose monthly salary you or I earn in a day.

The hand-operated red and white barrier swings open to let us through the checkpoint. Eager to make up time, I accelerate past a row of trucks, parked up alongside us. As I clear the last of these, a huge cow appears from behind it.

"MOOOOOOO!"

I slam on the brakes and swerve to one side, narrowly missing our surprise bovine guest. The hefty beast lollops away without batting an eyelid, leaving me in a state of slight shock.

Noisy crowds, painted concrete buildings and rusty tin shacks are now gone, as urban sprawl gives way to vast open countryside and pretty sugarloaf hills. The fields, semi-parched at this time of the year, are nevertheless punctuated with the occasional spindly tree or hardy shrub. Large crops of gourds – pumpkin-like vegetables two feet across – garnish the bland terrain with dashes of green. The road itself, though pitted with frequent potholes, is better than many I've encountered on this continent. The greatest threat to our suspension is actually the man-made speed bumps at the entrance to each village. Usually in groups of three, these irksome obstacles lie stealthily in wait for the unsuspecting motorist, cunningly blending in with the grey road surface. To add insult to (likely) injury, many of these *gendarmes couchés* now also have potholes in them, creating what looks like an elongated volcano with a potentially tyre-ripping crater.

The villages occur every fifteen minutes or so. Most are tiny, with no more than a couple of dozen houses, a mango grove and a small mosque, identifiable by its mint-green dome, topped with a crescent moon. The houses are mostly square, concrete affairs, with small windows and tin or straw roofs; a rural variation on Keita's place.

It's late morning as we approach the first built-up area since Bamako: the pretty riverside town of Ségou, three hours to the north-east. Dark-green, spindly trees plentifully adorn the fields here, each around 12 feet tall and vaguely resembling upside-down Christmas trees in both shape and texture.

"Those are the famous *balanzan* trees," says Keita, pointing eagerly. "They have spikes instead of leaves. During the cold season, balanzans lose their needles and look like they're dead. Then, during dry season, the green spikes begin to grow back."

"Their needles grow back during *dry* season?"

"Yes! *Incroyable, n'est-ce pas?*"

"*Oui!*"

"The balanzan is the tree of Ségou," he continues, "and there are exactly 4444 *balanzan* trees in Ségou. All the locals know this." I can't help thinking that one may have died since the last count and spoiled their nice symmetrical number.

Being one of only a handful of towns on the road from Bamako to Dogon Country and eventually Timbuktu (Mali's top two tourist attractions), Ségou gets a fair trickle of Westerner visitors; mostly Americans, French and – of course – Germans. There are always German tourists wherever you go in the world. Not quite sure why; I guess they just like to travel.

As the *Lonely Planet Guide* states, Ségou is 'strung out lazily along the riverbank' and 'has a languid slow-paced charm'.[14] It also manages to

---

[14] West Africa Lonely Planet Guide 2006, p.501

create a pleasant, touristic atmosphere without ever feeling busy or overbearing. There is a good range of decent hotels serving excellent food, a bustling market and some interesting museums of local art. The three-wheeled taxis here are curious, and unique to Ségou: imagine the back of a pickup truck with a motorbike stuck on the front. Cheap, fast and convenient, these bizarre contraptions can carry up to eight people, ten at a push.

We stop off at the *Auberge de Ségou*, a popular hotel on a dusty road junction, a stone's throw from the riverbank. It is owned and run by a short, friendly Lebanese chap, who always has a smile and a warm greeting for his visitors. He's often to be found in the hotel's lobby: a long, narrow bar area reminiscent of an English pub, covered from floor to ceiling with beer mats, pictures and other knick-knacks. At the far end, a pair of saloon-style louvre doors swing open to reveal a large, sunny courtyard filled with an abundance of tropical plants and a cool, blue swimming pool. In one corner, an African grey parrot is squawking away in its cage, intermittently shrieking '*Bonjour*' or '*Comment ça va?*' at passing guests. Although pretty deserted today, all the other clientele are Westerners. A bearded German chap in one corner is typing furiously on his laptop computer, stopping occasionally for a sip of his large black coffee. By the pool, three young American women are chatting and laughing together. Each of them has plaited 'African style' hair and they are sharing a 1.5 litre bottle of mineral water and a couple of croissants. I overhear one of them say the words 'my host family', and my suspicions are confirmed: these are *Peace Corps volunteers*. The Peace Corps is an amazing American organization, which allows young folk to travel to far-flung places for a couple of years to work on development projects. They manage to exist on an incredibly low budget (hence their economy breakfast), and their living conditions – with African families – are often basic by Western standards. It's seriously character-building stuff, though, and I've scarcely met a Peace Corps volunteer who isn't genuinely caring, thoroughly interesting, and delightful to chat to.

After we've had our cups of coffee and pastries, Keita asks:

"Robert, have you seen the Niger River in Ségou?"

"I've seen the Niger River in Bamako. I imagine it's pretty similar."

"No, you must see this one! It's *très, très joli!*"

We wander 100 yards from the *auberge* down a sandy dirt road to the river, in the now blistering heat. This short road is strewn with touristy stalls selling just about every kind of African souvenir: traditional wood carvings, tablecloths, jewellery, paintings, bowls, musical instruments and brightly coloured clothing. Many of the stalls are kept by Tamasheq people, like my friend Youssouf on Badala Market. These turban-clad, tea-drinking, semi-nomadic merchants are among the more persistent salesmen in Africa, always ready to sell the unsuspecting tourist one of their famous embossed leather-clad boxes, trays, bowls – even chess sets. The basic raised design of these is cut out of cardboard, which is then glued onto the wooden items. A damp leather sheet is then stuck on top and pressed in place, so as to take the shape of the card beneath it. The more intricate detail – dashes, ovals, diamonds and wiggly lines – are then hammered into the leather using small metal dies, many of which seem to be made from recycled car or bike parts. This attractive leatherwork comes in a range of vivid colours: emerald green, deep red, purple, navy blue – even orange – but only ever one colour per item.

The salesmen are quick to spot a potential customer:

"*Mossieu, Mossieu! Venez regarder!*"

"*Non merci!*" I reply, walking resolutely forth, fixing my glance on the river ahead.

"*Mossieu! Entrez voir! Venez regarder, pour le plaisir des yeux!*"

'Come and look, for the pleasure of the eyes'? That's an interesting turn of phrase! I do my best to politely refuse, making excuses such as: 'I live here', 'I've already got lots of those', or: 'I don't need any today'. This does little to assuage their incessant onslaught.

"*Venez voir! Venez voir Mossieu!*"

The Tamasheq people get a bad press, largely due to the so-called 'Tuareg Rebels' in the north of the country; I've seen Westerners quake with fear at their sight, wrongly assuming them to be terrorists. And there was recently an American tourist who called his embassy in great fear, saying: 'a man with a turban is on his phone outside my hotel room'. But Tamasheq folk I've met (and actually spent time with) are peaceful, hospitable people, who like to drink tea and have a jolly good chat.

Today, we've only time for the briefest glance at the Niger River before continuing our journey. Beyond its gently sloping, sandy banks, this vast watercourse flows majestically northwards, as fishermen in carved-out canoes punt their way across the waves and pied kingfishers hover in expectation; both parties vying for the same fishy reward. The Niger is almost a mile wide here, and on the opposite bank a luxury hotel is just about visible; its round, straw-topped huts poking out from behind the trees, and a swanky restaurant perched on stilts in the river itself. A free river taxi from this side is laid on for its wealthy clients.

Ségou's tourism is significantly boosted once a year by the *Festival Sur Le Niger,* a three-day event showcasing music, dance and arts from Mali and beyond. It takes place in February each year, and the main stage actually floats on the river, while the audience sits on tiered terraces on the riverbank. During the event, Ségou's dozen or so hotels are packed to the seams with tourists, often fully booked months in advance. This renowned festival, second only to the *Festival au Désert* in Timbuktu, attracts many big names in African music. Toumani Diabaté, Salif Keita, Habib Koité, Oumou Sangaré and Nigeria's Femi Kuti have all taken to this iconic floating stage.

Just upstream from the stage is a large blue and white steamer, three decks high and almost 100 feet long, docked beside the river. A narrow deck, encircled by rusty railings, runs around the entire vessel which, besides a few dents in the hull, looks in pretty good shape. The ship is guarded by a single security guard who, seeing my fascination, invites me aboard for a quick tour. The *Kankou Moussa,* I learn, is named after a fourteenth century emperor of the ancient kingdom of Mali, a realm which extended way beyond the country's current borders. The ship is one of several which make the 1200-mile journey from Bamako to Timbuktu and back on a regular basis during rainy season (when the river is deep enough); a round trip of six days. Although far from a luxury liner, each deck provides a different class of travel, all priced accordingly. The cheapest, and lowest, is nothing but a large metal deck, open to the elements on either side, where impoverished travellers doss down wherever they can. Climbing the rusty staircase to the deck above, we reach the second-class cabins, with two or four pairs of bunk beds sleeping up to eight people. Shared toilet facilities – albeit somewhat foul-smelling – are provided at the rear of this deck. The first class rooms on the top deck contain two single beds or one double, an en-suite toilet, air conditioning, and a small fridge.

Coulibaly and Keita are standing on the shore looking decidedly bored by now, so I disembark and join them on the dirt road.

"Why did you go on that old boat, *Monsieur Robert?*" asks Keita.

"I thought it looked interesting."

"Interesting – that old thing? I've travelled on the lower deck at least ten times, since I was a baby. The memories are not good!"

"I hope you took some beans along to cheer you up."

"Ah, Traoré! You are understanding the Malian culture now!"

The Niger River in Ségou

Chapter Six – Mac's Refuge

"Good old Mac saves the day."

THE FIELDS BECOME progressively more yellow as we continue northwards, and the villages less and less frequent; each equipped with a green-domed mosque or, occasionally, a church. Most have a small marketplace too and some have schools. The village well – often the only source of water – is an important social focal point, as is the shade of plentiful mango trees. And the further north we travel, the more buildings are made from *adobe:* mud bricks covered with a thin, smooth layer of mud, giving the exterior an altogether more aesthetically pleasing look than breezeblocks or brick. Known locally as *banco,* adobe protects from the heat more effectively than other materials but needs reapplying every couple of years; otherwise it will invariably crack and drop off in the heat.

"These days, banco is the choice of only the very poor or the very rich," says Coulibaly.

"Why is that?" I ask.

"Well, the poor can afford nothing but local mud to build with, while the rich have enough money to recoat their mansions every year, and they prefer its look."

Who'd have thought a glorified mud hut could become a status symbol?

After a couple more hours dodging potholes, goats, donkeys and dogs, we reach the bizarrely named town of Bla, which contains little of interest besides a road junction. Here, you can turn right for southern Mali (Koutiala and Sikasso), or continue ever northwards like we are. An hour beyond Bla is San, a slightly larger town with a decent market and a couple of passable hotels. The midday sun is now directly overhead, and the Hilux is becoming unbearably hot, in spite of its white colour and powerful air-conditioning. We're also getting rather peckish, so pull over in the shade of a huge baobab for a break. Stepping out of the vehicle, the full force of 46-degree midday heat hits us like a giant hairdryer. The humidity is almost zero here, so my mouth, eyes and nostrils dry out in seconds, leaving me instantly parched. Bizarrely, I don't appear to be sweating at all, as it evaporates the second it appears, leaving nothing but a few salty deposits on my skin. In this part of the world, you can hang your wet washing out at 8pm (after sunset) and it will be bone dry within an hour. And if you open a stale bag of soft crisps, they will return to their original crispiness within a few minutes, dried out by the air surrounding them. One final advantage of this climate is a lack of almost any mosquitoes, as the wee beasties can only breed in standing water.

I once met a Dutchman who drove his Citroën 2CV across the Sahara from Brussels to Benin. A crazy, crazy idea, but he evidently lived to tell the tale. Rudi told me: "In the middle of the desert we had to drink eight litres of water a day, and I never had to go pee once." We're not in the Sahara yet, but it's certainly getting close.

From the baobab to our hotel is a further two hours of almost utter desolation. Flat, bone-dry fields stretch endlessly in every direction, with very little to break up their monotony; just a few shrubs and trees, and the odd hamlet. The road here is still tarmacked and, rather surprisingly, has very few potholes. By late afternoon, almost nine hours since our departure, we arrive in Sevaré, the gateway to Dogon Country and the only sizeable town between Ségou and Timbuktu – each now five hours' drive in either direction.

The town of Sevaré grew up around an important crossroads: left takes you to *Mopti*, a key fishing port on the banks of the Niger, just a few miles away. A right turn leads to pleasant-sounding Bandiagara on the edge of the Dogon Cliffs, where we'll head tomorrow. Straight on takes you further north, past elephant country (Douentza) and all the way to the legendary Saharan city of Timbuktu. Such a long way from Bamako, yet Timbuktu is still only midway between Mali's southern frontier with Côte d'Ivoire and its northernmost point bordering Algeria and Mauritania.

It's almost dark now, so time to find our accommodation – a lovely little place called *Mac's Refuge*. Just a block from the main road, it offers decent accommodation and affordable prices, making it a popular choice for passing backpackers. Almost every tourist visiting Mali will pass through Sevaré en route to Dogon Country or Timbuktu, so Mac enjoys an almost constant flow of American and European guests. The wealthier ones arrive in heavily laden, dust-covered four-by-fours, wearing beige safari gilets covered in pockets, matching Tilley Hats and sleek Ray-Bans. The younger, more frugal travellers opt for public transport – sweaty, crowded buses and bush taxis – carrying nothing but small rucksacks of sun cream, insect repellent, malaria meds and a couple of spare T-shirts. They're invariably unshaven with a demeanour which says: *we're experts on this part of the world already*, even though they arrived last Thursday. Neither kind has ever lived in – or truly understood – Africa; they're here for the thrills and spills, before returning to their Western luxury. Unfolding a dog-eared Malian map over the boot of a car, they'll eagerly point out every junction, landmark, village and cliff-top they intend to visit. And if you meet them on their return, you'll get the blow-by-blow account of their adventures, coupled with plenty of advice on where you 'really must visit' because it's 'the coolest place ever'.

Quietly spoken, understated and a man of few words, Mac is certainly not your stereotypical American. Now in his mid-sixties, he grew up as a child of American missionaries to Dogon Country, so knows this area like the back of his hand. I'm told that, as a young adult, he tried living back in The States but never really settled, so returned 'home' to Mali, eventually opening this place – the only English-speaking, American-run hostel in the country. We pull up outside his imposing red metal gates and within seconds a friendly face appears.

"Welcome. I'll get the guard to open the gate and you can bring your car in."

I drive the Hilux through the small gap into a narrow space between two buildings: to the right is Mac's house, to the left the hostel. The rooms are basic but comfortable; some even have an en-suite. There's also air-conditioning; a near necessity in this climate.

Messrs Coulibaly and Keita are not staying at Mac's tonight. Although reasonably priced by Western standards, it is still more than they could afford. I offered to treat them to a night here, but Coulibaly has a *grand frère* in town, who has offered to put them up. This is a common practice among Africans, as family and relationships are paramount in this culture; they would also see it as a waste to pay for accommodation when a free bed is available.

Under Mac's watchful eye, the cook is currently preparing a delicious and copious feast in the kitchen. Each night of the week, Mac lays on a different themed meal. Tonight is Moroccan Night; other nights include traditional African, Indian, Mexican and good old American burgers with fries. Refreshed from a cool shower and change of clothes, I wander over and take my place around his long rectangular table, which seats up to 14. Tonight, there are eight of us including Mac. Opposite me sit three young Americans, two girls and a guy: more Peace Corps volunteers. To my right, the three remaining guests have just arrived: a middle-aged white lady and two young African men. After the customary *what are you doing here* questions, I establish that these three work for a large charity and are here to carry out polio vaccinations in the region. The woman is French and, although she's never lived in Mali, has made almost a dozen trips here over the past twenty years, and seems pretty fluent in Bambara as she chats away to her colleagues.

To my immediate left, Mac himself is sitting at the head of the table.

"Welcome everyone. Serve yourselves."

We tuck into delicious couscous with chunky vegetables and lamb – excellent quality food and huge portions; there are even cold beers straight from the fridge. The male Peace Corps volunteer is still wearing his baseball cap even though the sun went down a good hour ago; a lapse in mealtime etiquette Mac is not willing to tolerate.

"Take your hat off, please," he says quietly.

"I'm sorry?"

"Take your hat off at the table. I can't see your face properly."

Peace Corps Guy awkwardly obliges, his blushing (or perhaps tanned) face emerging from beneath his *Boston Red Sox* headgear.

The dinnertime conversation revolves around the usual kind of topics for such a gathering:

"Have you been to Africa before?"

"How long are you here for?"

"Are you enjoying it?"

Hatless Peace Corps Guy, whose name is Charlie, speaks up:

"It's mostly been great so far, but there should have been four of us on this trip. Our colleague, Dan, got really sick a few days ago…" His voice begins to falter, and I notice his hands are quivering slightly.

"What happened to him?" asks Mac, after an unnaturally long pause and a mouthful of couscous.

"We went swimming at a waterfall near Bamako. The water was cool and deep – it was awesome. But a couple of weeks later, Dan started feeling real sick. He had bad aches and pains, and a weird-looking rash all over his body. His temperature shot up to 104, so we tested for malaria, but it came back negative. We thought it must be some kinda virus, but he just kept on getting worse, then…"

Another awkward gap as Charlie composes himself.

"Then few days later, he was…he was peeing blood."

"Bilharzia?" the French lady and I ask, almost in unison.

"Yes, bilharzia."

A decidedly nasty tropical disease, bilharzia – or schistosomiasis – is caused by tiny worms which live in stagnant water, and is almost exclusively limited to the African continent. All it takes is for someone already infected to urinate into the water, and a load of schisto eggs are released. After 'hitching a ride' aboard passing water snails, the eggs hatch out into small worms, each no more than half an inch long. It is these worms which penetrate the skin of unsuspecting bathers and, once inside the human body, head straight for the bladder, where they lay their own eggs, ready for the whole cycle to begin again. But not before causing significant illness and damage to the bladder – hence Dan's symptoms.

"Where is he now?" I ask.

"They had to Medevac him out", one of the two girls replies, "just a couple of days ago. He was really looking forward to this trip."

I think of my colleagues Coulibaly and Keita: if they get sick, they have no such luxury as being flown out the country, nor would they be able to afford treatment in Mali. In this respect, Dan is very lucky indeed. The world has come a long way in the past few decades: Apartheid has fallen, Fairtrade goods are on the up, and aid is helping to eradicate polio and reduce malaria. But here still remains a vast chasm between the consumer-driven, prosperous West and the breadline existence of much of the developing world.

I call Lois before bed. The mobile phone signal is remarkably good here. Today, she and the kids went back to Broadway Café, this time with Doctor Dave and his family. They've also found a good tailor, just round the corner from our house, who is currently making outfits for the children. Chao Cheng is still fitting the replacement cylinder head on the Mitsubishi, so no further news there. Besides this, all is well. Abdoulaye cooked them chicken curry tonight – his repertoire of exotic dishes is broadening. Maybe I should teach him how to make Moroccan lamb and couscous.

At breakfast the next morning, Mac shares some disturbing news: a French scientist has been taken hostage in northern Mali.

"Where did it take place?" I ask, stunned.

"In Ménaka, beyond Gao. Not far from the Niger border."

That's roughly three days' drive from here, or two from Timbuktu, so is unlikely to affect anyone round this table. But this is by no means the first kidnapping to take place in Mali's remote desert regions, where bandits, smugglers and Al Qaeda-linked groups operate.

After a tasty breakfast of pancakes and syrup, I take a stroll into Sevaré. Although the town's main roads are tarmacked, its side streets are typical African dirt tracks; bumpy, stony and decidedly dusty during dry season.

A simple donkey cart passes by, manned by a young boy – no older than twelve – wearing a *Toronto Blue Jays* baseball cap. The cart itself is a simple affair: two old car wheels welded onto either end of a metal pipe, with a couple of V-shaped brackets joining this to the rest of the cart: a wooden platform made of planks. On top sit a dozen sacks of onions, as the weary, off-white donkey drags the cart slowly forward. Donkeys are popular in Mali, but there are virtually none south of Bamako; the tsetse fly killed them all off decades ago and they have never returned. So the entire West African coast (from Conakry to Lagos), and the region 400 miles to its north, is entirely donkeyless.

On either side of the dirt road there's a mixture of housing; some concrete, some adobe. Boundaries are marked either with stone walls or fencing made from woven dried grass. Bent over ladies are sweeping their thresholds with short straw brooms, and an old man is sitting on a low wooden chair outside his home, watching the world go by.

Two young boys run across the road without even looking, the younger narrowly missing the wheels of a passing motorbike. He falls to the ground and rolls over, springing back to his feet in a split second. The old man looks up at me and utters wise words:

"*Les enfants cherchent la mort, mais ça les fuit,*" meaning 'children seek out death, but it flees from them'.

"*Ah, c'est vrai!*" I respond. He looks up at me:

"*Toubab! Vous-êtes Américain?*"

"*Non, Anglais.*"

"Ah, verrry gooood! God sev za Kwin!"

I laugh, impressed at his attempt to speak my language.

"Sit down, toubab," he orders, as though it's my name. I perch myself on the only spare seat in front of his simple banco hut, beneath a palm-leaf shelter.

"My name is Amadou Diallo."

"I'm Robert Traoré."

"Pleased to meet you, Traoré."

From Amadou's surname, I can tell he's *Fulani:* semi-nomadic cattle herders, jokingly referred to as 'milk-drinkers' locally. His courtyard – if you can call it that – is no more than a tiny plot between two larger houses. A small sand-coloured puppy is tied to his flimsy shelter, with a skinny-looking goat tethered to the opposite corner.

"What is your dog called?" I ask.

"The dog? Wulu!"

"But, that just means dog."

"Yes!"

"But what is its actual name? I'm Robert, you're Amadou. What's the dog called?"

He pauses, confused and thoughtful.

"Why would a dog have a name? It's just a dog."

Amadou is typically tall and thin, and has the characteristic finer features of the Fulani. His heavily wrinkled face smiles warmly at me, revealing roughly eight yellowing teeth. I sit for a few minutes, as Amadou grills me about my country, what I think of his, and what I'm doing here.

"I have never been to your country. I went to Senegal once though," he says. Not quite the same.

"Tell me, toubab, is it true that white flakes fall from the sky there?"

"You mean snow, *la neige?*"

"*Oui, la neige.*"

"Yes, but only in the winter."

"And what happens when it falls? Does it kill people?"

"Not usually. It just covers the ground with a white layer, and it's very, very cold."

"Fifteen degrees?" he asks, in complete sincerity.

"No," I laugh. "Where I live, fifteen degrees is a nice summer's day. Zero degrees, minus five, maybe even minus ten."

"*Oh là là, mon ami! Ce n'est pas possible!*"

It's almost 10 o'clock, the time I told Coulibaly and Keita to meet me at Mac's, so I politely ask for the road and thank Amadou for the chat. As I get up, I reach over to pat the cute little puppy.

"*Au revoir, petit chien!*"

SNAP! In an instant, the anonymous canine has bitten a small chunk out of my right hand. Ouch! I'm bleeding slightly, and Monsieur Diallo looks concerned.

"Sorry, toubab, sorry!"

"It's just a scratch – I'll be fine," I respond, with typical British understatedness.

I reach for the bottle of hand cleanser in my pocket and rub it into the cut. It stings terribly but seems like a good idea at the time. Applying pressure, the bleeding soon stops, and I bid Amadou farewell, unable to offer the customary handshake.

Back at Mac's Refuge, there's no sign of my Malian colleagues, but it's only ten past ten. The place is all quiet now and Mac has gone to market. The Peace Corps volunteers left at the crack of dawn to make the most of their Dogon trek. 'Team Polio' are still here though, getting ready for another day's vaccinating in the local village.

"What 'as 'appened to your 'and?" asks the French lady, her trained eye immediately noticing the traces of blood.

"Oh, it's nothing. A small dog just nipped me."

"A dog bite?"

"Yes. Nothing serious though. Don't worry."

"*Mais non! C'est très sérieux!*"

"No, honestly, it doesn't even hurt…"

"*Mais, monsieur, la rage, la rage! Pensez à la rage!*"

What's she going on about? Rage? I'm not angry about it; neither was the dog. Then I remember: *la rage* is French for 'rabies'.

"If the dog was infected, you could die *monsieur*."

"Really?"

"*Mais oui!* Rabies is a very dangerous thing indeed." I can feel my heart beginning to pound as the reality sets in.

"What should I do?"

"You need a *piqure*, 'ow do you say…a prick."

"An injection?"

"*Oui,* an injection. You must have one in ze next few hours, then another one in two or three days. Otherwise, even in five years' time, ze rabies could appear, and then you might die suddenly."

I'm sold on this, but worried that my Dogon trip might now have to be postponed – even cancelled.

"Will I have to go back to Bamako for the injections?"

"*Ah, non.* You can get ze rabies injections in the local *pharmacie* 'ere in Sevaré."

"Okay, and is there a clinic where they could administer the injection?"

"Monsieur, as long as you go to the pharmacy right away, I will give you ze injection, but you must hurry – we 'ave work to do in ze village."

The chemist is on the crossroads in Sevaré, about half a mile away. I decide to take the Hilux to save time and because, somewhat bizarrely, I now feel quite nauseous. Driving down the main street in Sevaré, I notice my hands are trembling at the wheel – only a result of fear and shock, I'm sure, but my more paranoid side is beginning to fear the worst. What if they have no vaccines in stock? What if I take too long and the nurse has left? I don't want to get rabies and, though the risks are low, that slim chance is playing on my mind and I'm finding it hard to focus.

"*Avez-vous un vaccin contre la rage, s'il vous plaît?*"

"*Oui, monsieur.*"

Well, that's a relief. I buy two vials and return to Mac's as fast as I can, where Marie the French nurse awaits. In a matter of seconds, she has injected the contents of the first vial into my left upper arm.

"Now, monsieur," she says sternly, "You 'ave to 'ave ze second injection in two days."

"Okay. But I'm leaving for Sangha in a few minutes and plan to stay there for several days."

"Well, there is a clinic in Sangha which can give you the second injection."

"That's good. I'll take it with me, then."

"*Bonne idée.* But you need to keep it refrigerated; it will not survive in ze 'eat 'ere."

The plot thickens. *Now* what do I do? Sangha has no mains electricity! Just then, and only half an hour late, Coulibaly and Keita, turn up, and I fill them in on my predicament.

"Pasteur Thomas has a fridge in his house," says Keita

"And where does he live?"

"In Sangha."

"Do you have the pastor's mobile number?" Most pastors I've met own at least two phones.

"*Oui,* I will call."

I listen as Keita bellows down the phone in Bambara, scarcely understanding a word, besides *toubab, wulu* (dog) and something that sounds like clinic. He's nodding enthusiastically for the first half of the call, then his face changes, and he begins to shake his head. He ends the call, and turns to me.

"Pastor Thomas has a freezer but no refrigerator."

A freezer? That would most likely *freeze* the vaccine, which surely wouldn't be good. It's my only chance, though.

"It is a gas freezer, but his gas bottle is empty."

Calamity upon calamity! I decide to look for a gas bottle in Sevaré, to take with us in the Hilux. In Africa, most major petrol stations sell gas bottles, so I try the *Total* station round the corner. The metal cage where the gas bottles normally live is empty, and the pump attendant confirms my fears:

"*Le gaz, c'est fini!*"

I try a second station, then a third: no gas. I ask where else I might find a gas bottle in Sevaré and am told there's been a general shortage for several days, and the next consignment will not arrive for another week. I'm really wishing I'd never touched that dog now.

Drastic measures are called for: either I drive three hours south to San – with no guarantee of finding gas there – or I find another way of getting a gas bottle. Just then, I have a brainwave and return to the hostel, where Mac has just got back from the market.

"You still here?"

"Yes. Listen, I'm in a spot of bother. Do you happen to have a spare gas bottle?"

"Yes, I always keep two spares. They're both full right now."

"Can I ask you a huge favour?"

Good old Mac saves the day and lets me borrow one. Not only that, he also lends me a small round cool box to put the vaccine in, to prevent it from actually freezing.

Without further ado, the three of us load the bottle into the back of the truck, wedging it between the four sacks of charcoal, which I'm now strangely grateful for. My vial of rabies vaccine I keep with me in the cabin, turning the air-conditioning up full blast to keep it cool. We take a right turn at the crossroads in Sevaré, then continue straight towards the Cliffs of Bandiagara. The road here is one of the best in all of Mali: smooth, broad, flat, and not a pothole in sight.

"*C'est pour les touristes,*" says Keita.

"But what about the eight hours of driving to get this far?"

"Well, the richest tourists fly directly into Mopti." I'm surprised to hear that such a small town even has an airport.

"But the last charter flight from Mopti is next week," adds Coulibaly. "After that, they will have to come by road."

"And then will the government repair all the potholes?"

"Ha ha! Not necessarily, *mon ami!*"

Bandiagara is the final frontier before departing 'normal' Mali for the mysterious and culturally rich Dogon Country. As we pass through, several Toyota four-by-fours are being loaded up outside a pleasant hotel, ready for an outing to the cliffs. A little further on, a message has been painted across a wall in huge white letters:

MONSIEUR LE PRESIDENT, MANQUE D'EAU. POURQUOI?

Which means: 'Mr President, lack of water. Why?'

I ask Keita what this is all about.

"ATT came to visit Bandiagara last week," he explains. "Someone wrote this message for him to see. This is a town, not a village; people expect water to flow when they turn their taps on. Recently, this has not been happening."

From Bandiagara, the road is much narrower and noticeably inferior in quality, made up of a curious mixture of surfaces, which change frequently: sandy track, concrete, bare rock, washboard. I notice that the road dips down briefly in certain sections, before suddenly rising again.

"In rainy season the road regularly floods at these sections," Keita tells me.

"So, why don't they build bridges instead?"

"It would cost too much. The roads go down so that the rivers can keep flowing."

"How do vehicles get across then?"

"Sometimes the cars cannot, but four-by-fours can usually just drive straight through. In rainy season, there is a man with a boat, to help people cross."

This doesn't sound like the best system ever.

"A few years ago, Kofi Annan was visiting Sangha…"

"*The* Kofi Annan, from the United Nations?"

"Yes, Kofi Annan came, and there was a big storm. The road was so flooded that he had to wait several hours before he could return, and so his flight out of Bamako had to be rescheduled."

Well I never!

Chapter Seven – The Legacy of the Fish People

"We Dogon have always been interested in the night sky."

OVER A HUNDRED miles long and 1500 feet high, the Bandiagara Escarpment snakes its way from the Niger Inland Delta north-eastwards through harsh, semi-desert terrain. This giant, craggy shelf stops just short of the Burkina Faso border where *Hombori Tondo* – Mali's answer to Ayers Rock – rises 3000 feet out of the ground, like a giant full stop. Steeped in rich culture and history, the Dogon cliffs are scattered with curious villages, each with distinctly African-sounding names such as *Dunduru, Yabatalu* and *Jigibombo*. South-east of the cliff is the vast Dogon Plain: flat, semi-arid and larger in surface area than the cliff itself. This entire area – clifftop and plain – is what we call Dogon Country, and covers a staggering million acres, containing almost 300 villages; none larger than a small market town.

The clifftop village of Sangha lies midway along the Dogon Escarpment and is a popular tourist destination due to its stunning views and relative proximity to Sevaré and Mopti. The landscape here is varied and interesting, composed almost entirely of solid rock: from light brown to blackish in colour; some smooth, some jagged; sloping in places, relatively flat in others. Wherever you look, there are boulders of every size, strewn – apparently randomly – across the hard, dry ground. Some have been hewn into 14-inch cubes for house building and lie in piles or rows at various points across the village, ready for use. There are also numerous half-built houses – a common feature in Africa – many remaining as empty, roofless shells for years. Yet none of this 'rubble' seems to make the place look untidy; rather, it somehow adds to the beauty and charm of Sangha, where rocky heaps are completely at home.

Out of the tiniest gaps in the rockface grow tufts of yellowing grass and small bushes; even the occasional tree. Some have cleverly adapted roots, which run down the cliffside for several feet to reach moisture. Huge crevasses in the rock – some over 100 feet wide and miles long – are Sangha's saving grace; the sandy earth gathered in these is the only place vegetation can properly grow. This is how the Dogon have managed to survive up here for centuries. Dark-green mango trees, majestic baobabs and the ever-present neem trees all provide important shade and sustenance, while crops of millet, cotton and onions all thrive in these neatly tended gullies.

Entering Sangha in our tired, dusty Hilux, we descend a narrow, winding track into one such sandy ravine, jagged rock faces rising up on either side.

"That's where they roast the pigs on market day," says Keita, pointing out a large open area to one side.

"And up there on the edge of the cliff," adds Coulibaly, "is Sangha's only protestant church, built by missionaries 50 years ago."

"It's such a pretty place – so peaceful and unique," I reply. "I've never been anywhere quite like this before."

"And you will come back here again, *Monsieur Robert*," beams Keita.

I certainly hope so. In the centre of the road ahead is a roundabout containing a large monument which resembles a scaled-down version of Bamako's Africa Tower. Made entirely from local stone, and roughly twenty feet high, a large African bowl adorns its pinnacle and a rusty tin sign at the base reads: '*Monument UNESCO*', celebrating Dogon Country's designation as a World Heritage site in 1989.

Putting the Hilux into second gear, we ascend one final steep, rocky hill. Over the brow is the church: an imposing building standing on its own in the centre of a large open square, with a small, pointy tower and a corrugated tin roof. Opposite the church is a larger, Western-looking house: my digs for the next few nights. We pull up between the two buildings and step out of our air-conditioned vehicle into the intense Dogon heat.

"*Bienvenue, Monsieur Robert!*"

It's Pasteur Thomas Ongoïba, our host. I've done my homework, so greet him in his mother tongue:

"*Sɛɛwo mã?*"

"*Ah?*" he responds, with a classic high-pitched African interjection. "*Mon ami! Sɛɛwo! Sɛɛwo!*" He warmly takes my hand in both of his, shaking it vigorously. I've only said 'hello', but he's clearly chuffed to bits. Just for fun, I throw in a Dogon 'thank you' too:

"*Bidepo!*"

"*Ah, vraiment! Monsieur est fort! Bidepo! Bidepo! Bidepo!*"

A short chap in his late forties with Ronnie Corbett glasses and a balding head, Pasteur Thomas has certainly given me a warm welcome. It's amazing how something as simple as 'hello' or 'thank you' in the local language always generates such a positive response.

"Let me show you to your house, Monsieur. Ah! *Bienvenue! Bidepo! Bidepo!*"

"That would be good, but first, can I put something in your freezer?"

"*Ah, oui! Le sérum.* Come!"

I grab the plastic cooler containing my vaccine, whilst Keita – true to form – offers to carry the gas bottle. Pasteur Thomas leads us down a narrow cutting in the relatively sheer rock face, to a stone-walled compound right on the cliff's edge. The courtyard is tiny and predictably rocky, with a solitary and rather spindly neem tree growing out of a crack on its boundary. The house itself is far from large, made up of just two rooms either side of a central door. But, as is the custom in Africa, hosting is done in the courtyard, where a covered area in one corner provides suitable shelter from the sun.

"Come, sit!"

It's normal here to offer someone a seat and a drink of water as soon as they arrive at your home; quite different from England, where I've often stood chatting to visitors on my doorstep for half an hour. The three of us dutifully sit down beneath the corrugated metal shelter, on what I like to call *washing line chairs*. These are among the most common chairs in Mali these days, and are both easy to make and ideal for the climate. Think of a tubular, metal-framed chair but without the upholstery. Now, take some plastic washing line, blue or green (you choose), and repeatedly wrap this between the two opposite sides of the seat area, leaving roughly an inch between each parallel line thus created. Continue until the entire horizontal square is covered. Now repeat the same process between the two rising vertical poles for a back support, but only for the top eight inches or so. Ta-da! You now have a well-ventilated, cheap and comfortable chair. In this climate, a solid surface would leave you sliding around in your own sweat, so this 'egg-slicer chair' is an ideal alternative.

As we sit and wait, Keita is busy tinkering with the gas bottle, attaching it to the freezer in the corner. With the vial still inside my picnic cooler, I carefully lower it into the small chest freezer, turning the dial down to the lowest possible setting. Let's hope this does the trick: keeping it cool enough to still be effective, but not so cold it actually freezes.

In the corner of the covered area is a large TV with a cable leading to a huge satellite dish on the roof, all powered by a pair of twelve volt car batteries. Hanging from the low corrugated ceiling, a small black fan is rotating – powered by the same batteries. Made from thick black plastic with no caging, and less than a foot in diameter, it's unlike any ceiling fan I've seen before, and yet looks strangely familiar. Its gentle breeze is greatly appreciated though, in spite of its nauseating buzz.

"*Messieurs, voici ma femme!*"

Madame Ongoïba, a short, cheery lady, appears.

"*Bonjour messieurs.* Welcome to Sangha!" She shakes each person warmly by the hand, curtsying humbly and smiling warmly.

"My wife has prepared some *punrun* for you."

"Ahh," says Coulibaly. "I like so much the punrun!"

"What's *poo-roon?*" I ask.

"Punrun!" clarifies Pasteur Ongoïba. Punrun is a Dogon drink. It's made from millet, tamarinds, sugar and water. Very good for you!"

"What is the alcohol content?" I ask, cautiously.

"Ah no!" he laughs. "Punrun is not an alcoholic drink."

Using a small tear-shaped gourd as a ladle, Madame Ongoïba pours some for each of us, using larger round gourds as bowls. The drink is served lukewarm and has the texture of a protein shake, but tastes more like porridge.

"Would you like a second gourdful?"

"Yes please!"

Pasteur Ongoïba turns to me.

"You know, *Monsieur Robert*, many Dogon drink this and nothing else from dawn till dusk."

"Really? And what about meat?"

"*Meat?!* Ah, that's something else! Meat is a luxury most Dogon do not often enjoy."

"Punrun is known as *The Serum of the Dogon,*" adds Keita, "it's like their medicine. If you are sick, then as long as you can take one ladleful a day, there is hope."

My house on the hill – three times larger than the Ongoïba's – was built by missionaries around the same time as the church, but now serves as a guesthouse. Stepping into its sizeable lounge, the first thing I notice is an upright piano along one wall – not something I was expecting. It's predictably out of tune and several keys don't work properly. This isn't a good climate for such an instrument, and the nearest piano tuner must be at least a thousand miles from here, probably more.

There's a three-seater sofa in the lounge, bedecked with chunky burgundy cushions and four armchairs, none of which quite match the sofa. On the stained pale-blue walls hang faded, warped paintings, two of which I recognize as Constable's 'The Haywain' and 'Flatford Mill' – a rather incongruous tribute to rural Suffolk in rocky Mali. A fluorescent strip light is hanging almost diagonally from loose wires in the centre of the room, though there's no power at the moment. Frilly red curtains frame the archway leading to the dining room, where a dark rectangular wooden table is surrounded by six more washing line chairs.

In the long, narrow kitchen sits a wooden unit containing old-looking pots and pans, a tarnished double sink and a tiny gas stove. By Western standards, it is decidedly rudimentary, but compared to Pasteur Ongoïba's tin shelter, this is luxury (and he's a relatively rich Dogon).

After a short (and extremely sweaty) siesta in my comfy bedroom, I rouse and take a cold shower in preparation for my first bit of research. As an ethnomusicologist, I'm keen to find out all I can about Dogon music: instruments, types of song, scales, lyrics, and the status music has in this society. In some cultures – such as the West – talented musicians are hailed as celebrities, almost worshipped. Other cultures see music as a frivolous activity and rank musicians as the lowest of the low.

My first interviewee is a very old chap called Siméon: tall and slim with cloudy eyes and approximately five teeth. Old people are often the best sources for research as their knowledge spans so many years. Sat on a rickety wooden bench beneath a mango tree, we begin to chat.

"What were your early memories of music?"

"Well, I am a Christian and I grew up here. When I was small, we used to sing *your* songs in the church, accompanied by the harmonium."

"And did you like the hymns?"

"Yes, but the tunes were difficult because they were foreign to us. And they would sing just five verses, then suddenly stop and sit down."

This would certainly be unusual in an African context, where a single refrain can easily be repeated 50 or even 100 times.

"What about your local music?"

"Our Dogon instruments were forbidden by the missionaries. 'It's for pagans' they told us. No clapping or dancing was allowed: we just had to stand still, face the front of the church and sing your white songs."

"And is it still the same today?"

"Well, in the Sixties, we started to use the square drum, which came from Burkina Faso. The round drums were all considered demonic, but the square drum was okay." I can't help pondering why the addition of four right-angles would somehow rid a drum of evil.

"Then we also began to use the *gomboï* - the talking drum."

Shaped like a sand-timer, the double-headed talking drum is a common sight across West Africa. When squeezed under the arm, lateral leather cords tighten both skins, raising the pitch and creating a sound which resembles speech; hence the name. And its Dogon name*, gomboï,* is of course onomatopoeia for this voice-like sound.

"We also have the *barɔ,* a drum made from a large gourd with skin stretched over the top." [15]

"And has the *barɔ* ever been played in church?"

"We tried it for the first time in 2010, but some people didn't like it, so we haven't used it much since."

Early missionaries in much of Africa outlawed local music and dance, considering it too pagan for God's liking. Then from the 1970s, Africans slowly began to incorporate indigenous elements into worship, but only in a limited way. Since the 90s, there has been an explosion of local arts, as many African churches have begun using local instruments, song-styles and dance like never before.

"The barɔ is a very ancient instrument," he continues. "It was played by a man called Abirɛ, long, long ago, when the rocks were still wet."

"The rocks used to be *wet?*"

"Long, long ago, yes. Abirɛ travelled from village to village singing songs and playing his barɔ. He was born blind, and many of his songs were prophetic – he even prophesied the arrival of the *toubabs,* the colonisers."

---

[15] In the Dogon alphabet: 'ɔ' is as in 'hot' and 'ɛ' as in 'egg'.

"Really?"

"Yes, he sang: 'Many red-skins will arrive, and we will not be able to overcome them'. And it was Abirɛ who told the story of why people die."

I love a good African legend, and this one doesn't disappoint:

"There was once a woman called Yassama," he tells me. "She was very poor and had nothing to eat. So one day she asked God for a cow. God replied: 'I will give you a cow, but there is only the cow of death'. Yassama was so hungry that she accepted this cow. However, she now feared that God would kill her husband, so built seven barns to hide him in, so that God would never know which one he was in. Then one day, God came looking for Yassama's husband. 'Where is your husband?' he asked. Yassama lied and said 'he is dead'. Then God made her husband cough so that he could hear where he was. This gave Yassama's husband a bad chest and he died coughing. And that is why people die."

I enquire about other songs in the culture.

"There's *Emuna Ni*. It is sung to sit the dead person down."

"Sit them down? But wouldn't they be lying down dead already?"

"*Non, monsieur*," he laughs, "I'm talking about the *au-delà*. How do you say – the other side."

"The afterlife?"

"*C'est ça.* The song honours the dead person and his ancestors, so that he will be at ease in Heaven. They sing about the good things he did during his life, so that he doesn't harm them now he's dead."

I stay with Siméon for roughly three hours, audio recorder in hand, avidly listening to him reel off song after song, all accompanied with many more fascinating stories and facts; songs for weddings, songs for hunting, songs for greeting the king...

"Don't wander from the main path," he advises as I leave. "There are sacred areas on the edge of the cliff, where no foreigner must ever set foot. If you do, they will make you pay the price of a cow to rectify your error."

Not the cow of death, I hope.

"Once, they made a Western tourist pay 250,000 francs for kola nuts." That's 300 pounds!

I take a cautious stroll back through the town, careful not to stray off the beaten track onto anything that might incur me a penalty, bovine or caffeinated. Across the plains below, the plump, crimson sun is slowly descending, casting its amber light onto the rugged clifftop. Folk are heading wearily home from a long day in the fields, carrying tools, buckets, even crops on their heads. Excited children – some no more than two or three years old – are playing in the dusty streets. One is pulling a battered yellow jerrican along the ground with a ragged piece of string, as though it were a toy car; another is pushing an old moped tyre along with a small branch, hoop-and-stick style. Seeing me, he calls out:

"*Toubab! Toubab!* Do you want to see the cliffs?"

"No thank you. I'm not a tourist."

This stalls him for a few seconds: *White man, but not tourist?* He then continues:

"There are pretty waterfalls, *jolies cascades.*"

"No thanks."

"Are you alone, *mossieu?*"

"No, I am not alone!" though I'm beginning to wish I were right now!

I tentatively navigate the twilit stone steps to Thomas' courtyard. His concerned face greets me at the bottom:

"Robert, did you stray from the footpath at any point?"

I reassure him, and he invites me to sit down to dinner with Coulibaly and Keita. In the centre of our circle is nothing but a small wooden stool; no sign of a table, plates or cutlery, so I'm wondering where – and how – we're going to eat. My curiosity is soon gratified as Madame Ongoïba appears carrying a large metal bowl, which she places on the stool in front of us, removing the lid to reveal a huge quantity of steaming white rice. She returns with a second smaller bowl containing beef stew in a spicy peanut sauce, which she pours onto the rice. Finally, she brings out a box of *Omo* washing power and a blue and white stripy plastic watering can, shaped like a kettle. She tips a small amount of powder into her husband's hands then pours water over to rinse it off, proceeding round the circle in the same manner. I'm still waiting for my knife and fork when Mrs Ongoïba announces:

"*Bon appétit, messieurs!*"

And with that, my colleagues quite literally *dig in* to the bowl, using their hands to make a small ball of rice and sauce, which they place into their mouths. I see why we had our hands washed now. I tentatively reach into the bowl, plunging my fingers down under the food and bringing my hand back towards me, like a digger scooping earth. Ouch! I flinch and wave my upturned hand around in the air to cool the food down. My friends watch and laugh, realizing I'm new to this.

Hand-eating comes with its very own table-time etiquette: firstly, you only take food from the imaginary triangle directly in front of you; never straying beyond this imaginary 70 degree sector into either of your neighbours' zones. Secondly, any food on my 'plot' that I don't want is placed in the very centre of the bowl: a sign to other diners that it's up for grabs. Keita takes a large red chilli pepper and plonks it in the middle – clearly not a spice fan. Coulibaly almost immediately grabs the chilli, squeezing its potent juices all over his section before returning it to the centre. One final rule: you must only eat with your right hand; the left is reserved for less sanitary tasks, such as blowing one's nose or going to the toilet. I often wonder how left-handed people cope in Africa, as it is a serious cultural no-no to use one's left hand for anything formal or public here: shaking hands, giving and receiving money, even pointing at something or someone.

As we munch away, a question occurs to me:

"Is there any crime here?" Sangha feels so calm, friendly and unspoilt that I can't imagine anything negative happening (besides the occasional extortion for trespassing).

"There never used to be," Thomas replies, "but since tourism has developed, there have been one or two criminal acts here. One tourist had his camera stolen recently, but years ago there was nothing like this and Sangha was just a peaceful village. Now it is becoming more like a town."

"Yes," adds Coulibaly, "in the past, the missionaries had no compounds, everything was just open. They would store their belongings in open garages. But now, they have locks on their doors."

It saddens me to think that, because of tourism, Sangha is slowly morphing from a friendly open community into something less personal, driven more by greed and materialism than the needs of society as a whole. This, of course, happened in the West decades ago, but it's grim to see somewhere as idyllic and cohesive as Sangha gradually become a victim of its own beauty.

Darkness has now fallen, and I look up to see a million stars, standing out against Sangha's pure, unpolluted skies.

"Beaucoup d'étoiles ce soir."

"Oui!" agrees Thomas. "When there are many stars in the sky, the Dogon say that there has been much money made at the market."

And the Dogon have an impressive knowledge when it comes to stars: back in the 1930s, they somehow already knew that Sirius had a partner star, forty years before Western telescopes proved this to be true. And for centuries they have celebrated the paths of these two stars in an elaborate ceremony, taking place every 50 years – the very duration of Sirius B's orbit. They also knew it to be 'a very heavy star', a fact now also recognized by Western science.[16] I ask Thomas about this strange and mysterious phenomenon.

"We Dogon have always been interested in the night sky, and we have ancient knowledge passed down from our ancestors. You toubabs like to think you discovered everything in the world, but not so with the stars: the Dogon were far ahead of you! Long ago, we knew about Jupiter and its moons, we knew about Saturn, and we knew about Sirius and its two partner stars."

"*Two* partner stars?" I query, astonished.

"Yes, my friend. Your Western telescopes haven't found the other one yet, but the Dogon have always known there are *three* Sirius stars, not just two."

"But, how can you have access to this knowledge without telescopes?"

Thomas goes on to explain the Dogon belief that amphibious aliens, known as the *Nommos*, came to visit the cliffs thousands of years ago from a planet which orbits *Sirius C*. The Nommos, I'm told, lived in the water and taught humans how to drink. And, though scaly and fish-like to behold, they were also friendly and informative, referred to as civilizing gods by the Dogon, also called 'watchers', 'teachers' or even 'saviours'.[17]

"Saviours?" I clarify.

"Yes, legend says that The Nommo broke his body to feed men," Thomas explains, "and we say that the world drank his body.[18] The

---

[16] http://www.unmuseum.org/siriusb.htm
[17] http://locklip.com/the-dogon-tribe-and-their-nordic-alien-gods-from-sirius/
[18] Marcel Griaule Et Germaine Dieterlen, 'Le Renard Pâle', Institut d'Ethnologie, 1965

Nommo was sacrificed on a tree but was then resurrected and returned to his home world."

This is all sounding rather familiar, though I'm slightly confused by the fish-like features.

"Dogon tradition also says that the Nommo will return in the future to revisit the Earth in a human form."[19]

There's little more satisfying for an anthropologist than stumbling across a gem of this kind, which clearly echoes Christ in many ways. Was this God's way of revealing himself to the Dogon? Was The Nommo a pre-incarnation of Jesus, or have folklore and Biblical stories merely intermingled over the centuries?

It's been dark for over an hour now and, as though on cue, a huge amber moon slowly rises on the eastern horizon, illuminating the clifftop and casting faint moon shadows across the parched rockface. I notice the temperature has not dropped since nightfall, which is curious. I soon discover the reason: hanging my rice-coated hand down beside the chair, I feel heat radiating from the rocks below. Like a storage heater, the clifftop has been warmed by today's sunshine and will continue to give off heat until dawn. Sounds like a good night's sleep might be tricky.

---

[19] http://www.crystalinks.com/dogon.html and also: http://in5d.com/dogon-legend-of-the-nommos-fish-people/

The Dogon Cliffs

Chapter Eight – Clifftop Escapades

"The Tellem were pygmies and they had the power of flight."

I WAKE SWEATY, groggy and semi-dehydrated after what can only be described as a lousy night's sleep. The lack of electricity or any airflow, combined with midnight temperatures exceeding 30 Celsius, made sleep something of a challenge. In desperation, I drenched my bath towel in cold water then lay down with it draped across my entire body. The resulting evaporative cooling worked very well for roughly five minutes, after which the towel began to warm up and was bone dry again within fifteen. At 1am, I took a further cold shower then went back to bed undried, managing to fall asleep for the first time.

Then around 3am, I was woken by a repeated scratching noise from the kitchen, which seemed to be coming from the small gas oven in the corner. Torch in mouth, I tentatively pulled the rusty door open to reveal a tiny pair of terrified eyes staring back at me. I almost jumped out of my overheated skin when the brown mouse dived out and scurried off into the dining room, hiding beneath the large wooden dresser. Rather ironically, he was probably cooler inside the oven.

Today is another sunny, hot day (just for a change) and my hosts have already been into the dining room to leave me a typical *white visitor's breakfast*: locally made French bread, a tub of Blueband margarine and a jar of *Bonne Maman* strawberry jam. And to drink, none other than the ubiquitous Nescafé with Nido powdered milk and cubed sugar from France in a neat blue box. This may seem rather basic compared with bacon, eggs, fried bread and filter coffee, but to have this – rather than a gourdful of grainy punrun – is a real luxury in these parts.

A face appears at my window; one I don't recognize. I peer out through the dusty grille to see a man holding a ladder while his companion climbs up onto the roof.

"*Sɛɛwo mã?*" I call out.

"*Sɛɛwo! Aga po!*" I assume this to mean 'good morning'.

"Is everything okay?"

"Yes, *monsieur*. We're filling your water tank."

Using a pair of old buckets, these two have brought my water from the well a hundred yards down the hill and are pouring it into the large plastic tank on my roof. The buckets are not huge and the square tank, which holds a good fifty gallons, is already a third full. I had no idea my 'running water' was a result of such effort and feel somewhat guilty at my nocturnal shower (just to cool down), as they toil in this heat. As I finish my second slice of bread and jam, I hear a familiar scratching sound from the oven. I decide it's best ignored.

This morning, I'm off to meet another old chap by the name of Allai, who lives on the edge of the cliff and knows a lot about traditional Dogon music and culture. Thomas has agreed to take me, as the route is *un peu compliqué*, and he doesn't want me straying into forbidden territory. Wandering eastwards on the undulating dirt road, square stone dwellings give way to a desolate, rocky, almost lunar plateau, with the occasional hardy tree breaking up the monotony of brownness. We approach a broad gully where farmers in ragged clothing are throwing rusty bucketfuls of water over their dark-green crops.

"Onions," Thomas explains. "Dogon onions have a special flavour unlike any other. Once you know the Dogon onion taste, you will always recognize it, for the rest of your life."

"Do they sell the onions to the surrounding villages?"

"Oh yes, lots! And we send them down to Bamako in large trucks, and even export them to Senegal, Côte d'Ivoire and Burkina."

Onions were introduced by the French colonial powers in the 1930s[20] – I suppose all those anthropologists needed a few home comforts to supplement their rice and punrun. And it turns out they grow extremely well here.

"People love our onions. One charity even tried drying them and exporting them to Europe, but this worked for a short time only."

"Why was that?"

"The rules there were too strict. The onions were dried but had too much dust on them, so did not meet with European standards."

What a shame; Europe could otherwise be dining on some of the

---

[20] http://www.crystalinks.com/dogon.html

world's tastiest onions, while also providing much-needed income for a struggling economy.

Just beyond the plantation, several indented areas in the rock face have been marked out by neat lines of stones; some square, some triangular.

"That's where someone is going to plant more onions," says Thomas.

"But it's all rock. How can you grow onions there?"

"They'll bring earth from far away and fill in this whole area. That's how most of the fields here have been made."

"But the soil would only be about thirty centimetres deep."

"Yes, but that's enough. They have to water it every day, though."

"And where does the water come from?"

"We are very blessed up here on the cliff: our wells are only twelve metres deep in Sangha and never run dry."

Although 1500 feet high, the Dogon cliffs have a raised water table, allowing them easier access to water than those down on the plain.

A small path, distinguishable only by its lighter shade of brown and the occasional row of stones at its boundary, leads into a narrow, rocky ravine. We clamber down through semi-darkness; at some points the gap is less than two feet wide, and the ground underfoot is stony and uneven. A few more steps and the chasm opens out onto a ledge no more than twenty feet deep, beyond which the jagged cliff plummets into nothingness. The view from here is truly impressive: the vast plain below stretches as far as the eye can see, punctuated with round, green trees, more rocks and the occasional tiny village. To the north, undulating sand dunes break up the monotony, rolling off into the hazy distance to join the mighty Sahara.

The cliff itself is an impressive sight: completely vertical but dipping in and out along its jagged hundred-mile course. To our left, a rocky promontory reminiscent of the Wild West extends almost half a mile into the plain, a zigzagging dirt track winding precariously down its steep sides. Perched on this jutting cliff are dozens of small square adobe houses, quite different from the buildings in Sangha; eight feet wide at the base and mostly two stories high, tapering in slightly at the top. Flat roofed with tiny, square windows in their sides, these houses sit on two or three rows of thick wooden beams, laid in perpendicular lines like a giant game of Jenga. Branches are used for the upper floor and roof, protruding from the sides of the mud walls at regular intervals.

"The cliffs are famous for these houses," says Thomas, "but the Dogon do not live in them, and we did not build them: the *Tellem* did."

"The Tellem? Who were *they?*"

"The Tellem were pygmies and they had the power of flight."

First fishy aliens, now flying pygmies.

"The Dogon came here hundreds of years ago. Some of us took the Tellem dwellings, but most settled on the plain or the clifftop."

"And are there still Tellem in those houses?"

"Ah no, my friend," he laughs. "The Tellem disappeared many many years ago."

"What happened to them?"

"Nobody knows."

Maybe they simply intermarried with the Dogon and were thus absorbed into their ethnicity. This might account for the diminutive stature of the Dogon, many of whom do not exceed five feet.

As we continue along the narrow pathway, I see what look like small cairns: pyramid-shaped mounds of stones positioned on the edge of the precipice.

Thomas explains: "These show where someone fell off the cliff and died."

A timely reminder for us to tread carefully, if ever there were one. But round the next corner, a young boy – no older than twelve – is climbing down the sheer cliff face using nothing but a thinnish pair of ropes, tied round a solitary tree trunk beside us. He's perched literally hundreds of metres above the plain with no safety harness, but doesn't look remotely frightened. On his back is a small woven bag, into which he deposits a handful of what, from a distance, looks like chalk. But these are not chalk cliffs.

"Pigeon dung, *Robert*. He's collecting it to sell at the market."

"What for?"

"It makes good fertilizer for plants."

As the boy descends further, the cliff curves inwards leaving him literally hanging there on his ropes, swinging from side to side until he reaches a small ledge 30 metres below.

"Is the rope secure?" I ask, slightly concerned I might witness a horrific event.

"Oh yes – it's made from woven baobab bark and is very strong."

"And how much will he get for his dung at market?"

"If he fills his bag, perhaps 250 francs."

That's 30 English pence for risking life and limb.

"But sometimes, he will also find an old Tellem treasure, and this will be worth a lot of money."

"Treasure?"

"They used to make ornate statues out of brass or wood, usually depicting people. These are worth much money, and sometimes white people buy them for museums in their countries."[21]

Allai's village is not like the Tellem ones, but also quite different from Sangha. It is made up of single-storey Bethlehemesque houses with flat roofs and adobe walls. Each roof has a foot-high wall round its perimeter for storing or drying crops, and is accessed by a typical African *log ladder:* a thick Y-shaped branch with deep notches cut out at regular intervals as steps. The split near the top of the 'Y' enables the branch to be safely leant against any wall; an ingenious system, much simpler than a Western ladder and largely maintenance-free.

As we enter the village, a large round hut – quite different from the other buildings – catches my attention. It has a broad open doorway and its adobe walls are decorated with many embossed symbols.

"That is the *ponulu,*" Thomas informs me.

"The what?"

"The *ponulu.* The house of menstruation. Don't you have those in your country?"

"No, I can't say we do."

"The ponulu is the house where the women come for five days every month, when they are menstruating."

"Why can't they stay in their own homes?"

"Stay in their homes? Never! They are unclean, and must stay in the *ponulu* until they are finished."

"So, who cooks the dinner while they are in the *ponulu?*"

"Their sister or a neighbour. Everyone looks after each other's needs in

---

[21]http://www.crystalinks.com/dogon.html

a Dogon village."

We pass through narrow, dusty lanes between the adobe houses, most only just wide enough for cattle to pass. There are a few square Tellem-like buildings in the village, tall and narrow with pointed straw roofs. These are not houses, though, but granaries. Stone walls, about four feet high, bridge the gaps between buildings at various points, creating boundaries between properties and further defining the path through the village.

"*Bidepo! Sɛɛwo mã?*"

An old man sitting beneath a curiously low shelter calls out to greet us. The roof above his head is a staggering four feet thick and is made of branches, twigs and millet; highly effective in keeping the midday sun at bay. The entire structure is rectangular and roughly ten feet by six, its hefty roof suspended four feet above the ground by pillars of boulders and the occasional sturdy branch.

"This is a very important place," Thomas tells me. "It's called the *tɔguna,* the house of words. This is where two men come if they have a disagreement. They sit here and talk until they have settled their differences."

"Why such a low roof?"

"It forces the men to remain seated, so they cannot stand and fight each other." That's clever.

"And is this old man the village chief?"

"No. The Dogon do not have village chiefs."

"Really?"

"Well, they do now, but it was Westerners who introduced this concept."

"So, who was in charge before that?"

"Well, the *hogon*, of course."

"A hogon was in charge of the Dogon?"

"Yes. We still have hogons. They oversee traditional religious rites such as weddings and fertility rituals.[22] He has a special hut where he carries these out." This does not surprise me.

"The hogon wears a red hat and a special bracelet, and nobody is ever allowed to touch him."

---

[22] Dieterlen (1956). "Parenté et Mariage Chez les Dogon". Africa. **26** (2): 107–148

"Why not?"

"Because he is sacred. The Dogon believe that the first hogon was descended from *Lɛbɛ,* the snake god of the earth. And *Lɛbɛ* was descended from the Nommos."

"The fish-like aliens from Sirius C?"

"Yes. Legend says that *Lɛbɛ* was eaten by a Nommo, and so their spirits fused together. After eating him, the Nommo vomited him up, but now Lɛbɛ was part spiritual and part human."[23]

"And part snake?"

"No, not part snake. But he became the first hogon. The Dogon believe that the hogon is visited by Lɛbɛ every night. He comes in the form of a snake and licks the hogon's skin to purify him and infuse him with life force."[24]

I didn't think snakes had the ability to lick people, but Lɛbɛ was a *special* snake, after all.

"Does one need any specific training to become a hogon?"

"Once chosen, they spend about a year in the initiation process. During this time, they may not shave or wash at all. The hogon must never marry, and he always lives alone."

The midday sun is relentless as it approaches its zenith, so I'm grateful when Thomas announces our arrival. Allai's house is quite literally on the cliff's edge. I peer over his relatively low wall and gulp at the thousand-foot drop.

Shaking his bony hand warmly, I greet Allai with a hearty *"Aga po!"*

"Aga po toubab. Sɛɛwo mã?" replies the croaky, feeble voice of Allai, already in his late 80s. As I shake his hand, I grasp my wrist with my left hand: an important mark of respect when greeting an old man here. He offers us a seat in the courtyard, on a low, naturally occurring rock at the base of his house; not the most comfortable of seating, but shaded at least. Frail-looking and the usual five feet tall, Allai still has lots of energy for his age. Wearing a green and white bobble hat, a long white smock and a pair of red Crocs on his feet, he brings us a large metal goblet of water, from

---

[23] Imperato, Pascal James (2001). Legends, sorcerers, and enchanted lizards: door locks of the Bamana of Mali. Africana Publishing.

[24] http://www.crystalinks.com/dogon.html

which we each take a welcome sip. As he greets us, I notice Allai's teeth are very brown, and that those on his lower jaw are protruding unevenly from behind his bottom lip. A spindly beard, mostly white, covers part of his chicken-like neck, and his dark, piercing eyes stare constantly and warmly at me. Next to him sits one of his many grandsons, Benjamin, who is shredding an old rice sack into strips.

"What are you doing with that?" I ask, via Thomas as translator.

"I'm making rope," replies the teenager.

He strips away the plasticky strands one by one, then weaves them together to make rope one centimetre thick.

"Ask him how much of this rope he makes in one day," I say to Thomas.

"He says each length of rope is roughly five metres long. He usually makes three of these in a day."

"And what does he do with them?"

"He sells them. Each length of rope sells for 300 francs here in the village, or 500 francs if he sells them at the market in Sangha."

This kind of rope is much thinner than the baobab rope used by *pigeon dung boy* and is reserved for less risky tasks, such as tethering livestock or tying a door shut.

Allai has some traditional Dogon songs for me, so I hold my MP3 recorder a few inches from his mouth and he begins singing. What I hear next is astounding: this chap is almost twenty years older than my dad but has one of the strongest voices I've ever heard in Africa. Not a perfectly rounded timbre, and his diction is impaired by his lacking dentition, but still an incredibly powerful voice which moves me to the core. The melody of the song is undulating and pentatonic but also heavily ornamented, somewhat resembling Indian or Arabic chant. After roughly seven minutes of non-stop singing, he finishes and breaks into a laugh. We all laugh too – I'm not quite sure why, but it certainly helps break any remaining ice.

"What was the song about?" I ask, eagerly.

Thomas replies: "It's a song about a turtle dove who is a bit deaf. He cannot hear what the other doves are saying…"

But before Thomas can finish his explanation, Allai has launched into a second song, equally beautiful but sounding almost identical to the first (to my non-Dogon ears, at least). This one lasts only five minutes and – like the first – includes fast, intricate melodies, as well as some long notes and pauses.

"What was that one about?" I enquire, wondering if all Dogon songs depict disabled animals.

"Ah, this one is quite well known," says Thomas, animated. "It tells the story of a porcupine who gets caught by a hunter and put into his bag. Then the hunter finds a larger animal and because his bag is small, he cannot carry both. So he lets the porcupine go."

"That's nice."

"The refrain is the song of the porcupine. He sings *I went into his bag, but then I said the name of God.*"

He proceeds to sing me song after song, including one which talks about women at the market wearing indigo cloth and how fine they look, all clad in blue.

"*Robert*, these songs are all *buloni*," Thomas tells me.

"Baloney?!"

"No, *buloni*. It's a Dogon song we sing when sowing seeds in late May or early June. *Buloni* songs are accompanied by the *boiná* and are used to worship *Lɛbɛ*."

"The snake god, who was swallowed by a Nommo and licks hogons on a nightly basis?"

"Yes."

The *boiná*, I discover, is a double-headed barrel drum – quite a common sight in West Africa.

I ask about other Dogon instruments, and Allai mentions the *kɛbɛlɛ*.[25]

"What's one of those?"

"There are many *kɛbɛlɛs* in our village," says Benjamin, as he rounds off his first five-metre length of rope. "I can take you to see some now." And with that, he rises to his feet and heads off.

"Come!"

Navigating more narrow passageways – and at great speed this time – Thomas and I follow our young, energetic guide out to the far edge of the village, passing more tall Dogon granaries, large piles of wood, an ornate adobe mosque, and the occasional mango tree. In one narrow street,

---

[25] Pronounced [keh-beh-leh]

various touristy items – bags, hats, wood carvings and wall hangings – are laid out on the dusty ground, as a couple of white back-packers admire them. In spite of its relative remoteness, this small village gets a fair trickle of intrepid young Westerners, some daring to trek the entire length of this 100-mile escarpment in a matter of days. The carvings, I notice are mostly of lizards, snakes and houses, as well as several depicting bare-chested women with pointy breasts.

"The Dogon have a well-known proverb," adds Thomas. "It says: *The breast is second only to God*."

There are also a couple of iconic Dogon doors: thick, dark wood ornately carved with a range of images, rather like a cathedral door back home, though much smaller. One creature I wasn't expecting to see depicted here is the fox, as I've never encountered one in Africa. Benjamin notices me run my finger over the dark wooden fox head on the embossed door.

"*C'est le renard, monsieur* – the fox. He tells the future for the Dogon."

"How can a fox tell the future? What does he say?"

"He doesn't speak, *monsieur*, but his pawprints tell the future."

"His pawprints?"

"Yes. First, the hogon draws squares in the sand."

"Like a grid?"

"Yes."

"How large is the grid?"

Unable to answer in any Western unit of measurement, he crouches down and draws a large rectangle, roughly one metre by four.

"This is divided into lots of small squares," he adds, etching these into his box, "and in these boxes are small mounds of sand and sticks, or drawings."

"What do the boxes mean?"

"Each box is a question or answer. Who should I marry? What job should I do? Should I grow onions or kola nuts? Then the priest calls upon the sacred fox to come and mark the sand with his feet. They also leave him some milk or peanuts."

"To make sure he comes?"

"Yes. But he always comes late at night. Then the next morning, everyone comes to see where the fox has trodden. This tells the future and gives answers to the questions."[26]

Benjamin is eager to actually show us a *kɛbɛlɛ*, so races off through more narrow passageways, as we attempt to keep up with his disappearing figure. After a steep climb, we reach our destination just outside the village on another exposed ledge, where a steep cliff wall rises upwards some thirty feet.

"Where are we going?" I ask Benjamin, intrigued.

"To the blacksmith's."

"What for?"

"*Toubab*, don't you know anything?! The blacksmith does all the male circumcisions in a Dogon village. It's his job."

Curious indeed. I know barbers used to carry out surgery back home, but blacksmiths circumcising is a step further still.

"I thought you were taking us to see a *kɛbɛlɛ*."

"I am! All *kɛbɛlɛs* are kept with the blacksmith, of course."

I'm none the wiser, but I'm sure all will become clear.

---

[26] http://www.crystalinks.com/dogon.html

Tellem cliff dwellings, Dogon Country

Chapter Nine – Circumcision

"When he has healed, he stands naked by the roadside."

AS WE APPROACH the steep cliff wall before us, I am struck by an impressive sight: a multitude of wall paintings extend roughly 40 feet across this entire section of cliff. They remind me of prehistoric cave drawings, and use just three colours: red, white and black. No single image is more than a couple of feet across, but there must be more than 300 pictures painted here, rising to a height of around 15 feet. Although aesthetically very pleasing to the eye, many of these etchings are quite hard to identify. Some look like drums, some vaguely resemble Dogon granaries, some look like people and others depict lizards – an important symbol in many African traditions. One or two images, I shiver to admit, resemble detached foreskins. The blacksmith, a plump middle-aged chap, emerges – Fagin-like – from the smoky doorway of his hut and greets us warmly. He's wearing a pink ladies' nightdress over his torn, fawn-coloured trousers, though has no idea of the garment's original purpose. As Benjamin heads back to his rope making, the blacksmith shows us a large circular area beneath the wall paintings, marked out with yet more stones on the ground.

"This is where the circumcisions take place," he proudly announces, sitting on a big square rock in the centre of the area. "I have performed over four hundred circumcisions here."

I ask for more detail, cautiously intrigued.

"When a boy is ten or twelve years old, he is brought here, and I use this knife to cut off the skin." He pulls out his weapon of choice from a leather sheath hung round his waist and waves it at me, its point almost touching the end of my nose. I gaze cross-eyed at the rusty blade, twelve inches long and surprisingly narrow. A tarnished brown colour, it doesn't even look particularly sharp. The handle, I notice, is made from wood carved into the shape of a man.

"The boy sits here on this rock and I cut, cut, cut!" he explains with great energy, using the knife to mime a curved cutting motion with each utterance. "Afterwards, the boy bleeds a lot, so he goes to that hut next to mine. It is called the healing hut."

The Dogon really do have a hut for every purpose.

"When he has healed, he stands naked by the roadside shaking a kɛbɛlɛ. Passers-by will give him money or gifts. He does this every day for a month."

"Completely naked?"

"Yes. This is so that people can admire him and see his newly cut…"

"I understand," I quickly respond, shuddering. "Can I see a *kɛbɛlɛ* now?"

"Follow me!" He heads round the corner of the painted cliff wall on a path so narrow it scarcely exists, with a sheer drop beneath us. Here, there is a wedge-shaped opening to a small cave.

"Look, here are all the *kɛbɛlɛs*!" he declares, pointing inside.

I tentatively step through the entrance of his dingy grotto, unable to see much initially. Once my eyes have adjusted, I make out at least thirty odd-looking gourd shakers piled on top of each other, coated in a thick layer of Dogon dust. I'm thinking there must be a lot of circumcisions in the village to need all of these.

The kɛbɛlɛ is a simple instrument, made from local materials. First, you take an L-shaped stick, roughly two feet long in one direction, slightly shorter in the other. The shorter end is your handle. Now get a smallish whole gourd (4-6 inches in diameter), make a hole through opposite ends and hollow it out. Thread this entire spherical vegetable onto the longer side of your stick. Now cut small disks from other gourds, make holes in their centre and thread these on in front of the sphere. The disks tend to go onto the stick in the following order: two small, two large, two small, two large, until about twenty have been added. A piece of string is tied around the end to stop the disks falling off, and the instrument is played by being shaken forwards and backwards, causing the gourds to collide and vibrate. I reach down to pick one up.

"STOP!" he shouts, waving his hand furiously at me. "This is strictly forbidden! You may never play or even touch a kɛbɛlɛ unless you have just been circumcised."

As much as I'd love to play this fascinating instrument, I'm not quite prepared to make such a sacrifice, especially having seen the state of his knife.

"Can I not just give it one little shake?" I ask, tentatively.

"Never! If anyone plays the kɛbɛlɛ at the wrong time, then a pregnant woman in the village will lose her baby."

I certainly wouldn't want to be responsible for such an occurrence, so resign myself to merely looking and imagining what these curious idiophones must sound like. He does let me take photos, though, as this will not cause any grief in the village. Thomas and I bid our knife-wielding metalworker farewell and I instinctively turn towards the path along the ledge, clearly the shortest route back to Sangha.

"No!" he shouts, vehemently. "You cannot take that path – it is sacred land."

We climb up through the narrow gulley to the rocky plateau we crossed this morning. Midway across, I notice two middle-aged white men using some sort of laser device to measure distances. I approach and greet them, intrigued by what they're doing.

"We are here to find uranium in the Dogon cliffs, so we can build a nuclear power station here," the taller and slightly older Frenchman replies.

"A WHAT?" I exclaim, furious at the very thought.

Just in time, his colleague smirks, and I'm relieved to realize they're joking.

"We're actually planning to build a hotel complex right here on the cliff."

"You're serious this time?"

"Yes, completely."

"It would have a fabulous view!"

"Yes, that's why we are considering this location. It's also right next to Sangha, which is a popular destination for tourists but only has a few small hotels."

"And you think that a larger hotel like this would draw more tourists?"

"That's our plan."

I wish them all the best with their elaborate enterprise, somewhat ambivalent as to the effect such a development would have on the local landscape and culture.

Back at Thomas's house that evening – and after another towel-soaked siesta – we sit round our communal bowl for *fonio* with beef, carrots and cabbage. I quickly place most of my cabbage into the centre.

"You like the *ponio*, Robert?" Fonio is a local cereal, a bit like couscous. The Dogon make no distinction between the sounds 'F' and 'P', and so frequently interchange them in French.

"Yes, it's good. *C'est très bon!*"

As we eat, Thomas shares some tragic news: a young child died in Sangha today. Wandering through the village thirstily, he came across a tin of what looked like water in a mechanic's workshop shop and drank it. It turned out to be battery acid. By the time he – or anyone else – had realized, it was too late.

"It's very sad," says Thomas, "but also very common. In the past, some mothers would give birth to ten children and lose every one of them."

"Really? Why?"

"Because they were undernourished so could not produce enough milk to keep their babies alive. Things are improving these days, and more children survive."

"That's good. Do you celebrate Mothers' Day here?" I ask, naively.

"The Dogon don't have such a celebration."

"What about birthdays?"

"No, this is a toubab thing. We do not celebrate birthdays, and we do not even know the date or year most people were born."

"So, how do you know how old someone is?"

"We guess."

"And how does that work for schools?"

"They guess too, but most parents roughly know the age of their child. You see, *Robert*, keeping the child alive was always more important here than the luxury of remembering its date of birth."

It strikes me how much of our culture in the West is built upon unnecessary luxuries which, over time, we have come to regard as essential: television, eating out, tourism, sport, photography, cars, theatre, and even birthdays. Most Dogon experience none of the above and have struggled to survive in the past. And yet, why is it these people still seem happier and more fulfilled than the average Brit? Their society is more cohesive, and theft, murder and suicide are virtually unheard of. No drug addiction and, whilst they have alcohol, their society would frown upon the mindless binge-drinking seen as 'normal' in many Western societies. Could it be that the Dogon's hardships have strengthened and united them? Meanwhile, the West has had it easy for so long that our cultural and societal 'muscles' have withered away, rendering us no longer capable of achieving a society which functions as one. We've built walls, hedges and fences, we've put locks on our doors, and we often don't even greet the neighbours on our own street any more. This has done away with accountability – still very prevalent in African society – and, as a result, we have graffiti-covered walls, mindless muggings and old people who die alone, undiscovered for days. Although clearly not without its dangers, none of the above happens in Sangha.

Once we've finished our '*ponio*', I take the opportunity to look inside the gas freezer: my vial of rabies vaccine is nicely cool inside its tub but definitely not frozen, which is good.

Thomas's small black fan is still whirring furiously on the ceiling, providing a much-needed breeze. It still looks strangely familiar to me, but I can't quite work out why.

"I like your ceiling fan. I'm not sure I've seen one like that before."

"*Ah oui,*" replies Thomas, "it came from a Land Rover engine. I've had it up there for ten years and it has never gone wrong."

There's a bit of quality British engineering for you, and the reason it looks familiar – I drove a Land Rover for almost four years in Benin.

The next day is Sunday and I'm off to investigate the music at the church on the hill. Traditional African music tends to be dumbed down when used in church, so I'm keen to see if that's also the case here.

At the door, I'm welcomed by a short chap wearing a Western shirt, smart trousers and sandals.

"*Aga po!*" I say.

"Ah!" comes the usual surprised response. "*Sɛɛwo mã?*"

"*Sɛɛwo!*"

It's a typically rectangular church with a concrete floor and a raised platform at the front, upon which stands a wooden lectern. Beneath the building's tin roof is a white painted wooden ceiling where half a dozen fans are rotating noisily. The congregation are sitting on straight benches, all painted bottle green: men to the right, women to the left. I've never found out why they separate the genders – or who introduced it – but it is terribly common in Africa. Between the congregation and the stage, a small choir of twelve stands at right angles.

The service starts only fifteen minutes late, and worship begins with three very Western songs, one of which I instantly recognize as *Amazing Grace*. The fourth song sounds much more African and uses a vaguely pentatonic scale with call and response. Two further semi-Dogon songs follow, all accompanied by the *gomboï* talking drum, a gourd shaker (always played by women), and the 1960s 'demon-free' square drum. It's encouraging to see these instruments, but the church still bears a massive imprint of Western missionaries and has become a hybrid of two cultures, rather than being genuinely Dogon. There's no dancing or moving about to the songs, just people standing still in straight rows like white people would.

Time for the offering, and everyone processes up to the front of the church to put money in one of *three* wooden containers. One is for the tithe (a tenth of one's income), the second is for building work, and the last one is for the poor. This procession is accompanied by a strangely familiar melody, which I quickly recognize as *Auld Lang Syne*. How on earth did *that* make it over here? And they're singing it so slowly I fear they might actually grind to a halt midway through. I'm guessing some well-meaning missionary taught them it decades ago as 'the collection song' and it stuck. But, like *Amazing Grace*, Auld Lang Syne uses the pentatonic scale, as does most Dogon music. So these songs may not be as foreign as you think. There are many hymns and spirituals based on African pentatonic melodies, taken over to America with the Slave Trade. So, in a sense, this morning's songs have come full circle – back to their roots. But in the process, they have become so Westernized they no longer sound like any of Siméon or Allai's *real* Dogon songs.

Next morning, I wake from a reasonable night's sleep, somewhat disrupted by more scratching from the mouse in the oven. I'm just out of the shower when the young house-help arrives with my breakfast: more jam, bread and Nescafé. While he's here, I decide to mention my stove-dwelling rodent.

"Ah yes, *monsieur*. The mouse lives in there. But if you light the oven, he leaves."

"Why don't you remove him permanently from the oven?"

"It's his home."

Coulibaly and Keita arrive. Today, we will cross the flat, sandy Dogon plain all the way to *Koro*, roughly 70 miles south-east of here, then head back to Bamako tomorrow. Before we leave, I have one very important task to carry out, so carefully remove the rabies vaccine from Thomas's freezer, ready to visit the clinic on the hill. It's only a few hundred yards away, but I can't risk the serum getting too warm, so take the Hilux, air-con on full blast. The pastor comes with me to show the way and to introduce me to the staff there.

Comprising two simple rooms, the clinic is compact but well-equipped, the entire single-storey building no larger than a single garage. The waiting room – should one ever be required – consists of half a dozen *egg-slicer chairs* lined up across the front of the building, beneath a narrow veranda – just large enough to keep the sun off. Inside, the walls are clad with shiny, aqua-coloured tiles from floor to ceiling.

"Bienvenue messieurs!" The Dogon nurse greets me

"Sɛɛwo mã?"

"Sɛɛwo, sɛɛwo! Asseyez-vous."

I hand her the vaccine, which she takes to prepare. As we sit and wait, I notice a large poster on the wall showing Dogon people dancing round the rocky clifftops in curious fluffy red costumes. The masks they are wearing are equally strange: some look like cows with horns, others have long 'trunks' like an elephant, and several are topped with a two-foot symbol resembling a skinny lizard. Many of the masks are decorated with cowrie shells round the eyes and mouth, giving them a rather spooky appearance.

"That's the *Fête des Masques,"* Thomas tells me. "Every April, the Dogon celebrate this, to give thanks for the harvest and to honour their ancestors."

The strangest costume of all is a hat with a fifteen-foot extension, which rises vertically to the sky but is no more than ten inches wide. Striped from all the way up with alternating foot-long brown and white sections, the top is adorned with a red pom-pom.

"That's the plank mask, or *sirige*," Thomas explains. "During the ceremony, the dancer leans forward until the top of his hat touches the ground. This symbolises the heavens meeting the earth."[27]

Out of the corner of my eye, I see the nurse holding a syringe vertically, slowly pushing the plunger upwards. Turning to dab my left arm with antiseptic, she then jabs the needle in with no warning. Ouch! However, my momentary pain pales into insignificance when I ponder the horrors of contracting rabies.

"Au revoir mes amis!" Thomas and his wife wave warmly as I crunch the Hilux into gear and bounce my way out of town. Before us lies the sight I spotted from the clifftop a couple of days ago: a narrow road which zigzags gradually down to the vast plain below. The views are spectacular as ever, the morning mist hanging mysteriously above this semi-desert landscape. Some of the road has even been clad with concrete here – for the tourists, of course. After a dozen hairpins, we finally reach the bottom. This is where I fully grasp the sheer size and majesty of the cliff itself: 1500 feet high and continuing fifty miles in each direction, with tiny box-like Tellem dwellings hanging onto this massive craggy wall for dear life. In front of us, the road peters out, and I'm struggling to see which way to go from here. Keita notices my confusion:

"Straight ahead, Monsieur Robert. That's the road."

"That?!" Before me is a sandy channel ten feet wide, the same beige colour as everything else on the plain and only marginally flatter and smoother than its surroundings.

"This is the road, *monsieur*. It was created by Mr McKinney's parents."

"Mac's parents?"

"The missionaries, yes. Roughly fifty years ago they attached a heavy log to the back of their tractor with ropes. Then the Reverend McKinney drove the whole 100 kilometres across the plain, dragging the log behind him all the way."

"Just the once?" I ask, dumbfounded.

---

[27] http://www.afrique-annuaire.com/musique/mali.html

"Well, he came back again the same way, of course."

It's a tricky surface to drive on, as the sand is so dry and soft that my wheels are in danger of becoming embedded. The technique is to maintain an optimum speed: not so slow as to get stuck, but not so fast that I lose control. Keeping the steering straight also helps, though this is not easy as the road frequently turns or splits in two, rejoining itself further on. We pass several donkey carts, horses and even motorbikes, all of whom are struggling somewhat too. One motorcyclist has his legs splayed out like stabilizers, to avoid falling off his bike.

I suddenly find myself driving through a deep channel with sandy walls several feet deep on either side, and am grateful nothing is coming the other way. Further on, a solitary camel is blocking the road, eating what little leaves it can find from a wizened *balanzan* tree, stretching its long leathery neck upwards in an almost giraffe-like pose. I swerve to avoid its hefty body, and the Toyota veers off the road onto the bumpy plain. I desperately try to regain control, but the rear wheels spin outwards as we career sideways, eventually colliding with a large bush, bringing us to an abrupt stop. For a moment, we all just sit there in a stationary stupor, stunned and dismayed.

"*Ça va, Robert?*" asks Coulibaly after a long pause.

"*Oui, ça va!*" No damage done, apart from a small dent on the driver's door.

As I try to move off, the wheels spin frantically and a stench of melting rubber radiates from the engine as it screams louder and higher. The car is now moving slowly forwards, and gradually picking up speed. We've still got 45 miles of this terrain to go, so I'd better get into the swing of it soon. Dodging more bushes, motorbikes and donkeys, we enter our first village.

"This is a Christian village," says Keita, proudly. In its centre is a square-towered church, not unlike the one in Sangha. Five miles further on, we reach another village, which I'm told is Muslim. Its mosque is not dissimilar from the church building in the previous village, apart from its domed top, adorned with a crescent moon.

"What about African traditional religion?" I ask.

"Oh, there's plenty of that too, often blended with one of the two religions."

In this village, I notice a large open square with a well in the centre. A camel is running away from the well, with a little Dogon man on its back, beating it with a stick. A long rope runs from the camel's harness all the way into the well.

"This is how they get the water from the well, Robert," Keita explains. "There's a bucket on the end of that rope, so they make the camel run to raise the water."

"And how deep is the well?"

"On the Dogon plain, the wells are very deep. 60, 70, or 80 metres. Some even a hundred metres deep."

"That's very deep!" I can see why they use a camel.

We speed off back into the wilderness, and I realize I'm actually quite enjoying the challenge of this road now. It's a constant adrenaline rush, but one I'm finding quite rewarding: folk back home would pay good money to spend a day *off-roading* in a four-by-four, and we're not even off the 'road'.

"Woohoo! This is fun!" I shout, slithering adeptly round another abrupt corner.

"Fun? What do you mean?" asks Coulibaly, frowning.

"I'm enjoying myself – this is exciting!"

"But this is a bad road, *monsieur*. Why would anyone like it?"

And there's another huge cultural difference: life in Africa is already difficult enough; nobody seeks out additional struggles for fun. But back home, life has become so comfortable, that we inflict difficulty upon ourselves just to be able to experience the struggle in a controlled environment. But we have a choice *not* to do so; the Dogon only have this road and so using it is understandably arduous.

A few miles from our destination, the flatness of the plain is broken up by sand dunes – this is the edge of the Sahara after all. The road mostly circumnavigates them, but there are a couple of slopes. I can't resist pulling over at one point, just to clamber up the steep dune edge, to its curvy ridge, feeling like Lawrence of Arabia. In terms of vegetation, there's nothing but the odd tuft of yellowing grass here, but the view from the dune is worth the climb, with the entire length of the Dogon cliff now visible in the distance.

We make it to the town of Koro as the sun is setting in my rear-view mirror. After a luxury meal of goat and fonio, accompanied by copious quantities of punrun, we all hit the sack. Tomorrow, I will travel back to

Bamako alone, as my two colleagues are staying in Koro for some meetings.

"Are you alone?"

"Yes!"

"Please, join me for dinner."

"Thank you."

"My name is Hans, from Germany."

I've made a detour to the riverside resort of *Terya Bugu*, located on the Bani River some distance west of the main road between San and Bla. It was created in the 1970s by French priest Bernard Verspieren who, having trained as an agronomist, developed the site after the great drought of the 60s, building invaluable irrigation canals and carrying out eco-scientific research. He lived in a house beside the river and had a great interest in renewable energy, going on to install solar-powered water pumps across Mali, as well as developing wind and biogas technologies. His philosophy was: 'No evangelism without development; no development without evangelism', and he once said: "It's all well and good to celebrate the Eucharist with bread and wine, but the Africans have neither!"[28]

In neatly organized orchards, grapefruits, mangos, oranges and lemons all bloom in Terya Bugu; a thriving oasis of natural beauty. The site also includes a school, a clinic, a library, a bakery and a workshop. The hotel is a relatively new addition, having been added after Verspieren's death in 2003.

"So, what are you doing in Mali, Hans?" I ask, after ordering a *poulet-frites* from the menu.

"I drove here."

"From Bamako?"

"No, from Germany."

"What?!"

"*Ja ja!* I came viz my Volkswagen Bulli."

Sure enough, just behind the restaurant sits a somewhat beaten-up VW campervan, hand-painted in faded orange and green.

"Why didn't you fly like everyone else?"

"Because of ze Mayan Prophecy. On 21st December zis year, ze

---

[28] www.jeuneafrique.com/54744/archives-thematique/bernard-verspieren-le-malien-blanc/

magnetic field of ze Earth is going to change, and all electrical devices will fail. Our brains will also become more powerful."

"Really?!

"*Ja ja!* So, I quit my job and drove out here. I plan to be somewhere I can survive vizout ze modern appliances in December. Maybe India."

"That's quite a drive! Have you had any problems on your journey so far?"

"*Ja ja!*" He seems to like this short phrase. "I had several flat tyres, and zer was one road in Mauritania where I could hardly pass and thought I would have to turn around. I also ran out of water once, and was quite dehydrated."

A few months later, I bumped into Hans at a resort near Bamako. I spotted his distinctive vehicle first, and there he was sitting behind the wheel.

"You look unwell, Hans."

"Ja ja! Ich bin sehr krank."

Gaunt and skinny, he'd had malaria, amoebas and various other ailments, and was unsure he would be able to continue his journey. That was the last I ever saw of him.

Chapter Ten – Turkey Twist

"An artificial tree will have to suffice this year."

Have you ever had a serious accident with a gas oven? I don't recommend it. The other day, I was in the middle of baking some potatoes (on Abdoulaye's day off) when the gas bottle ran out. Thankfully, we had a spare one in the yard, so rushed out to change it, not wanting to delay dinner. But I made one crucial mistake: I forgot to turn the oven *off* first. This meant that when I returned to the kitchen to light it with a match, the oven was already oozing fresh gas, just waiting to be ignited.

BOOOOOOOOOOOOM!

A wall of intense heat rushes over my head and the noise – albeit short-lived – is intense. I fall to the ground in shock, still unsure what has just happened. Lois rushes in and helps me up. My face is a little red, my eyebrows non-existent, and the front inch of my hairline has completely singed away. Other than that, I am, thankfully, unscathed. Probably a good thing I wear glasses, though.

Afterwards, I mentioned the event to Doctor Dave, who told me: "A few years back, a guy here died from a similar incident. You were very lucky, Rob."

Today, I've been invited on an early morning bike ride. Bamako is surrounded by pleasant countryside and rolling hills, which turn from yellow to green in rainy season. A Dutch missionary called Henk organizes the rides every couple of weeks, but seven o'clock on a Saturday morning is not an hour I generally relish. There's a good reason for the timing though, as the heat becomes too intense for sport after 10am. Henk's e-mail read:

Meet at start of Sotuba Canal, south of river by Pont Submersible. 7am.
Route: Along canal, then up to Kangaba and back. Duration 90 mins.

As you may recall, this is also the point where the third bridge is currently being built by the Chinese. Already, huge concrete pillars rise into the sky across half the river, neatly aligned in two parallel rows. The horizontal floor of the bridge is also in place for the first few metres, jutting out across the Niger like a super-sized jetty. Thankfully there's a barrier in place to stop cars driving on and taking a nasty plunge.

As well as Henk and Doctor Dave, other blokes on the ride this morning include a couple more US Embassy staff, a Norwegian aid worker and a Brazilian missionary. There's even another Brit: a portly redheaded chap who vaguely resembles an overweight Ed Sheeran.

"Mornin' boyo!" he calls, cheerfully.

"Are you from Wales, by any chance?"

"Ow d'yooo guess?" he replies with a smile, sweat pouring down his ruddy face. "Merthyr Tydfil. The name's Gareth, but most people call me Gary."

"Pleased to meet you, Gary. What are you doing here?"

"Ridin' my bike, innit?"

"No, I mean in Mali."

It turns out that Welsh Gary is here because his wife, Sally, works at the British Embassy. She's spent almost half her life on this continent, is fluent in Bambara, Shona, French and Swahili, and was previously married to a Kenyan. Newly wed though both in their 40s, she and Gary met on a mountain in the Brecon Beacons.

"There I was sat on top *Pen-y-Fan*, exhausted and sweatin' like a pig, and she appeared. We 'it it off right away and were wed last Christmas. She said I'd 'ave to live in Africa with 'er, and I thought I'd rather be hyur with 'er than in Glamorgan without 'er. So hyur I am!"

"And where do you live in Mali?"

"Hyur in Bamako. In Boudalabago."

"You mean Badalabougou."

"That's it. Over near the Old Bridge."

The ride starts alongside the Sotuba Canal on a red dirt track which is surprisingly smooth, in spite of the dust our tyres are kicking up. We're on a narrow strip of land, with the canal to the right, and the broad Niger River to the left, its gently sloping banks decorated with vegetation. Henk is keen and rides fast, his long Dutch legs and athletic figure putting chubby Gary and me to shame, as we bring up the rear, desperately trying to keep up.

The canal starts here and runs roughly 15 miles northeast, towards the small town of Tyenfala. Back in the 1920s, when Mali was still called French Sudan, colonial powers had it built at great expense; not for transport but for irrigation. Their aim was 'to transform the plains of the mid-Niger into a new cotton-growing Egypt.'[29] The plan clearly worked, as Mali now produces half a million tonnes of cotton per year – more than Côte d'Ivoire to the south and almost as much as Burkina Faso to the east.

After a couple of miles, we take a right and cross a rickety bridge, which could feasibly date back to the canal's construction. From here, a steep path ascends through tall green walls of maize plantations, emerging at a tiny village, where locals stare incredulously at their transient, pale-skinned visitors. It's hard work and I'm sweating as much as Gary now. We chat away, trying to forget the pain in our calves.

"You know," says Gary, "there's a lot about this country that makes me angry. Yesterday, I saw a chap ridin' a donkey cart. He was hittin' his donkey hard to make it go faster. Now that's not on, is it? So I shouted out at him: 'NO! Stop hittin' that donkey!' and I waved my fist at him furiously."

"How did he respond?"

"He just looked confused and carried on hittin' the poor animal."

"That's what they do here. In Africa, an animal is either meat still alive, or a workhorse."

"Doesn't make it right, though, does it?"

Sensing his anger rising at the thought, I change the subject: "What are you going to do here work-wise, Gary?"

"Oh, I dunno really. I was thinkin' of offerin' Welsh lessons."

"Do you think there'd be a call for those in Mali?"

"Maybe. It's a language, isn't it?"

I decide not to comment.

Just then, Doctor Dave calls out:

---

[29] http://www.aventures-motocyclistes-dun-broussard.fr/2016/04/bamako-le-canal-de-sotuba-et-le-fleuve-niger.html

"Look down there guys! That's the *Campement de Kangaba*. You two new Brits should go there some time – it's very nice!"

At the base of the cliff is a lush, green rectangle roughly 500 metres across, contrasting starkly with the arid, russet landscape surrounding it. Perched on the hillside amid this verdure are quaint thatched huts, which surround a turquoise L-shaped swimming pool beside a rustic restaurant. A clearly marked footpath leads from this Eden up the slope, crossing our path and finishing at an imposing, Lion-Kingesque rock on the hilltop, adorned with a single baobab. In 2003, there was nothing on the plain below but barren scrubland and the occasional goat. Then a Frenchman bought the plot and began planting trees and building huts, and the *Campement* was born, opening its doors to delighted tourists in 2007. It offers wealthy expats the ideal get-away: peace and quiet, comfort, nature, excellent food and a warm welcome. And all just a stone's throw from bustling Bamako.

As we pass through our final village, the cogs on my rear wheel give way and my pedals rush forwards from lack of resistance. I lose control and career off the path, tumbling violently to the ground with a bang. Stunned, I dizzily open my eyes to see half a dozen blurry faces peering down at me.

"Are you okay Rob?" asks Henk, his brow furrowed with concern.

"I'll...I'll be fine, but I think my bike just died."

"That was quite a tumble, boyo!" says my newest friend.

I've grazed my leg and elbow and wrenched my shoulder muscle quite badly. Thankfully, our starting (and ending) point is now only a few hundred yards away, so I hobble back, a couple of chaps staying with me. The grazes heal up after a few days, but my shoulder will take a couple of months before I can even lift it to head height. On the plus side, a chap in town mends my bike for less than ten pounds.

It's Christmas time, and the best present of all is finally getting the Mitsubishi back on the road. I smiled the biggest of smiles when I got the call last week: "*Culasse, c'est bon! Culasse, c'est bon!*" I thanked Chao Cheng and proudly drove the vehicle out of his workshop, where it had spent a total of five weeks and had its engine dismantled and rebuilt *four* times. The total cost was £600, way cheaper than in the UK, where the repair costs would most likely have written the vehicle off entirely.

One positive offshoot of the car saga is that we've found a delightful African restaurant not far from the workshop. *Le Petit Gril* does the tastiest beef kebabs I've had anywhere in the world, so we're sure to be using this place quite often from now on. That said, Vietnamese *nems* are still our top fast-food snack here. Yes, for reasons I am yet to fathom, Bamako is littered with a dozen or so blue wooden shacks selling these yummy spring rolls. Goodness only knows why, or how, so many Vietnamese ended up in Bamako; they can't have arrived by boat. But their nems, served with a sweet chilli sauce and wrapped in lettuce leaves, are truly delicious.

Navigating the colourful, fly-infested aisles of Badala Market on my way home, I pop in to see Youssouf, who offers me a seat and a warm handshake as usual.

"You want tea?"

"Just the second and third cups."

"Ah yes! Traoré does not like the bitter one."

"*Sanbé sanbé!*" I say, proudly.[30]

"What do you mean? We do not celebrate this!"

"But, you believe in *Nabila Isa*,[31] so why not remember his birth?"

"We call him *Isa Al Masih* in the north. It means *anointed one.*"

"And it's his birthday! Isn't that a good thing to celebrate? We believe he was God's son..."

"NO! Isa cannot be the son of Allah. Here's your second cup, my friend."

"Thank you. Isa is in the Koran..."

"Yes, but Allah cannot have a son. He cannot have sexual relations..."

"I agree. Jesus came from God but not through sexual relations. It's a bit more like...like...a banana plant."

"My friend, what are you saying?!"

"Well, a baby banana plant just grows from the root of the big plant. Jesus came from God a bit like this."

"But what about Mary? She is your god too!"

"No, there is only one God. We both agree on that."

"But you Christians have *three*: the Father, Jesus and Mary."

---

[30] 'Merry Christmas' or 'Happy Festivities'
[31] Noble Jesus

Oh dear! He thinks Mary is part of the Trinity.

"We believe Isa is fully God and fully man, and that he came to save the world. How are you reconciled with Allah if you sin?"

"Through good works, through discipline, through *Islam* – submission to Allah. Third cup?"

"Yes please. I believe in submission to God too. But I also believe Isa was a sacrifice for our forgiveness."

"You Christians always talk about forgiveness. But what about working out your faith?"

"We do that too, but faith and forgiveness come first."

An African expat Christmas is, in some ways, a rather empty experience, yet refreshingly undemanding compared with one back home. It's a time you miss your extended family the most, but is also a blank canvas to create the Christmas *you* want, with very few demands or obligations. And best of all, nothing Christmassy happens here till mid-December, allowing one to enjoy September, October and November untarnished by nauseating adverts, overcrowded shopping malls, premature fairy lights and the same old wall-to-wall cheesy hits. Then, around December 10th, you'll receive a text message from some other expat, saying:

Christmas stock has just arrived at Azar's

All five Bakers dive into our newly repaired Mitsubishi and rush off to find the supermarket packed with tinsel, baubles, balloons, fairy lights, party poppers, hideously over-priced board games and endless tacky toys from China. French cheeses, exotic looking pâtés, boxes of chocolates, wines and spirits all proudly adorn the shelves (and even a Methuselah of champagne!) Artificial trees – green, white or silver – take up a significant area of the shop floor, ranging from cheap and nasty to huge and expensive. There's even a *real* Norwegian spruce for sale: seven feet tall and decidedly bushy, it looks, smells and feels exactly as it would back home. It has no roots though, and costs 300 English pounds, so I think an artificial tree will have to suffice this year.

In England, it's frosty windowpanes, log fires and snow-covered landscapes which trigger that warm 'Christmassy' feeling. Here, the job is done by the *Harmattan* – a cool, dry, dusty wind, which blows southwards from the Sahara every December. After a couple of years in West Africa, that fuzzy festive feeling fills you the moment you open your curtains and see the air clouded with thick Harmattan dust. An almost tangible dryness to the air (and your throat), a dusty beigeness in the sky, and the fact you can no longer see the opposite bank of the river all tell you it's Harmattan season and Christmastime is here.

Our first Malian Christmas will be extra cool, as we've just had a *swamp cooler* installed. Bought from a Belgian family, we had it fitted yesterday by Monsieur Coulibaly (another one), who knocked a two-foot square hole in our lounge wall to do so. Although common in other parts of the world, I'd never heard of a swamp cooler before coming to Mali. Essentially a crude predecessor to the air-conditioner, it works by humidifying the air, so is only effective in very dry climates like this one. From the outside, it looks like a giant, cube-shaped beehive, with louvred metal vents on its three vertical sides. Inside this box is an enormous bladed cylinder, which rotates to draw air through the lateral vents, pushing it into the house through the open fourth side, which is fixed to the wall. But here's the clever bit: water is pumped to the top of the three sides and trickles down through straw matting before being pumped back round again. So, as the dry air is sucked into the box, it becomes humidified, and evaporation causes cooling. So this damp air brings chilled moisture into our lounge, and at a faster rate than any air-conditioning unit could. Cool in more ways than one, and an almost vital addition to help us survive the coming hot season.

Tonight, we have a bono fide pop star coming to Bamako! Jamaican singer and rapper Sean Paul is actually doing a concert here in Mali. It's a charity gig to help combat malaria, and is being held at the *Stade Modibo Keita,* Bamako's main football stadium (named after a former president). This is a rare occurrence in these parts, so I'm taking Madelaine – now twelve – to her first ever live pop concert.

We catch a taxi to the venue: a Mercedes 190D with a rare *blue* stripe down the side, splayed wheels and a hole in the exhaust which makes it sound like a dragster. It is driven by Monsieur Doumbia, who has eight children and greets me in Arabic, mistaking this bearded, tanned Brit for a

Lebanese. When we arrive at the stadium, it's more chaotic than I could have imagined: people everywhere, pushing, pulling and vying for a space around the entrance. I'm wondering where we get tickets, when a tout approaches me:

"*Monsieur*, you want ticket?"

"Yes, where do I buy them?"

"I have! I sell good price!" Here we go…

"Where is the ticket office?" I persist, keen to do things properly.

"There is no ticket office. I sell!"

"Okay, how much?"

"5000 francs, one ticket."

"I was told they were 2000 francs."

"Tickets for 2000, *c'est fini!*" None left at that price. I reach for a 10,000 franc note and he hands me two tickets. I immediately notice they are both labelled '2000 CFA'.

"*Monsieur!* Come back! These are 2000 franc tickets!"

"No, my friend. 2000 francs, it's finished. This is a 5000 franc ticket."

"But look, it says 2000…"

"2000, *c'est fini!*"

WAWA! West Africa wins again.

At the entrance, crowds are still pushing furiously and, to my horror, a bouncer on the gate is literally whipping members of the public with a large leather belt, beating them into submission to prevent illegal entrants.

"GET BACK! GET BACK! YOU MUST HAVE TICKET!" he shouts, angrily.

I wait until he has stopped, then we cautiously edge our way forwards.

"I have tickets," I say, holding them high. He grabs them.

"Come!" He ushers us safely through the frenzied maelstrom.

Inside the stadium is somewhat less chaotic, and we find two seats on the risers with a decent view of the stage. The place is pretty full when the artist finally comes on stage, amidst tumultuous cheers and applause. From where we're sitting, the sound quality is poor; the mix seems all wrong and, whilst I can hear the bass and drumbeat clearly, Sean's voice is almost inaudible at times. I confess I don't know a single song by this guy, but what I can make out sounds decent.

After about 45 minutes of Caribbean rapping and grooving, unrest breaks out on the pitch, where the audience are beginning to push and shove, sometimes quite harshly. I've no idea what has triggered this, but it seems to be escalating by the minute. A handful of riot police, with shields they hardly know how to use, are deployed in an attempt to maintain order. I decide it's time to leave, before things deteriorate further, so Mads and I make our way back towards the entrance.

Meanwhile, Sean attempts to start another song, hampered by severe moshing on the lawn below. People are now throwing cans, stray clothing or anything they can get hold of, and a policeman is beating fans with his truncheon as they surge angrily forwards.

Sean stops mid-song. "Hey people!" cries the Jamaican rapper. "Y'all want more music, right? Keep it low."

This has little effect on the angry mob, as chairs begin flying across the stadium, injuring several fans in the process.

"Hey, don't do dat! Don't do dat! You all came here to have a good time, not start a riot," urges shocked Mr Paul. Meanwhile, his stage hand has taken hold of a second microphone:

"Easy, easy! Hold it! Hold it! Everybody stop!"

"We believe in peace on earth" adds Sean. "Everybody give a peace sign!" he urges, but to no avail. And with that, a van rushes onto the back of the stage and the door swings open. Sean is bundled aboard and whisked away in seconds.

Mads and I are now outside the stadium, pushing through the already gathering crowds, leaping into the first taxi available before we get stampeded. What mayhem! It turns out folk on the pitch were peeved they couldn't sit on the risers where wealthy VIPs were, and so turned to violence. Shame on you, Bamako! Poor show, Mali! An international star came all this way in aid of a good cause and this is how you repay him.

It was the Santa Market in Bamako last weekend – a genuine German Christmas market, in the grounds of the *Palais de la Culture* by the river. Alongside the mandatory giant sausages and beer, fifty or so stalls were selling jewellery, place mats, wooden carvings, paintings, clothing, tablecloths, dried mango chunks, peanuts – anything these 'rich foreigners' would spend their money on. There was even the chance for our kids to go and see Father Christmas – a treat I never expected them to have out here. The queue was short and we were soon stepping into his tinsel-filled grotto.

"Bienvenue les enfants! Venez vous asseoir!"

I shouldn't have been as surprised as I was to see a black Santa – this *is* Africa, after all. But I'd never seen one before, and consequently suffered a minor culture-shock at the sight of this skinny, dark-skinned chap, sweating profusely beneath his red and white coat and fake beard. He wasn't smiling, and he didn't even say 'ho, ho, ho'. Mads, Ruth and Micah, having grown up in Africa, didn't bat an eyelid at this Afro Kris Kringle – why would Santa have to be white anyway? I decided against explaining to them what a native of Greenland ought to look like; they were happy, he was happy, and my kids went away clutching three gifts with a combined value of less than half the entry fee. Fun times!

As a family, we've always managed to recreate a pretty passable Christmas Dinner in Africa. Veg is easily available from any market: carrots, potatoes, beans – sometimes even broccoli. Brussels sprouts are something of a challenge though, as they only come in the tinned variety. We persist in buying them every year, even though they ooze out of the can, soft, brown and squishy, smelling vile and tasting even worse.

Our turkey was 'interesting' this year. I bought it from Azar's all wrapped up, and put it in the fridge ready for the big day. On Christmas morning, Lois was alone in the kitchen when she unwrapped the bird. From the lounge, I heard a loud scream, as she came running through, crying:

"You do the turkey! You do the turkey!"

Intrigued, I rushed in to take a look: there lying on the worktop was an *entire* turkey – head, beak, claws; the lot. It looked just like, well, a dead turkey. After half an hour of twisting, dislocating and chopping (while Lois recovered in the lounge), it finally looked more like a meal than a farmyard fowl. We got less meat than expected though: I had paid for five pounds of 'turkey', but wasn't expecting the first pound to be nothing but inedible body parts.

Chapter Eleven – A Flying Visit to Timbuktu

"A constant convoy of sturdy camels processes in from the desert."

"THIS IS A POSH old do, innit?"

"It certainly is, Gary."

It's the annual New Year's reception at the Hotel Salam, a swanky bright pink place beside the river. Through its ever revolving doors is an enormous vestibule with polished marble floors, high ceilings, comfy seating and carved wooden sculptures. There are even two *real* palm trees growing in the centre of its classy restaurant. Less than 500 yards from here, Malians are living in single-room corrugated shacks on a mud road next to one of the city's largest refuse tips.

"Ow about another glass o' bubbly, Rob?"

"I'm okay thanks."

Welsh Gary is here, as it's a British Embassy do. He's settling in to life in Mali, though still struggles with the culture on many levels.

"I 'ate it when they call me toubab. Just because I'm white – it's racist."

"They don't mean it insultingly, Gary. It's just what they say here."

"I'm not 'avin it, and I tell 'em. I say: *No! Don't call me toubab! It's not my name.*"

"And how do they respond?"

"They just look confused or sad."

A smartly dressed chap of Chinese descent approaches us.

"Ray! 'Ow are you, boyo?" Gary clearly knows him. "Rob, this is Ray. He's a pilot here!"

"Air France?" I ask, shaking his hand.

"No, nothing so grand. I fly small planes to remote parts of Mali."

"For medical purposes?"

"Sometimes, but it's mostly charities, businessmen or folk working at the gold mines."

"Gold mines?"

"Yes, Mali has plenty," Ray explains, "mostly over in the West, towards Kayes."

"Shouldn't Mali be richer than it is, then?" I enquire.

"Almost certainly, but the mines are mostly run by South Africans, who take the lion's share."

Gary's wife Sally has flown with Ray for work on numerous occasions, which is how they know each other.

"Gary, are you sure you can't come on the flight tomorrow?" asks Ray. "It would be a shame to have an empty seat..."

"No, sorry. My wife's birthday. I could send 'er instead, but then we wouldn't be together either."

"Where are you headed?" I ask.

"Timbuktu, just for a few hours."

"Wow! I've always wanted to go to Timbuktu!" I respond, almost leaping in the air. "It's such an iconic place; half the world thinks it's fictitious, the other half think it's an island."

"Ha ha – that's true!" says Ray, smiling.

"Well, I nominate Mr Rob Baker for my place," adds Gary ceremoniously.

"Any chance you're free tomorrow Rob?" asks Ray.

I certainly can be, if there's a *free* trip to Timbuktu involved, but my Britishness obliges me not to accept immediately.

"Really? Are you sure? I wouldn't want to impose! And we've only just met…"

"No problem at all. I'm going anyway; it would be a shame not to fill that jump seat. And you seem like a fun guy to travel with!"

"Thanks. Okay then. I'd love to come. How long's the flight?"

"An hour or so, as long as there are no haboobs."

"No what?"

He laughs, "Haboobs. Dust storms. They're very common up there, especially at this time of year. See you in the morning, eight o'clock prompt at the airport."

"I'll be there with bells on!" I reply, excitedly.

"And don't forget your passport."

The domestic terminal of Bamako Airport is just beyond the international one and has a disconcertingly derelict feel to it, with several disused planes sitting haphazardly beside a pair of hangars. Ray met me at the entrance a few minutes ago and ushered me quickly through security.

Although of Chinese heritage, Ray grew up in France and went to uni in the UK, so is fluent in French and English. He's flown planes in these parts for the several years, also in Senegal, Niger and Cameroon.

"Hey, you wanna see the view from the control tower before we fly?"

"If there's time…"

Ray takes me through a strong metal door, where a spiral staircase leads all the way to the top. The tower is a four-storey, square pillar with a wide hexagonal glass control room perched on top. Inside, a couple of blokes – one white, one African – are sat at computers which display various dials and data only they can interpret. The view is a tad disappointing: nothing but a long, flat runway and a couple of stationary planes. I'm figuring this must be one of the easiest air traffic controller jobs in the world, with little more than half a dozen flights daily.

"This is my friend Rob. He's coming to Timbuktu with me."

The guys shake my hand in turn.

"Will you visit the festival while you're there?" asks white control guy.

"What festival?"

"You didn't know, Rob?" interjects Ray. "The Festival in the Desert starts tonight."

Every January since 2001, the *Festival au Désert* has drawn punters and artists from across the globe to perform in this unique and atmospheric setting. I hadn't realized it was this week, but it's definitely an unexpected bonus for me.

Our plane is a white and blue Beechcraft Super King Air – a twin prop affair with seven round windows down the side. Ray's co-pilot, Vincent, is a tall Nigerian who says very little indeed. Together, they pull open the curved door in the side of the aircraft, which swings down to reveal the steps to the cabin. I climb in after Ray, feeling like James Bond.

Inside the Beechcraft, there is seating for only nine passengers, with a luggage compartment in the tail, separated from the cabin by criss-crossed netting. I'd assumed my jump seat would be in the cockpit, but I'm actually given the front seat in the cabin itself.

"Once we're in the air, you can come through and chat to us," says Ray, kindly.

"Ladies and gentlemen, please fasten your seatbelts and prepare for take-off."

Joining me on this flight are a pair of French diplomats, three Tamasheq guys, one Tamasheq lady, and a couple of Norwegian soil scientists. I think back to the last time I flew and hope this one won't be nearly as turbulent. We're almost 100% certain of not having rain or a thunderstorm at this time of year, though.

After a short but noisy burst along the runway, we're airborne, passing over the hills of knowledge and power, and the ever-meandering Niger River.

"You can come through now, Rob," says Ray, poking his head out from the cockpit, where there's only just enough standing room for me between the two pilots. In front of me, I count 29 different dials, along with dozens of switches and buttons – how on earth do these guys know what's what?

"Ségou," says Vincent after a few minutes. I peer forwards, careful not to press anything: the *Kankou Moussa* and the festival stage are clearly visible on the river, as is the road of Tamasheq souvenir sellers, like tiny ants from this altitude.

Beyond Ségou, you may recall, is little besides pale-brown wilderness littered with dark-green dots for trees and the pale outline of a solitary tarmac road. Directly beneath us, the Niger River flows ever northwards; having begun its journey in northern Guinea, it will eventually pass through Timbuktu and Gao, before curving southwards through Niger and then Nigeria, where it finally enters the sea.

As we near Mopti, the Dogon Escarpment appears to the east, tapering off into the distance. North of Mopti is the region where, at this time of year, there's a good chance of seeing the Gourma Elephants – Mali's only herd – who migrate from Burkina Faso in search of watering holes every January. No such luck today, though.

We cross the Niger River once more, this time at right angles, and Ray calls out:

"There it is, Rob!"

On the horizon lies the legendary city of Timbuktu. Its perpendicular streets of square, beige houses give it the allure of a Biblical epic. In the 18th and 19th centuries, many European explorers risked – and lost – their lives in the quest to 'discover' this mythical place. Now, I get to fly there in an hour – and for free.

Outside the city is nothing but desert dunes, scattered with dark, spider-like bushes. A small train of camels is crossing the desert beneath us, the morning sun elongating their shadows in picture-postcard fashion. A five-mile-long channel can be seen winding northwards, linking the Niger River with Timbuktu city. This was formerly a busy canal used for hundreds of years to transport goods, but is now permanently dried up due to the advancement of the desert.[32]

"Here comes our first haboob!" says Ray, calmly, pointing to a large brown cloud in the distance, at ten o'clock. "No need to panic, Rob, we'll be landed long before this guy gets near us. That's a good 40 miles away, and it looks like a small one."

We bounce down onto the tarmac airstrip. No applause today – I guess the plane is just too small for that kind of thing. The airport is a simple affair and formalities are quickly dealt with. Ray, Vincent and I board a taxi and make the three-mile journey into the city. En route, we pass through a large stone gateway with the words *Bienvenue à Tombouctou* standing proudly across its archway. A little further along the road, another sign reads:

Tombouctou, Cité des 333 Saints

We're staying at the Hôtel Bouctou, a grand-looking stone building this side of the city. Its large inner courtyard has two storeys of tall, ornate arches which lead to the rooms and give it a mosque-like feel. The helpful receptionist offers me an air-conditioned room on the first floor, right next to Ray's. It's bizarre to think that yesterday at this time I hadn't even *met* Ray; now, he's just about the only person I know within a thousand-mile radius.

The name of the hotel – Bouctou – is, of course, significant. The story goes that, almost a thousand years ago, some Tamasheq nomads were offered hospitality in these parts by a woman with a very large belly button. So they called her *Bouctou*, which means 'big navel'. The Tamasheq word 'tin' means 'well', so this was originally the place of Bouctou's well: Tin-

---

bouctou. When the French arrived in the late nineteenth century, they changed its spelling to 'Tombouctou', though most other nations still use the African spelling of 'Timbuktu'.

After freshening up, I take a stroll into town. The first thing that strikes me is just how *beige* everything is here: the streets, the buildings, the desert beyond; even the camels. The occasional neem tree breaks up this monochromaticity with a dash of green. Even the streets, apart from a single tarmac road through the centre, are dirt or sand. No larger than a small English market town, Timbuktu has a population of just 50,000. Back in the sixteenth century, it was home to three of the world's first universities and was, in some ways, more civilized than Europe at the time. Thousands of ancient manuscripts from this era still exist today, covering broad topics of learning from astronomy to philosophy, trigonometry to medicine.[33]

There's a mixture of opulence and poverty here: some important buildings have ornate arched doors, fashioned in smooth, fine wood with embossed metal inlays, so common among the Tamasheq. Other buildings remain unfinished or are crumbling with neglect. Circular dome-shaped bread ovens at the roadside stand ten feet tall every few blocks, their semicircular openings resembling the nails of giant thumbs sticking out of the ground. Electric power lines dangle between knobbly wooden posts, and high TV aerials protrude from the roofs of square, single-storey homes. In places, these dwellings are joined together in a long row, almost like terraced housing back home, many finished off with a smooth layer of adobe. There are relatively few cars about; those I see are either white Toyota pick-ups or Mercedes Benz. There are also donkeys and camels everywhere you look; some pulling carts or carrying goods and people, others standing tethered to posts or buildings, enjoying a well-earned break. They're all single-humped dromedary camels in these parts of course, the twin-humped Bactrian being native to Asia.

I stumble upon an adobe building with a grey stone plaque fixed on its wall, which reads:

---

[33] As referred to by Joshua Hammer in *The Bad-Ass Librarians of Timbuktu*

To the memory of
MAJOR
ALEXANDER GORDON LAING
2nd. WEST INDIA REGIMENT.

The explorer who, at the cost of his life,
reached Timbuktu in 1826.

Erected in his honour by
THE ROYAL AFRICAN SOCIETY
in 1963.

Laing was a British Army Officer from Scotland, who somehow made the arduous journey across Europe and the Sahara to Timbuktu almost 200 years ago. His journey was not without difficulty, and he was attacked by the Tamasheq at various points, one such assault resulting in him losing a hand. In spite of all this, he made it here and was one of the first Europeans to do so. He stayed in Timbuktu for about a month but was murdered shortly after leaving; a sad, sad story certainly worthy of this plaque, honouring a brave and, some would say, foolhardy adventurer.

A little further on is a large, ornate building with sloping adobe walls, in a vaguely pyramidal form. Carefully positioned branches protrude several inches out of the walls at regular intervals, making the whole building resemble a giant pin cushion; these are partly for stability, partly for aesthetics. The building, I discover, is the Sankoré Mosque – almost as old as the city itself and part of the original university. On all four sides of its vertical tower sit grey loudhailer-style speakers for announcing calls to prayer.

"Impressive, huh?" says a voice in English. I turn round to see a skinny, scruffy-haired guy in dark glasses, whose accent I immediately recognize as Australian.

"Yes, it certainly is."

"UNESCO World Heritage Site, you know!"

"Really?"

"Brad. Brad Gordon."

"Rob Baker. Pleased to meet you, Brad. You're an Aussie, right?"

"Correct, Pommy! But I live in Burkina Faso. Been there...what...five years now."

Brad, who somewhat resembles Shaggy from Scooby Doo, works for an NGO in Ouagadougou, and travels over here by road every year for the festival.

"Hey, come and see this cool monument!" he says, beckoning me onward.

I follow Brad as he rushes down a nearby side street, crossing a small market square, where tattered, sun-bleached parasols protect tomatoes, okra, onions, spices and some meats. Here, I spot a slim white lady, sitting in one of several tents, drinking tea and chatting with local Tamasheq folk.

"That's Beatrice," Brad explains. "Met her a couple of times before. She's a Swiss missionary – been here for years."

In just a few months' time, Beatrice will be taken captive by Islamists: briefly in 2012, then long-term in 2016. To this day, she is still being held hostage somewhere in the Saharan region.

"Here you go, Rob. Look!"

Resembling a giant square crown composed of three huge interlocking arches, the *Flamme de la Paix* monument is situated in the north of the city in a district called *Abaradjou*. Four metal globe-like spheres adorn the pinnacles of its corner towers, and a large flame-like sculpture sits on the very top. But the most important symbol lies in front of the monument itself: dozens of Kalashnikovs embedded into the concrete. Built in 1996 to mark the end of the Tuareg Rebellion, these are the actual weapons laid down at the time; and there are hundreds more buried beneath the monument's pedestal as a testimony to the cease-fire. Very moving indeed.

"Come see the desert, Rob!" My new austral friend is tireless in his enthusiasm. We walk no more than a couple of hundred yards from the monument and are instantly surrounded by flowing dunes, undulating magically as far as the eye can see. It's no wonder the desert – and particularly the Sahara – has been the subject of so much art and literature over the years. Seeing it is a truly breathtaking experience; one which inspired Norwegian composer Edvard Grieg to compose his famous 'Morning Mood'.

"Hey mate, look at this!" And with that, Brad takes off one of his flip-flops and places it vertically in the sand.

"That's the tallest structure for the next 1000 miles!"

"I suppose it would be."

Suddenly, the wind grows stronger and an enormous dark-orange cloud looms to the west, rolling quickly in our direction.

"Mate, we've gotta take cover fast!"

Rushing back into the town, we dive into the first available doorway, as the foreboding ochre shroud – almost half a mile high – surges menacingly closer. This doorway is thankfully quite deep and faces away from the storm.

"Cover your mouth, mate, and shut your eyes; or squint 'em if you wanna see this!"

I gladly oblige, pulling my T-shirt over my mouth and nose, and cupping my hands in front for extra protection. Then it happens: in a matter of seconds, the entire city is cloaked in semi-darkness as a tsunami of sand and dust rushes through the streets, eclipsing the sun and filling every crevice. The peace monument, no more than 50 yards away, is now completely invisible, enveloped in muted umber hues. Across the road, a small herd of goats huddle together against a wall, and the thumb-shaped bread oven beside them – smoking away healthily seconds ago – is now completely dead. I glance up at the thick, bronzen sky, where black plastic bags – the bane of West Africa – are circling madly, rising and falling at the whim of this violent, turbid tempest. And whilst you'd expect a wind of this strength to be cold, this air is hot and desperately dry. After a couple more minutes of squinting, shutting my eyes, and mostly facing the inside corner or the doorway in desperation, the haboob vanishes, almost as quickly as it had appeared. I uncover my mouth as the bright Saharan sunshine returns amidst blue skies.

"You're brown everywhere mate!"

"You too!"

Before heading to the festival itself, Brad has one more sight to show me: Timbuktu's salt market, where a constant convoy of sturdy camels processes in from the desert with huge salt slabs lashed awkwardly on either side of their humps. Each of these coarse, off-white tablets measures four feet by two and is a couple of inches thick, weighing in at 50 kilos. They've been carried an arduous 500 miles from the mines in Taoudenni to the north, where deep pits are dug by hand using Medieval-style tools. Salt has been mined in these parts for at least 1000 years and was once traded for gold, ivory or even slaves.

One such hump-backed beast passes in front of us and, as though disapproving of our spectatorship, opens his mouth and lets out the ugliest roar ever – a cross between Chewbacca and the loudest burp you can imagine.

"*Ca va, monsieur*?" asks its Tamasheq owner, seeing my flabbergasted pale face.

"Yes, I'm fine. Does he often make this noise?"

"Yes, often. I am used to it."

"How was your journey?"

"Long and hot, but I am used to this too. I live in Timbuktu – the trip to the mines and back takes 45 days."

"45 days?! But what about your family?"

"They too are used to it. This is our way of life; it is how we make money. I will now chop the slabs into small pieces to sell at the market."

"Who buys them?"

"Everyone! We are the source of salt for Mali and all its neighbours. These slabs will supply West Africa's needs."

And with that, he rapidly chisels a tiny corner off one of his slabs.

"Here you are, toubab," he says handing me the sugar lump-sized piece of salt. "A small gift for you."

In the past few years, hefty yellow trucks have begun to replace the camels, making the round trip in just one week instead of six. These clearly save time and money, but they are also destroying an important part of Tamasheq culture. So, many still choose the traditional camel method they have known for generations.

Chapter Twelve – Desert Music

"Through our music, we are messengers."

A MILE OUTSIDE dusty Timbuktu, surrounded by nothing but sand, lies an unexpected, somewhat incongruous sight: on a large stage perched amidst undulating golden dunes, musicians from Africa and beyond entertain international audiences for three consecutive days and nights. Huge *Marshall* speakers are stacked up in threes on either side of the performance area, and a tent-like awning is draped over the top to protect artists from the incessant 45-degree heat. A slope in the dunes opposite forms a natural terrace where around 2000 spectators are sitting, split almost evenly into three categories: black Africans, white people and, of course, the Tamasheq. Also known as Tuaregs, these proud, turban-clad, camel-riding nomads are neither Arabs nor black, yet tend to consider themselves superior to both. They enslaved black Africans in the past and, while also Muslim, maintain a certain degree of mistrust of the Arabs. With a reputation for being austere and emotionless, and for staging multiple revolts, the Tamasheq are often feared by Westerners, but not always with good reason.

Behind the crowd, on the dune's ridge, several dozen Tamasheq sit astride majestic camels, whose tails are swaying from side to side, almost in time with the music. The richest Tuaregs have the ultimate vantage point; sat atop their sand-tainted Toyota Hiluxes on the ridge, they look on with a dauntless air of superiority.

On stage at the moment, a large Malian woman in white robes is swaying her arms as she bellows powerful lydian airs into the microphone, accompanied by a pair of guitars, various drums and some well-synchronized dancers. This, I discover, is Khaira Arby, a renowned Malian *griotte*, or professional singer. Her resounding melodies ring out across the sands in a mixture of Tamasheq, Bambara, Songhaï and Arabic.

Surrounding the arena, and in a vaguely circular formation, lie dozens of cream-coloured tents – many too low to stand up in – each adorned with a Persian-style rug at the threshold and a simple vertical stick holding the draped tarpaulin open. Many of them are selling the usual Tamasheq souvenirs: heavy silver pendants, bangles, earrings, daggers and sabres in leather sheaths, as well as the iconic embossed leather boxes in various sizes and colours. In other tents, Tuareg men and women sit in small circles singing and clapping, as they rock gently left and right, swaying their arms slowly in time to the rhythm of guitars or *ngonis*. There's even a large medical tent, mostly attended by Tamasheq from remote desert parts, making the most of this rare opportunity for treatment. And, of course, there's plenty of tea-pouring – and slurping – going on too. At various points to the edge of the crowd, men can be seen knelt on small roll-away mats in the sand, facing east as they carry out their five-times-a-day prayers, bowing their heads reverently to the ground.

The Tamasheq women are all wearing full-length robes, their heads decorated with sparkling coin-like sequins atop dark headscarves. The men are robed too, also wearing the characteristic desert turban, or *tagelmust*. The colour of the robe and turban doesn't need to match, and rarely does. Glancing around, the most popular combination seems to be a pale-blue robe with a black tagelmust, though brown or beige robes are common too, often accompanied by white headgear.

The entire scene covers no more than a couple of acres, beyond which dunes extend in every direction. Even the road from Timbuktu is nothing but a sandy track, accessible by four-by-four or camel only. I turn to my new Aussie companion:

"This is quite a sight."

"Isn't it fantastic? But it was even better in the middle of the desert, mate. The remoteness out there was just awesome...like being on another planet."

Billed as 'the world's most remote festival', it all began in 2001, when concert organizer, Manny Ansar (himself a Tuareg) invited two or three bands and a few journalists to a desert gig. The staging was basic and the sound equipment rudimentary, but word of mouth nevertheless brought a crowd of 500 to this initial event.

"We had just been through some terrible years of rebellion," said Manny, "I wanted to have a festival which would be a weapon of peace."[34]

And each year thereafter, numbers continued to soar, peaking around

---

[34] http://africultures.com/festival-au-desert-peace-and-love-7581/

the ten thousand mark. The larger the festival became, the bigger the names it attracted: Toumani Diabaté, Robert Plant, Ali Farka Touré and Blur's Damon Albarn. Originally, Ansar had planned for it to be a nomadic festival, roaming the desert to different locations each year, rather like the Tamasheq people themselves. But once the gathering gained popularity – especially with the West – a fixed location was deemed more appropriate.[35] Until last year, the festival was held in the oasis town of Essakane, 40 miles west of here, but moved south this year amid fears of terrorism; such remoteness would make Westerners an all-too-easy target for kidnappers.

"The turnout's not as high this year mate," says Brad, "and not as many white faces."

"Why's that?"

"Well, many Western embassies have warned their nationals not to come – too risky, they say. Tour companies all over the world used to promote the festival, and the West poured in shed loads of money too. Not so much this year."[36]

On stage, Khaira finishes her final song, amidst tumultuous applause, screams of admiration and standing ovations.

"Merci...shukrun...aelbaerka!" she calls out, thanking the audience in French, Arabic and Tamasheq.

Between acts, Brad and I stroll round the stalls, which takes a lot more effort on hot, dry sand. In terms of sustenance, grilled mutton and goat are the main meals on offer, served with rice or couscous. And as a matter of necessity, there's plenty of water on offer too, along with Coke, Sprite and even beer. We sit on a sandy rug and tuck into dinner, surrounded by hungry Tuaregs doing the same, chatting amongst themselves in odd glottal syllables and paying little attention to their two pale-skinned guests. The Tamasheq are descended from the North African Berber people, and can also be found in Niger, Algeria and all the way to Libya.

"Bon appétit!" I say, holding up a handful of goat and couscous in their general direction. They nod but say nothing. Determined to break the ice, I turn to the least scary-looking chap, on my left:

"My friend, how do you say *'bon appétit'* in Tamasheq?"

---

[35] https://mg.co.za/article/2008-09-20-the-tuareg-export
[36] https://www.youtube.com/watch?v=xox44sMi-wo

He slowly finishes his mouthful, then says:

"We don't say this in Tamasheq."

"What about 'the food is delicious'?"

"We don't say this either," he munches.

Apparently, the Tamasheq don't express emotion in speech; for them, it is actions that really count. I can't help wondering whether having much of the face almost permanently covered has contributed to this lack of emotion, or perhaps it's a survival thing: in the harsh desert heat and dust, the last thing you want is someone going all gooey on you.

A couple of tents beyond our eatery is one draped with long pieces of coloured fabric.

"What do you suppose that is?" I ask Brad.

"Mate, can't you tell? Those are the tagelmusts unwrapped!"

Of course! Not selling turban fabric in the desert would be like a British seaside resort without ice cream; both are culturally specific ways to combat the heat.

"I'm buying one, mate. How about you?"

At roughly eight British pounds for a fifteen-by-two-foot piece of fabric, it seems rather expensive, but it's a fun cultural thing to do. Brad goes for the classic black; I opt for a palish blue hue. Donning a tagelmust is not as easy as it looks, but thankfully our stallholder – now £16 the richer – shows us how:

First, bring the fabric flat over the top of the head, under the chin, then back over the head a second time. At this point, I look ready to play the Virgin Mary in a nativity pageant. Now comes the clever part: under the chin again, then round the *back* of the skull passing above one ear and crossing the forehead horizontally. The now scrunched fabric is then wrapped around the rim of the head a couple more times, finally passing flat over the mouth and chin, the remaining material left hanging over one shoulder. This last piece is removed from the mouth when eating or drinking and, although useful for keeping sand out, was originally designed to prevent evil spirits from entering through the mouth or nose.

"You buy *kitab* too, my friend. I give you good price!"

The kitab is an ornate leather or metal pendant, which most Tamasheq wear around the neck. Although highly decorative, these too were originally designed to protect the wearer from evil. I politely decline this somewhat cumbersome addition.

Before night falls, there's one more event at the festival we have to see: the camel race. On the edge of the festival area is a flatter piece of desert where, right now, around twenty camels are lined up in the sand; some beige, some white, others dark brown. There's no track to speak of, just more sand, with excited crowds gathered along either side of what is about to become the race arena. As we approach, a group of four Tuaregs are dancing in a circle, each wielding a two-foot sabre, swinging them above their heads in swashbuckling fashion, as onlookers clap and cheer. They then crouch down and move round in a circular formation, still waving their swords as they kick each leg forwards, Cossack-style.

Each racer is sat on their camel's single hump, most with an ornate U-shaped saddle, their feet resting precariously in front of them on the low part of the animal's neck. Most riders are Tamasheq of course, but some black Africans are taking part too; no Westerners have the courage, or experience, to attempt this exotic sport. A couple of official looking chaps in indigo gowns walk in front of the line to inspect each camel and rider. I'm expecting a pistol to go off to start the race, or at least a loud 'on your marks...' type call. What actually happens is rather inconsequential: one of the officials says a couple of words in Tamasheq and they're off! Each rider has a tree branch in one hand, which they use to beat the side of their camel in an attempt to make it run faster. This has a variety of outcomes: some camels barely move, others walk on begrudgingly, and a few – but only a few – run from the start, their necks jolting forwards with each step, as their riders bob energetically up and down. Other camels begin to catch on and join in running, and the crowd is going wild, as clouds of sand fly from dozens of cloven hoofs. One rider is most disgruntled when his stubborn beast decides to run in the opposite direction, out into the desert. The finish line, marked only by another official standing by, is roughly 250 metres away, and the first camel makes it over the 'line' in a little over 30 seconds, which is impressive. Others take two or three minutes, while several never complete the race. None of this seems to matter; it's an exciting event for all concerned, the likes of which I've never witnessed before, or since.

Back at the main stage, we're in for another treat:

"*Mesdames et messieurs,* please welcome two legends of Malian music, deeply loved by the entire world: Amadou and Mariam!"

Applause even more enthusiastic than the last erupts across the crowd, as the couple are led on stage, wearing their usual matching robes and dark glasses. Tonight they are sporting costumes with a pale-green diamond design embossed with gold. She's wearing a matching headpiece; he has his usual black and white Stratocaster hung round his neck.

"Bonsoir le Festival au Désert! Bonsoir Tombouctou! Aw ni ce! Aw ni ce!"[37]

Six-foot-three Amadou enthusiastically greets the crowd in French and his native Bambara, then they instantly launch into one of their best-known hits: 'Beaux Dimanches', which talks about Sundays in Bamako being the day to get married.

Just about everyone in the crowd is singing along with the chorus, many dancing joyfully as Amadou punctuates the music with funky pentatonic guitar riffs. They follow this with another favourite song: 'Taxi Bamako', whose simple but catchy two-note melody describes a speedy Bamako taxi that will take you anywhere you want, crossing the bridge on its way to Heaven. No mention of splayed wheels, cracked windscreens or whistling policemen, though.

In 1975, Amadou Bagayoko and Mariam Doumbia met at Bamako's *Institut des Jeunes Aveugles* (Institute for the Young Blind), though neither of them was born blind. They began singing and making music together almost immediately, and were married in 1980. Although known in Mali, it is only in the past decade or so – when the couple were already in their 50s – that they gained global recognition, partly thanks to collaborations with Western artists such as Manu Chao and Damon Albarn.[38] Their beguiling songs have matter-of-fact lyrics and are harmonically simple, usually based around just two or three chords, but with catchy Mandé hooks and bundles of charisma.

As the couple launch into their next song, Mariam calls out: *"Chaud! Chaud! Chaud! Chaud!"* in time to the beat, which whips the crowd up even more.[39]

Their set ends with a song you'd think they'd written for the occasion:

---

[37] Thank you
[38] https://www.allmusic.com/artist/amadou-mariam-mn0000013647/biography
[39] Hot! Hot! Hot! Hot!

Dek I Lalane says that if you go to the north of Mali, you will see the Tamasheq. It seems like this single line makes up around 90% of the lyrics, but the crowds love it, joining in loudly at the end of each line with: *'LES TAMASHEQ!'* Even the Tuaregs are getting excited about this one, as they twist and sway their long arms to this catchy song.

As the sun finally sets behind the western dunes, a single spotlight, perched on a tower amidst the crowd, whirrs into action, casting its light onto the entire stage, like an old-fashioned movie projector. An entire multicoloured line of square lights comes on at the back of the stage, and other lamps on tall posts light up around the festival's perimeter, giving the whole place a decidedly magical feel. The temperature drops several degrees within minutes and I begin to feel chilly, even though it's still in the twenties.

The evening closes with *Tinariwen*, a Tamasheq band who, over the years, have somehow managed to combine good music with genuine rebellion. You may think Billy Bragg or The Sex Pistols sang songs of protest, but these pale into insignificance in the face of Tinariwen's militant rantings. The band first came into being in the late 70s under the leadership of Ibrahim Ag Alhabib who, as a small child, had witnessed his own father's death during the 1963 Tuareg rebellion. Profoundly affected by this trauma, his life was set on a course of conflict but also one of musical creativity. As a boy, Ag Alhabib saw a cowboy film on one of the few televisions in the Sahara at the time, and was inspired by the music he heard. So he built himself a makeshift guitar from a tin can, a wooden pole and some wire, and began teaching himself to play. Later, growing up in a refugee camp in Algeria (following the Tuareg rebellion) he was given a guitar by an Arab, and was able to play a *real* instrument for the first time.[40] As a young man, he joined forces with three other Tuareg musicians, and they began to play at weddings and parties in the region, where they became known at *Kel Tinariwen,* or 'The Desert People'. Later, they dropped the 'Kel', so the band's name now simply means 'Deserts' or 'Empty Places'.

Besides their musical talents, the band had something else in common: an axe to grind against the non-Tamasheq world. Having seen their people

---

[40] https://en.wikipedia.org/wiki/Tinariwen

suffer and their land taken from them, this all-pervading cause drove the band ever forwards. The Tuaregs' own country, *Azawad*, covered much of the Saharan region, but when French colonial powers created Mali, Azawad was swallowed up within its vast borders; an engulfment similar to that suffered by Kurdistan, Tibet or even Catalonia elsewhere on the planet. But the Tamasheq are not quitters; they fought back – and continue to fight back – for the land they see as rightfully theirs. The three most notable Tuareg uprisings took place in 1963, 1990, and 2008.

Meanwhile, Colonel Gaddafi *loves* the Tuaregs, especially ones he can train to fight his battles. In 1980, he offered many of them places at his military training camp in Libya. Several members of Tinariwen accepted, combining war and music for years to come, apparently taking an active role in the 1990 rebellion. Cassette tapes of their political songs – bemoaning the Tuaregs' plight, or urging its people to fight for freedom – circulated in the region, adding extra fuel to the fire. The band's bassist, Eyadou Ag Leche, once said: "Since the independence of Mali in 1960, our people have endured humiliations and repression. Through our music, we are messengers."[41]

The band come on stage to tumultuous applause and launch into one of their funky 'Desert Blues' riffs. Each is wearing a shiny black turban, and white, gold or pale-blue robes. Two guitarists, a djembe player and – curiously – a left-handed bassist, form the band, creating a sound which is unique, haunting and strangely uplifting.

This is by no means Tinariwen's first appearance at the festival; they played here back in 2001, when they met and became friends with Led Zeppelin's Robert Plant, also performing that year. If you listen to Plant's song 'Mighty Rearranger', you'll instantly recognize Tinariwen-like riffs, as he was greatly influenced by their music when they met. Probably the first (and only) time a rock band has been influenced by the music of Timbuktu!

---

[41] http://afrique.lepoint.fr/culture/tinariwen-le-blues-de-la-nation-touaregue-19-08-2014-1857627_2256.php

Chapter Thirteen – Slow Train to the Gates of Hell

"Thankfully, we both brought plenty of water to drink."

"A SINGLE TICKET to Kayes, please!"

"Kayes? What are you going *there* for?"

Having fought my way through hoards of heavily laden Malians in this cavernous but semi-dilapidated railway station – the only one in Bamako – I'm finally at the front of the queue (if you can call it that). It's still dark, and mosquitoes are avidly nibbling at my calves.

"First or second class, *monsieur?*"

Amazed both exist, I'm roused from my astonishment by a portly chap leaning towards my ear from behind:

"First, *monsieur.* You want first class," he says, reassuringly tapping me twice on the shoulder.

I pay the equivalent to nine British pounds to make the 300 mile journey to literally the hottest town on the planet. Kayes (which rhymes with 'sky') is known locally as *Les Portes de L'Enfer,* or 'The Gates of Hell' and has clocked an astonishing 52 degrees Celsius[42] at its hottest, often remaining above 37 degrees even at night: the temperature of your own body. Because of its oppressive climate, the French army would send its officers to Kayes as a punishment during colonial times.

"We have a place like that in the States," Doctor Dave told me before I left. "It's called Death Valley, and nobody is dumb enough to want to live there!"

Reassuring indeed.

"I went there by rail during rainy season once," he continued, "and a flash flood literally washed part of the tracks away!"

"Really? What happened?"

"The driver noticed in time and stopped the train. Up ahead, there was a huge chasm in the earth where the tracks had been. We had to get out and walk half a mile to where the tracks were good again, but it took

---

[42] Or 125.6 Fahrenheit

around seven hours for a replacement train to arrive from the opposite direction."

"Sounds exciting!" I responded, somewhat naively.

"We were crammed in a hot carriage, and the aisles were full of sacks of rice and other produce, which I had to clamber over to get to my seat. Oh, and beware of thieves – they're rife on that train!"

I take my ticket and step through a large archway onto the vast, bustling platform which, I'm surprised to see, is equipped with a huge clock on the wall. And it's telling almost the right time: 6.55am. Departure is scheduled for 7.30am; no sign of the train yet, but I'm not expecting it to arrive – or depart – on time.

I sit down on a simple wooden bench overlooking the deserted tracks and wait. 7.30 comes and goes, but still no sign of a train. 8.30...9.30...still nothing. The platform is filling up with more and more passengers, each bringing with them an array of varied, bulky luggage: sacks of rice, yams, mangos, jerricans of oil, metal pots and pans, mattresses and fabric. There are even a couple of small fridges waiting to board our non-existent train.

The railway was built by the French in the late 1800s, when Mali was still part of French Sudan; a vast country running from Senegal in the west all the way to Niger in the east, also incorporating Côte d'Ivoire and Benin. Although not completed until the 1920s, the purpose of this line was to link the major port of Dakar with the Niger River in Bamako, allowing goods to be transported vast distances by boat and rail.

A skinny old man in long white robes sits down beside me.

"Toubab! Good morning," he says, shaking my hand vigorously.

"Is the train arriving soon?" I ask.

"Of course. *Tout-de-suite!* Have you travelled this way before?"

"No, this is my first time."

"The trains are not good here. Not anymore. Back in the 60s, when the French were still around, there were curtains in the windows and the toilets had running water. Not now. Since independence, the Malian trains have got worse and worse. Very bad, very bad!"

"Are you from Bamako?"

"No, I am a *Hausa*, from Niger. My name is Ali. I have lived in Bamako for many years. I came here for work, selling fabric and clothing at the market. My sons do most of this work for me now I am old."

"Why are you travelling to Kayes?"

"I am not. I am travelling to Dakar."

I thought *I* was in for a long journey, but this guy has the same distance again after Kayes, continuing westwards all the way to Senegal's capital; an arduous route through a dusty wilderness littered with cow carcasses and a few hardy shrubs.

"Why are you going to Dakar?"

"My brother lives there. Why are *you* taking this train?"

"I'm going to Kayes to do some research," I reply.

My plan is to find out about the music of the Soninke[43] people, a culturally rich ethnicity, almost all of whom are Muslim. I'm also intrigued to find out how they balance their Islamic beliefs with music – something which, in some branches of Islam, would be strictly forbidden.

It's now gone 10am and there's still no sign of our 7.30 train. My Hausa friend decides to relieve the boredom with some jokes from his culture. The Hausa, it emerges, make jokes about the Fulani (cattle herders), in the same way as the French have often joked about the Belgians, or the English about the Irish.

"I have a joke for you...it's about a Fulani man."

"Okay."

"A Fulani man goes to the doctors and sits in the waiting room. The receptionist appears and calls out his name. 'How does she know my name?' he cries. 'She must be a witch!'" He laughs uncontrollably at what, apparently, was the punch line. "A witch!! Ha ha ha, she must be a witch!"

Like music or dance, sense of humour is not a universal language. As a Brit, I only have to spend a short time with a Frenchman or an American to realize that we don't find the same things funny. So it stands to reason that West African humour would be different too.

"Here's another one," he continues.

I only hope it's funnier than the first.

"A Fulani man buys a box of matches. But before using them, he tries each one to make sure they all work. Ha ha! He strikes every match to check they work, but then they'll all be..."

---

[43] Pronounced: [so-nin-kay]

"I get it! Ha ha! He strikes them all!" I really hope my fake laughter is convincing enough; that was certainly no funnier than his first joke.

I hear a soft rumbling noise in the distance, getting gradually louder. Along the tracks, a hefty green and yellow locomotive thunders into the station, pulling a dozen or so carriages. I'm pleasantly surprised by its appearance, which is nowhere near as worn out as I'd expected. Just over a year ago, on 13th May 2009, this very train derailed in Senegal, killing five people and injuring thirty. Apparently, four carriages overturned. Nobody can tell me how or why this happened.

"First class is at the front, *monsieur*," says my joking companion as the huge train groans to a halt. He bids me farewell and disappears towards his carriage at the rear. Everyone piles on board, passing heavy luggage through doorways and windows. I climb the vertical metal steps to the carriage, where rows of shiny pale-blue faux leather seats run in pairs. A substantial chrome luggage rack runs along both sides at head height, and there are even ceiling fans in cages, some of which are working. Most of the seats are facing the same way, but some face each other over a small table. I opt for the latter option, where a bearded, casually dressed white guy is sitting.

"Welcome aboard!" he says, reaching out his hand. "Chuck. Chuck Anderson." I can tell he's American by both his accent and his propensity to give his full name upon meeting; something Brits seldom do.

"Do you live in Mali?" I ask Chuck.

"Yes. I'm with the Peace Corps – staff. I was here twenty years ago as a volunteer, then came back to Mali two years ago. You headed to Dakar too?"

"No, only Kayes. Why did you take the train, rather than flying?"

"I like rail travel – it's more relaxing than an airplane, and you can enjoy the view. I've travelled in trains all over the world."

"And how do Malian trains compare to those in other countries?"

He thinks for a moment, then replies: "Mali is the second worst I've travelled on."

"Really? And where was the worst?"

"Uzbekistan. They used to hide contraband under the floorboards there. But some of it was perishable food, which would rot during the journey. You could smell it through the whole train, and sometimes you'd hear it swashing about under your feet."

With a loud clunk, our colossal locomotive lunges into action, thundering slowly out of the station at 10.45am – just over three hours late. Our entire carriage, now almost full, rocks disconcertingly from side to side as we chug along the single track through Bamako's dusty suburbs, then climb steeply towards the town of Kati, 10 miles to the north.

"I was in Côte d'Ivoire last month," says Chuck.

"How are things there these days?"

"Largely peaceful and safe. But I had trouble getting my visa."

"How come?" It's usually a pretty straightforward affair.

"When I handed in the form at the embassy, they said: 'We don't accept photos with beards on.' I was amazed and asked: 'Doesn't it look just like me?' But all they could say was: 'No beards!'"

"What did you do then?"

"I had to go fetch an old photo from seven years ago, before I grew my beard. It looked nothing like the current me," he explains, massaging his bushy facial hair proudly. "But they accepted it."

At Kati, we make our first stop and are immediately descended upon by people selling goods on their heads, each loudly calling out the name of their product. It's a very gender-specific business here: the women sell fruit, peanuts, bread, grilled maize, dried fish – anything edible really. Meanwhile, the men tend to sell sunglasses, watches, towels, clothing, boxes of tissues and cigarettes. Young girls add to the cacophony, calling out: *Ji sumalen! Ji sumalen!* or 'pure water', which they sell in small knotted plastic bags. There's a loud two-tone HONK and the train sets off again. I ask Chuck how transport has changed since he was first here.

"Well, a decent road didn't exist until the late 90s, and there were no flights to Kayes, so the train was the only option. As a volunteer, I once took the freight train, sitting on the floor in a cattle car in the dark, with the side door open for ventilation. It was a 40-hour journey! There's a reason they call the freight train *petite vitesse* – it's soooo slow. The train we're on now is the *grande vitesse*, or 'high speed train', and still takes 12 hours to travel 300 miles. Go figure!"

"Have the trains themselves changed?"

"They're much shabbier now. They used to have air-conditioning back then, and the windows were all fixed shut. I remember the air-con breaking down once; it was unbearably hot, with no way to let fresh air in."

Talking of which, the midday heat is now streaming into our carriage and, in spite of the open windows, I'm sweltering as I slip around on my seat with sweat.

Last week, it was Mali's 50th anniversary of independence, known as *Le Cinquantenaire*. A lavish military parade took place on the *Avenue du Mali*, a broad, straight road two kilometres long, just across the river from us. There's a reason it's so long and straight: until 1974, it was the runway for Bamako Airport and became a road when the airport relocated.

The procession was impressive, with endless lines of soldiers, armed vehicles, camels, tanks, horses – even rocket launchers. It lasted two hours on the morning of 22nd September 2010, with brass band music, military fly-overs, and parachutists with green, yellow and red canopies; the colours of the Malian flag.

Gaddafi was there too, having spent the night in his enormous Bedouin tent on the edge of town; quite a hassle to erect, but it's how he prefers to sleep when travelling. As you'll remember, Gaddafi has had a hand in Mali for some time, building hotels, government buildings and schools here. Wearing lavish robes, he sat on the podium next to ATT, who was looking uncharacteristically casual in a simple dark-blue suit and baseball cap. Many other presidents were there too: Burkina Faso, Guinea, Niger, Senegal and Nigeria, but none got Gaddafi's seat of honour. Armed guards lined either side of the road and, I'm told, Gaddafi brought along his famous 'Amazons' (all female bodyguards), and had gunmen positioned atop various surrounding buildings.

The Aga Khan flew in too, and opened the brand new 'Parc National du Mali' while he was here: an impressive leisure facility of lawns, flowerbeds, streams, fountains and cafés that would put the average British park to shame.

"Why have we stopped? There's no station here, is there?"

"I wouldn't say so."

A glance out the window confirms my suspicions: nothing but yellow fields here. Just then, an official-looking chap in uniform passes through our carriage.

"*SORTEZ! SORTEZ!*" he bellows, ordering everyone to alight from the train at once. Chuck and I climb down and sit on the edge of the bank in the tiny strip of shade provided by the train at this hour. We're semi-stranded in an unknown location somewhere between Bamako and Kayes. Thankfully, we both brought plenty of water to drink.

"So, Rob, as an ethnomusicologist, what's your opinion of Malian music?"

"I absolutely LOVE it! I used to live in Benin, where the music was rhythmically very interesting but had little in terms of melodic instruments. Malian music is complex and deeply moving."

"You like the griots?"

"Griots are amazing, but there's so much more."

Griots (and female *griottes*) are the equivalent to medieval minstrels or bards, often heard performing at weddings and other large gatherings. You don't become a griot, you're born into a long lineage of griots. They sing stories in a strident but lyrical way; once you've heard a griot sing, you'll never forget their powerful, undulating airs.

"I met a Christian griotte the other day," I tell Chuck.

"How does *that* work?"

"Well, she looks like a griotte..."

"Big flowing dress, huge earrings, make-up..."

"You've got it. But she sings songs about Jesus in the griotte style."

"And how does that go down in a Muslim country?"

"Bizarrely, it's very well received. Because Malians respect the artform, they are happy to hear her songs."

"So Muslims listen to her Jesus songs?"

"They do! Sometimes hundreds. And they like them!"

"But Muslims don't like Jesus..."

"That's not true. *Isa* is a very important figure in Islam; he's in the Koran many times. Muslims deeply respect him, but they don't believe he's God's son, or a saviour."

"Do you play any Malian instruments, Rob?"

"Yes, I started having kora lessons a few months back."

The kora is a 21-stringed harp, commonly found in Mali, Senegal and the Gambia. At the base of the instrument is a large hemispherical gourd with goat's skin stretched across its opening. A four-foot pole protrudes from the gourd, forming the neck of the instrument. The strings, in two rows, run from the base of the gourd over a bridge (with 21 notches in it) and are then attached to the neck at intervals of an inch or so all the way up. Because the strings run diagonally into the neck – rather than parallel to it – the kora is considered a harp.

"Where did you find a kora teacher?" asks Chuck.

"It was Toumani Diabaté."

"What?! THE Toumani Diabaté? How did you swing that one?"

Toumani Diabaté is the most famous kora player on the planet and one of Africa's most widely known and celebrated musicians. Born into a family of griots, his father, Sidiki, recorded the first ever kora album back in 1970, when Toumani was only five years old. Surrounded by kora music from birth, he quickly picked up the instrument and mastered it by his teens. Allegedly, his family can trace their griot heritage back 70 generations!

In 1987, aged just 22, Toumani recorded his first album and has since gone on to produce a dozen more, touring the entire planet and bringing his lilting melodies to a world which, until then, scarcely knew the existence of such a beautiful and enchanting instrument. He has played with many big names in pop, classical and world music, and in 2006 won his first Grammy for 'In the Heart of the Moon'; a joint effort with Malian guitarist and singer, Ali Farka Touré.

"Quick Rob! It's moving!"

"What?"

"That train's starting to move. Come on!"

Sure enough, our train is pulling away, and *nobody* is on board! We're up in a second and, along with 400 others, scrabble for a doorway – any doorway – just to get on board. It's only moving very slowly, but there is still considerable chaos and a few failed attempts, where folk fall backwards and roll down the embankment. Within a couple of minutes, miraculously, everyone is back on the train. Further confusion now ensues, as almost nobody has had the fortuity (or opportunity) to get back on their original carriage. And so, for the next half hour, folk are wandering up and down the train, desperately trying to find their seat and luggage; all amid temperatures of 44 Celsius and a great deal of swaying. There's been no explanation as to why we stopped (or started again).

"So, how did you get your kora lesson with Toumani Diabaté?"

"Well, it all started on the Queen's birthday..."

The British Ambassador to Mali liked to throw a party every now and again, usually at some swanky hotel with endless cocktails and canapés. I met Ray the pilot at a similar occasion, of course, and got my free flight to Timbuktu. This time, the ambassador had decided the Queen's birthday was a good pretext for a shindig. Saturday, 12th June was the date, and he'd even booked a famous Malian kora player (guess who) to entertain us. Now, I'd already heard Toumani play at the famous Blonba club in Bamako a few months earlier, and even had my own kora made by one of his cousins. But I'd never met the man himself.

As he rounded off his epic solo performance, a certain Welshman turned to me:

"He's good, isn't he?"

"Amazing Gary. Truly spellbinding."

"He's the Eric Clapton of the kora! You should go and talk to him, as you're a music-ethnocology whatnot."

"I don't want to disturb him, though."

"Go on, boyo! It's your one chance."

So I plucked up the courage and tentatively made my way to the stage.

"Thank you for your music. It was wonderful!" I say, in French.

"Merci, merci."

I'm feeling brave, so continue: "I have a kora and can play a little."

"I can give you a lesson," he responded. Just like that!

"Really?" I say, in good British form.

"Of course. And it's free."

At this point, I feel as though I'm dreaming. Did THE world's greatest kora player just offer me a free lesson?

"Here's my number. Call me. I'm at home for the next week."

Chuck is listening in awe to my story, which has now gained the attention of four or five other passengers in our carriage.

"So, how was the lesson?"

"Excellent. I called him the next day and he said, 'come this afternoon', giving me directions to his house. It was tricky to find, but when I got near I just kept asking: *'Où est la maison de Toumani?'* Everyone in the neighbourhood knew, and pointed me in the right direction."

Most of the carriage is now listening into my tale; some have even turned to face me.

"What's his house like? I imagine it's huge?"

"No actually. It's relatively small, with a traditional African courtyard. We sat by the dirt road outside, on washing line chairs."

"I know the kind you mean."

"Toumani had brought in his relative, Boubakar to teach me, while he watched and commented, like a masterclass. But he also came over and demonstrated some techniques to me, and gave me exercises to do every day to improve my playing."

And with that, the carriage bursts into applause, and *I* feel like the star, for just a moment.

I had a second lesson with him the following week, then carried on learning the kora for the rest of my time in Mali with Boubakar, but still at Toumani's house. I'd arrive at 10am and Bouba would just be getting out of bed (kora players are notoriously nocturnal). Occasionally, the great master would be at home and would emerge from his room and compliment me on my progress.

After my first lesson, I said to Toumani: "Thank you so much. My friend says you're the Eric Clapton of the kora."

"I've played with Clapton," he replied, matter-of-factly.

Chapter Fourteen – Melting in Kayes

"I applaud as he finishes, and he smiles warmly."

THERE ARE AROUND 1.2 million Soninke people in Mali, but closer to two million in the world. Many live in Senegal and other neighbouring countries; others find temporary work in France, eventually becoming permanent residents there. And as is the custom in Africa, a 'rich' relative living in Europe will always send cash back to their family, a practice which has significantly boosted the income of the Soninke people for decades. They're staunchly proud of their ethnic roots and identity and, whilst being Soninke means to be Muslim, they also happily celebrate their Soninke-ness in music and song.

"Rob, wake up! We've arrived in Kayes!"
Chuck is shaking my shoulders to rouse me from a deep sleep in which I dreamed my kora grew matchstick legs and ran away from me. It's dark outside as screeching brakes bring us to a jerky halt. Bleary-eyed, I look at my watch: 12.07am. So, it's taken us 13 hours and 22 minutes to get here. I grab my bag and clamber sluggishly down to the bustling platform, heckled by a dozen cries of: 'Taxi! Taxi!'
Having bid farewell to my Peace Corps chum, I climb into a dented Renault 12 with half its windows missing and no upholstery on the ceiling.
"*Bonsoir* toubab!"
"*Bonsoir,*" I reply to my cheery driver. "What is your name?"
"Diarra."[44]
Excellent! As I'm a Traoré, Diarras are my joking cousins, so the excitement of some late-night bean banter suddenly wakes me up.
"My name is Traoré! If I'd known you were a Diarra, I'd have taken another taxi!"
"*I Traoré! Sho dun na!*"[45]
"No, Diarras eat all the beans!"
"NEVER! Beans are for Traorés. You even grow the beans!"

---

[44] Pronounced [ja-ra]
[45] You Traoré! You bean eater!

"Then we grow them to sell them to you Diarras!"

"No, you grow them to fill your own bellies!"

Diarra means 'lion', so I continue.

"What is Diarra doing in Kayes? The lion should be in the jungle!"

"But here the lion can eat the Traorés."

"Then Diarra is eating beans too!"

"Ah, so you admit you ate them, Traoré!"

"Then so do you, Diarra!"

Always such fun, day or night, and the Malians never tire of it.

Our rickety Renault creaks its way down a dry, sandy dirt track to my accommodation: a charity guesthouse near the river. The building is cleverly designed to withstand high temperatures, with a second wall built six feet outside the main one. This outer wall has holes in it to allow airflow whilst protecting the inner wall from the midday sun. That said, it's still 38 degrees outside (at 12.30am!) and my room is only equipped with a small fan.

I wake from a restless, torrid night, feeling as though a train (*the* train) has run over my head. I wander into the large kitchen area of the guesthouse, decked out with the customary dark wooden cupboards, luridly coloured curtains and an old fashioned kettle whistling away on the hob.

"Good morning Rob!"

It's Brenda, the guesthouse manager. From the USA, this short, jovial lady has worked in Kayes for over 20 years and is still smiling!

"I made you some yoghurt and granola. Help yourself!"

The morning air is refreshingly cool as I tuck into my brekkie (even though 28 Celsius would constitute a minor heatwave in the UK).

My first appointment of the day lives a mile or so from here, so I asked Mr Diarra to come and pick me up in his clapped-out Renault. In the light of day, I notice that his car has two gaping holes where air vents once sat, and a bare nut visible in the centre of the steering wheel.

"Traoré!"

"Diarra!"

"Have you had your *petit déjeuner?*"

"Yes, but no beans. They're for the Diarras!"

"Never!"

In a single-storey, tin-roofed shack on the edge of town lives Moktar – one of the Soninke's finest musicians, I'm told. I bid Diarra farewell and step out into an open area containing two huge piles of scrap metal, each 15 feet high and twice as wide. I can't help but wonder what they're doing here.

"Ko ko ko!"

A warm face appears at the door. *"Bonjour. Entrez!"*

As is the custom, I'm given a seat in his small, dingy lounge. Perched on the burgundy velour cushions of his chunky wooden-framed sofa, I'm served tepid water in a shiny metal tumbler, along with copious quantities of abnormally dry biscuits.

Moktar is short with a balding head and steel-rimmed glasses. Over the years, he has accumulated a fascinating range of musical instruments, all of which are stashed in a shed in the corner of his courtyard. Climbing up on a rickety stool, he reaches down specimen number one:

"This is the *dundunye* drum."

"Ah, yes, I know this one!"

Famous across much of West Africa, the 'dun-dun' is a double-headed barrel drum with a deep, penetrating tone. Here, they are worn on a strap over the shoulder when played, rather than on an X-shaped stand (as in many parts). The next drum he passes down (narrowly missing my head) is the *danye*, bigger than the first and only single-headed.

"This is a drum played only by young men. It is played with sticks and two people can play it."

"Two people at the same time?"

"Yes."

That's quite rare, but not unheard of. I'm relieved when he passes me a slightly less bulky drum.

"This is the *juburé*. It is played by blacksmiths and cobblers only."

He lets me play it, even though I've never been either. Almost five feet tall but with a small head, the *juburé* has a bright but resonant sound, which I really like. I think back to the blacksmith in Dogon country with his stash of kɛbɛlɛs, and wish I'd been allowed to shake at least one of those.

"I need to get higher for the next one. Can you pass that chair, *monsieur?*"

He puts the stool on the chair and clambers up into the roof space of this concrete shack, passing down a long thin instrument, resembling a sawn-off didgeridoo.

"Have you seen one of these before?"

"I think so...in Nigeria."

"It's called the *dunxunme*. Played only by women."

He sits to demonstrate the technique. The instrument is a hollow tube-shaped gourd, played by hitting one end against the top of the thigh, giving a hollow, bouncy kind of sound.

Rather like Mary Poppins' handbag, Moktar continues to conjure up more and more instruments from his tiny store: a bamboo flute, a small harp, a single-stringed lute and the ubiquitous talking drum. From his house, he brings out a four-stringed *ngoni* – the ancestor of the banjo.

"I play this one."

"The ngoni?"

"Yes."

"Can you demonstrate for me?"

Of course. Here is a traditional Soninke song, which has been passed down from griot to griot for generations."

I listen intently to his jolly, undulating melody, which I really like! The opening lines sound like the jazz song 'Frankie and Johnny', which is curious. It's not out of the question that these could be linked, though; my ethnomusicologist colleague Tom was in Senegal a few years back, when he was played a melody which matched note-for-note the song: *Mama's little baby loves short'nin' bread*. Astonishing, but it stands to reason that some of the songs taken over to the States by slaves would find their way into popular culture there, while also persisting in their homeland.

I applaud as he finishes, and he smiles warmly.

Moktar's final instrument is a broad, bowl-shaped drum, roughly two feet in diameter.

"This is the *taballe*. It is only ever played to signal war, theft or the death of a chief."

"How do you know which of the three it is?"

"From the beat."

"Can I have a go?"

"Of course not!" he exclaims, laughing. "You're not a slave!"

"A slave?"

"Yes, the *taballe* is only played by slaves."

"But I thought slavery was abolished."

"Monsieur Robert, in Soninke culture, we have three castes: nobles, griots and slaves."

"And is this still observed today?"

"Yes, very much indeed. But the slave caste are no longer enslaved."

"And which caste are you?"

"I am a carpenter, and all manual workers are in the griot caste. Blacksmiths, cobblers, tailors – all griots."

"Ah, so that's why you're such a good musician – you're a griot!"

"Yes, partly. But not everyone in the griot caste plays music these days."

"And what about the other castes – don't they make music too?"

"The slave caste all sing, but the nobles *never* sing."

"Never?"

"No! It would be inappropriate for a noble man to sing. He would never do such an undignified thing."

"Why not?"

"Because he's nobility. It would be degrading for him to sing like the slaves and griots."

As I bid Moktar farewell, I ask about the two mountains of scrap metal beside his house.

"Ah, those are for the Chinese."

"The Chinese?"

"Yes, the Indians too. Big trucks will come and collect it soon."

"And drive it all the way to China?"

"No my friend, to Dakar. From there it will travel by ship to India and China."

Who'd have guessed that's where West Africa's scrap metal ends up? And we're hundreds of miles inland here!

I've been told I need to book my return train ticket from Kayes, as places fill up quickly, so stop by the railway station on my way home.

"Bonjour!"

"Bonjour monsieur."

"I'd like a ticket to Bamako, for Wednesday."

"For Wednesday? This is not possible! It is Monday today."

"I know, but I'd like to buy my ticket in advance, to travel on Wednesday."

"No, you must come back tomorrow."

"But can't you just sell me one today to save me the taxi fare back tomorrow?"

"No!" he bellows, sliding his little window firmly shut. "Today we sell tickets for tomorrow's train only. Come back tomorrow and you can buy a ticket for Wednesday. This is our system!"

That evening, I eat with Brenda and her husband Dan in the guesthouse: goat curry with rice and okra.

"Do you like the food, Rob?" asks Brenda.

"Mmmhhhm!"

"I cooked it in my solar oven."

"Solar oven?"

"Sure! They work well here in Kayes."

After dinner, Brenda shows me the oven: a wooden box sitting out on the lawn, two feet by one, and eighteen inches deep. The solid lid is covered in aluminium foil and open at an angle to reflect the sun's rays into the oven. The inner walls are painted matt black to radiate the heat inside, and there's a thick horizontal sheet of Perspex covering the rectangular opening, to prevent the heat from escaping. An ingenious device indeed.

"This is where I cooked the goat. It took four hours and cost nothing." Ideal for this climate, but not something that would ever catch on back home.

The following morning after a much-needed lie-in, I take a stroll into Kayes as my next appointment is not until late afternoon. The focal point of the town is the serene, meandering Senegal River which, like the Niger, has its source in Guinea, and passes through Kayes a third of the way along its journey. From here, it will travel all the way to the Senegalese coast (near Dakar), forming a natural border between Mauritania to the north and Senegal to the south as it does so. On the river's dusty, litter-strewn banks, a couple of dozen African canoes (or *pirogues*) are moored at right angles, many used as water taxis, others for fishing. As I descend the sandy slopes, a young boy – no older than twelve – is pulling his boat out of the water, its floor writhing with freshly caught Nile perch.

"*Toubab! Viens acheter poisson!*"

"No thanks, I'm not a big fish fan."

"You don't have fish in America?"

"I'm British. We have fish, but I don't eat it much."

"Do you catch fish from your rivers?"

"Some people do. They use a fishing rod."

"A stick? How can you catch a fish with a stick?!"

"At the end of the stick there is string, and at the end of the string there is a hook. You hang a worm on the hook to attract the fish. It can take all day to catch one, though."

My young friend is wide-eyed with fascination. "All day? One fish?!"

"Yes."

"And then you eat it!"

"No. Then you throw it back into the water."

"Why would you do that? *Ça n'a pas de sens!* You toubabs are crazy!"

I take Kayes' only bridge into town; a simple beam bridge with criss-crossing iron trusses on either side. Shared by traffic and pedestrians, the whole structure vibrates beneath my flip-flops every time a truck passes. Some say its days are numbered, as it was only built to carry vehicles up to 40 tonnes. And since things went pear-shaped in Côte d'Ivoire in the early noughties, more and more goods have come through Dakar rather than Abidjan, putting an ever increasing burden on the bridge. The only alternative here is the *pont submersible* (like the one in Bamako), a stone's throw upstream. Navigable only when the river is low, this concrete structure is mostly used for washing things these days: cars, trucks, goats, clothes, oneself.

On the far side of the river, large squares of fabric are left to dry on the paved slopes approaching the bridge. As Kayes is north of the tsetse fly zone, there are plenty of donkeys pulling carts here, like in Sevaré. And there's a whole herd down by the river, where a young man has taken them to be watered.

As I'm passing, I call in at the railway station again to get my return ticket sorted.

"Bonjour monsieur. Welcome back."

"Can I please buy a ticket for Bamako, leaving tomorrow?"

"Of course!"

"What time does it leave in the morning?"

"I'm not sure." That stands to reason. "The train has not arrived at Bamako yet."

"Of course not, it leaves tomorrow!"

"No, yesterday's train. The train left yesterday morning. It has not arrived in Bamako yet."

It's 10.45am, so I make that 27 hours, assuming it left vaguely on time.

"So, you don't know whether it will make it back to Kayes in time tomorrow?"

"*Exactement!* There was a derailment, you see..."

"It derailed?!"

"No, the freight train derailed. It's always the freight train, because it is heavier. It derailed and the passenger train is behind it. This is what has caused the delay."

Upon further questioning, it appears that neither of these trains is even *halfway* to Bamako yet, so I can't see how mine could possibly make it back to Kayes by tomorrow. I'll take a bus home instead; a nine-hour journey on dusty, pot-holed roads. But a punctual departure is pretty much guaranteed.

The centre of Kayes has a much dreamier pace of life than other towns in Mali, probably due to the heat, and there are more motorcycles than cars on the roads. Straight ahead are some attractive but rather dilapidated colonial buildings with crumbling pillars, overhanging roofs, and balconies circling the entire upper floor. In spite of their condition, they still have a great deal of character and appeal. A little further on sits a rusty old yellow truck with no wheels, abandoned years ago in the corner of a sandy square.

They say it's only mad dogs and Englishmen who go out in the midday sun. I really should have known better, especially as Kayes is clocking a scorching 46 Celsius today. I feel myself teeter with dizziness and struggle to stay vertical, as the sun's heat scorches through my hat, burning my crown. I need water, shade and, most importantly, salts. All the sweating means my body is seriously low on electrolytes, and this is beginning to affect every joint and muscle. My knees give way and I crumble to the floor like a melting snowman, wrought with nausea and lethargy. A few feet ahead is the Catholic Cathedral; a simple, cream-coloured building with a large cross atop its square tower. I stumble to the door and try it. Locked.

"C'est fermé, monsieur!" a passing lady tells me. "But it's open on Sundays."

I sit on the threshold in the few inches of shade the archway provides, my head in my knees for several minutes. I'm roused by a passing motorbike carrying 12 large crates of eggs, held in place by just a pair of old bungees. Behind the motorcyclist – as though sent from on high – is a *Fan Milk* salesman, racing along on his blue bicycle. The plastic icebox on the front contains a range of refreshing frozen yoghurt lollies in plastic wrappers, terribly common in these parts. Seeing the toubab, he slows down, calling out his product's name loudly. For once, I'm glad to be badgered by a pushy salesman.

I muster up the energy to speak: *"Oui!"*

"Qu'est-ce que vous désirez?"

"One Fan-Ice, a Fan-Choco and a strawberry Fan-Yogo, please."

"Trois glaces?"

"Oui! Trois."

I eagerly bite the corner from the first packet in tears of relief, as my body welcomes this much-needed sustenance. The other two ice creams, I put under my hat to cool my throbbing skull.

Within a few minutes all three are gone, and I feel much better. I decide to head back, this time taking the *pirogue* across the river; it may even be slightly cooler on the water, you never know. As I climb aboard, a Coke salesman waves a bottle of brown fizzy liquid in my general direction. I buy that too, downing it in seconds.

There are no seats on board the pirogue; you simply perch on the rim of the boat, so there's no snoozing in this game. The boatman has a long pole which he pushes into the river, rather like a punt in Cambridge or a gondola in Venice. The experience is not as luxurious or relaxing as either, but definitely cheaper: to cross this 200 metre stretch costs 25 CFA, or four English pence. There are 17 people on board, evenly arranged on either side so we don't capsize. The boat swings out, its pointed prow narrowly missing the heads of passengers on the adjacent vessel.

"Il n'y a pas de freins!"[46] says the smartly dressed man next to me.

Our boat heads upstream so as to arrive at the right spot opposite once it hits stronger currents in the centre. In doing so, we narrowly miss another boat – by six inches at the most. Nobody on board seems remotely flustered.

"Il n'y a pas de freins!" repeats the businessman with a smile.

I'm feeling revived by the relatively cool breeze across the water, as my cocktail of caffeine and lactose begins to kick in. An old lady on board turns to me and utters something in Soninke.

"What did she say?" I ask the dapper chap.

"She said she wants to be your wife!"

"My wife?!"

"Yes!"

"Ah, no, no, no!" I exclaim, waving a furious finger. "I'm already married." And even if I weren't, she's 60 years old and we speak no common language.

"She says she can be your second wife: one white wife, one black." They seem quite serious about this.

"It's not possible, I'm afraid. Sorry."

This is not the first time I've had this kind of proposition in Africa. And of course, the motivation is largely financial.

"Traoré, are you *sure* this is the place?"

"That's what I was told."

It's 4pm and, following a much-needed siesta, Mr Diarra has dropped me outside a three-storey concrete shell with no doors or windows. This is where I'm meeting the *Troupe Tigadege,* a Soninke folk group, who perform at weddings and festivals across the region. I'm welcomed by an older man with one leg, who vaguely resembles OJ Simpson.

"I used to be the head of the troop," he tells me, "but my illness came back and I had the amputation last month."

We enter the building to the sound of drums and singing. Within seconds, I've got my audio recorder and notebook out, avidly taking all of this down. Every song genre has a purpose in Africa and is linked to a set

---

[46] There are no brakes.

event, occupation or ceremony. Before each song, they explain its significance.

"The next song is in the style *Nunu Wute*," says OJ. "We sing it when a boy becomes a man."

"Ah, yes!" I reply. "Most African cultures have one of these. What happens when you sing it?"

"We circumcise him, then we sing the song," he says.

More circumcision. "And what age is the boy when this happens?"

"25 years old."

Twenty-five! And I thought the Dogon were brutal waiting until twelve…

"We sing the song as we dress him in baggy trousers." I can imagine why he'd need those. "And we put a band around his head. Then the crowd lift him up in the air."

That could be a bit dicey. The song is rhythmic and catchy, with plenty of polyrhythmic drumming and claps. I like it!

"Next, we have *Yimbe*, which is for telling stories when sitting around a fire at night."

I'm wondering why they'd ever *need* a fire at night here. But storytelling is an important part of almost every African culture, and this one can be sung by men or women. Understandably, it's a quieter song, with no drums.

"That was nice. What else do you have?"

"There's also *Dosongoni,* which is for hunting. A retired hunter will always become a singer."

"What if he can't sing?"

"He will learn."

I ask how they reconcile music with their faith.

"Islam has not changed our musical culture!" responds one portly chap. "Just, we have to stop for prayer times now. We hear music every day."

"When you white people play your music, it makes people sin," adds OJ. "Your women dance in alluring ways with little clothing, and the men lust after them. This is sinful. In Islam, women are not like this; they cover their bodies and are dignified in front of men."

"So does Islam condemn music?" I ask.

"Music and Islam have co-existed here for centuries," he replies. "But now some complain when we make music."

The overweight chap chips in: "But how could we get married without music? Religion tells us to celebrate!"

At this, an elderly lady jumps to her feet and joyfully shouts: "*YULA YANKANDE!*" and the whole room erupts into cheers and applause.

"What did she just say?" I ask, as the noise dies down.

"*Yula Yankande,*" repeats OJ. "Wedding songs."

"Okay, what about them?"

The scrawny old woman turns to me: "There are many, many wedding songs and they are all sung by women, *never* men!" she says, waving a single spindly finger at me. "Here's a song about arranged marriage."

She launches into a joyous melody, which the rest of the women in the room echo. I notice that none of the men join in, obediently following Soninke convention.

The portly chap turns to me: "The words say: *My father has said it, so the marriage must happen.*"

The song ends and she segues into another equally joyful air.

"This is the song for washing the bride," says the round fellow.

"*Washing* the bride?" I clarify, bemused.

"Yes, before the wedding, the other women all wash the bride. In public. There's also a song for drying the bride."

"In public?"

"Of course."

Next comes a song for when the woman is taken to her husband's house, followed by one sung when she arrives at the door, which says: *The head of the family is coming in.*" The old woman shows no sign of tiring and has now been singing – virtually non-stop – for almost an hour.

"Thank you!" I say, as she finishes. "You have so many wedding songs!" I can see why they said: 'How could we get married without music?'

"We have one more song, which we sing when the bride enters her husband's bedroom," she proudly proclaims. "The other women crouch outside the door and listen..."

"Really? Is that not indiscrete?"

"No, this is what we do, to confirm the marriage has been consummated."

Curious indeed. With its non-singing nobles, piles of scrap metal, dodgy river taxis, colonial housing, oppressive heat and highly intrusive wedding songs, Kayes is indeed a fascinating place to visit.

It's still completely dark when the bus leaves the next morning; a sleek blue and white 'Gana Transport' vehicle with air-conditioning. Across the top of the windows is written *'El mejor camino para conocer Catalunya'* – the best way to know Catalonia. I'm pretty sure that's no longer the case…

Although the road is littered with potholes, the journey is largely pleasant, sat next to a Mr Maiga, who's heading to Bamako to begin nursing training there. At one point, a whole troop of baboons runs across the road at great speed, their long auburn tails waving behind them. The bus slows down as they leap across the rocks with great agility. Some of them stop to stare at us angrily with their long, protruding black faces; others raise their iconic pink bottoms in our general direction. I grab my camera and take some pictures; this is only the second time I've seen wild baboons.

Almost twelve hours later, we pull into the sandy bus station on the edge of Bamako. I catch a taxi home: another Mercedes 190D with one headlight out, the side mirror hanging off and a small hole in the floor; driven by a fellow Traoré.

Back in Badalabougou, a brand new supermarket – a stone's throw from our house – is almost finished. The broad, concrete building is painted bright yellow and is called *Shopreate Libre Service*. I think that's an attempt to spell 'shop-right' or maybe 'superette'; I'm not quite sure. It will be handy to have somewhere so close, as Azar's is a good 20-minute walk away.

The kids have spent most of today in the pool, which Coulibaly came to clean just yesterday. And we have a new addition to the family: Shiloh, a brown dachshund who recently travelled here with some missionaries from Benin. He's a friendly chappie, whose feet can regularly be heard pattering along the tiled floors after Lois. He has been known to bite strangers, though, and urinates everywhere whenever he gets too excited (which is quite often).

Mr Kouyaté has just arrived for his night shift. He and Shiloh have already bonded in my absence, and the dog toddles out to greet him, peeing everywhere.

"Shaaaayy-loooh! Shaaaayyy-loooooh! *Mon ami, ça va?*"

After petting the animal enthusiastically, he asks me about my journey.

"Et le voyage?"

I tell him all about my adventures on the train, the wedding songs and the boats on the Senegal River. Kouyaté was at Bamako railway station just this afternoon on an errand. Apparently, the train to Kayes (the one I was hoping to catch home) has *still* not left Bamako!

Chapter Fifteen – Bozo Bound

"It's somewhat disconcerting to board a boat you know is slowly sinking."

"WHERE ARE YOU going, *monsieur?*"

"Mopti."

"That's a long way. Are you travelling alone?"

"Yes, I am," I reply, rather stating the obvious; I clearly have no passengers in the Mitsubishi today. It's 7.05am at the city limits of Bamako, where I'm bracing myself for a 400-mile drive north to riverside Mopti. From there, I plan to catch a boat to Bozo Country as the roads are waterlogged this time of year. The Bozo are fishermen who inhabit the vast Niger Inland Delta, fifty or so miles northwest of Mopti. The guard at the checkpoint waves me on, wishing me a *bon voyage.* Let's hope so.

The purpose of this visit – like most – is ethnomusicology: finding out more about Bozo music and attitudes towards it. Like the Soninke, most Bozo are Muslim, which may mean music is not favourably viewed.

Roughly five years ago, an Austrian colleague lived in Diafarabé,[47] the Bozo's largest town and a thriving fishing port. Although not remotely musical (tone deaf actually), Stefan made dozens of recordings of Bozo songs for his anthropological archives. I got hold of this music and am taking it with me on an MP3 device. Unfortunately, Stefan made virtually no notes on these songs, so my plan is to play them to key individuals and find out more – a good starting point for my research.

The road ahead, pot-holed as ever, is empty at the moment. Just the occasional pigeon sitting in the road (one of which I accidentally squished a few miles back). It's February, a relatively cool, dry time of year. Pied hornbills swoop majestically from one baobab to another, drawing smiley faces in the sky, and dozy goats wander haphazardly into my path, narrowly avoiding death.

There's been lots of bad news in the region lately. Two Frenchmen were

---

[47] Pronounced [ja-fara-bay]

taken hostage in Niamey, Niger, last month. One of them was killed. This is the second case of hostage-taking in the country of Niger. A couple of days later in Bamako, a 25-year old Tunisian threw a hand grenade over the wall of the French embassy, injuring two Malian guards. He also fired several shots at the building and, when arrested, admitted being from one of the *katibas:* camps of AQIM.[48]   The embassy now has barbed wire fencing on all its walls, a taller entrance gate and huge concrete bollards along the street outside. The French Cultural Centre has made similar modifications, as has the American School, just round the corner from us.

Then last week, 36 people died at the *Stade Modibo Keita*, the very same stadium where chaos broke out for Sean Paul just over a year ago. Thousands of people had gathered to hear an important Imam preach and many were trying to get near enough to touch him. Panic broke out for reasons unknown, and many were simply trampled underfoot in the rush. 36 dead, 64 injured, most of them women. So, so sad. The Malian Hillsborough.

A few days before this, civil war broke out in Libya between Gaddafi and those seeking to oust him. And, more significantly for us, Gaddafi co-opted hundreds of Malians to fight for him – almost entirely Tuaregs.

On a more positive note, Bono (*the* Bono!) made a guest appearance at the *Festival au Désert* this year. It was something of a surprise visit, and very few people knew until he appeared on stage, singing with the band Tinariwen and also performing with Malian ngoni player Bassekou Kouyaté. He arrived in his own private jet, almost literally under the radar, and flew out again shortly after performing. I don't know what he was thinking, as the risks in Timbuktu are significant now; much higher than 12 months ago when I was there. Even Bozo Country is not entirely risk-free as it borders the zone where hostage-taking is happening and is also very remote.

When the fields of gourds and *balanzan* trees appear, you know that Ségou is not far away, and I make it to the *Hôtel de l'Indépendance* for a late breakfast: *omelette aux fines herbes* with the ubiquitous Nescafé and powdered milk. There are just three others in the restaurant, which overlooks the

---

48 Al Qaeda in the Islamic Mahgreb

river: a couple of rich-looking Tuaregs who arrived in an almost brand new Toyota Hilux and – you've guessed it – a German. The *Kankou Moussa* is still moored beside the Niger, but the hotel on the opposite bank is not visible today, cloaked in thick Harmattan dust.

Continuing north at 120km/h, something black steps out from nowhere, just feet ahead. It's a goat. I slam on my brakes, but it's too late. BANG! I hit the poor beast and hear my wheels go *gedung-gedung* over its body. What should I do now? Advice varies: some say stop at the next village and pay the price of the goat. I've never subscribed to this method, as it could go two ways, one of which might be very nasty indeed. So I just keep driving, figuring someone will find the animal soon enough. And when they do, the whole village will have a feast at its expense.

I wish I could say this was the only setback on my journey north; it was not. Half an hour later, the road ahead is blocked by a huge truck which has jack-knifed and overturned, landing at right angles across the entire road, its huge cargo of oil drums scattered far and wide. I pull up tentatively (but not too close) and take a look. The driver is nowhere to be seen, so I assume this happened a while ago. In the UK, there'd be police galore with flashing lights and everything. Nothing here, besides a few tufts of grass on the road as a warning. The only way round this obstacle is to leave the road and drive through the adjacent field. It's bumpy and very difficult to avoid the gourds growing there, not to mention the oil drums, which are everywhere. I hit a couple of gourds en route, which make a much more satisfying noise when squished than a goat does. Roughly a mile further on, I see a teenage boy rolling an oil drum along the road towards his village – not the most subtle plundering I've witnessed, but I'm sure it'll come in useful to him and his family.

Three more hours from Ségou and I once again pass through the inconsequential town of Bla. They seem to like short town names in this part of Mali; as you may remember, the next one is called San, still an hour from here. I'm making good time so far (goats and oil drums notwithstanding), and enjoy listening to Amadou and Mariam's CD, which I bought at the festival in Timbuktu last year.

I'm singing along to *Dimanches à Bamako* as I whizz ever northwards at some speed. The road is straight, the weather is pleasant and the view is flat and brown but not altogether disagreeable. I'm just thinking how lucky

I am to be driving this lovely Mitsubishi to another fascinating destination as part of my job, when I hear a loud and regular thumping noise from the rear of the vehicle. It takes me a while to slow down, and the frequency of the thuds decreases as I do so. Pulling over onto the sandy, red verge beside a vegetable stall, I step out to take a look. The driver's side rear tyre is completely ripped apart – so much so that strips of metal wire are protruding from the ten inch gash. Oh dear! The ladies selling veg look on in dismay but offer me little assistance – car maintenance is very much a male domain here. I pull on the dust-coated rear door, which creaks slowly open. I locate the jack and place it under the car, remembering to loosen the wheel nuts before raising the vehicle. As I'm on a sloping dirt verge, my first attempt fails terribly, as the base of the jack merely slips down the slope. I find a firmer bit of ground and try again. This time the car rises slightly but not enough, so I have to burrow beneath the wheel to remove it. No sooner have I done so, than the jack slowly sinks into the sand, leaving the now exposed brake disk embedded in the dirt. What now? I have one more idea: gathering half a dozen stones from the roadside and fields, I remove the jack and dig a small hole where it was. I now put the stones inside as 'foundations' for my jack. It works!

Just then, a minibus travelling south pulls in and a small Tamasheq man in a mustard-coloured turban gets out to buy veg. He sees the white man and offers to help.

"It's okay thanks – I'm almost done now."

"Are you going to San? I need a ride to San." He's just come from there, so I smell a rat. I'm always cautious of picking up strangers, especially ones who randomly appear from nowhere.

"San is not my destination," I tell him (which is true).

I lift the spare wheel down and put it on the car, having dusted the sand from the brake disk. It is now that I realize my next problem: the spare is almost flat and I have no pump. I've seen folk repair flat tyres by stuffing them with dry straw and it works quite well. But I have no way of even removing the tyre to do that, and there's no straw about. Mustard turban blokey (to whom I have just refused a ride), notices my problem.

"*Mossieu*, there is a pump at the next village."

"How far is that?" I ask, in slight embarrassment.

"About three kilometres."

I trundle off, the tyre barely holding up. I daren't exceed 20km/h, but eventually make it to the village where, sure enough, there is a small workshop, easily recognizable by the tall pile of tyres out front. The guy there charges me 200 CFA to pump the tyre up by hand, which takes him roughly seven minutes. From here, it's still 45km to San, where I must get a replacement tyre, or risk being completely stranded, should I get another puncture.

Sometimes, more haste means less speed; this was the case when I failed to check the spare tyre this morning, and is also the case when I arrive in San. Eager to solve my problem fast, I pull over at the first shop, wind down the window and call out:

"Do you know anywhere that sells tyres?"

Eager to help me (and possibly make a fast buck), he's straight on his phone.

"Yes, yes *monsieur!* It's coming right away!"

Amazingly, a young lad turns up just ten minutes later, rolling said tyre along the road towards us.

"Here you are, *monsieur!*"

I inspect the tyre carefully; it's not in bad shape. But my relief is short-lived, as I check the numbers on the side.

"No, this one is no good. I need 265, 70, 15 and yours is 255, 65, 15. That's not the same."

And, with that, he's straight on his mobile.

"It's coming, and this time, it's *definitely* the correct size!" he says, nodding rather unconvincingly. He offers me a seat, which I take; and some water, which I politely refuse. The second tyre arrives 25 minutes later and, I'm pleased to say, all the numbers match.

"How much?"

"40,000."

"That's way too expensive!" He wants 50 pounds for a bashed-up old tyre. "I'll give you ten thousand!"

We settle on 35,000, which is still too much. Using nothing but a crowbar and a mallet, he replaces my gashed tyre with this one, then inflates it.

HISSSSSSSSS!

"We can fix it! We can fix it!"

I don't think so: there's an inch-long slit in this tyre.

"Wait, wait! When I got this tyre, there was another one next to it just the same. Let me get that for you!"

I should have moved on after the first dodgy tyre, but I'm just too trusting, too optimistic and too gullible. Africans will bend over backwards to please you, even when there's little chance they can actually come up with the goods. Tyre number three has no tread whatsoever. Time to move on. I thank him for his time and drive away looking for more piles of tyres, which always denote a workshop. To save time, I simply slow down and call out: '265, 70, 15' – quite a mouthful in French.

Most respond negatively: *"Il n'y en a pas!"*[49]

On the fourth attempt, I get a positive response and the numbers are *almost* the same.

"It *will* fit, monsieur, it will fit!" the guy assures me.

He has no fitting equipment at his workshop, so trundles off down the road with my wheel. I follow him along the main street, where most of the metal shacks are painted either orange or blue and red, to advertise the local mobile phone networks: blue and red for 'Malitel' and orange for...well...Orange. Distracted by this tricolour onslaught, I manage to lose sight of my *tyre blokey*. I search every alleyway, but to no avail, so have little option but to return to his workshop and wait. After 25 minutes, he is still not back. His assistant gives me his phone number. No reply.

"Where is he? Has he stolen my wheel?"

"No, of course not! He is an honest man."

Just then, a chap from *another* workshop I'd called at en route arrives on a motorbike.

"Come with me, *monsieur*, we've found you a tyre."

"But I'm already having one fitted." At least, I hope I am.

"No, no! I've seen that one – it's the wrong size." News travels fast in these parts. "Jump on: I'll take you to see mine."

I trustingly hop on the back of the motorbike with a complete stranger. Amazingly, he has the right-sized tyre. A tad beaten up, but definitely useable. It's 3pm now; I don't want to arrive in the dark, and beggars can't be choosers.

---

[49] There aren't any!

"How much?"

"25,000."

"Deal!"

All sorted, but I still have nothing to put the tyre onto.

"Where is my wheel hub?"

The guy shakes his head nonchalantly, saying nothing. If it's taken me this long to find a tyre, imagine the fun and games I'd have trying to find a replacement Mitsubishi wheel hub here.

"Try calling him," he suggests.

"I've tried *three times* already! Look, I need my wheel now, so I can continue my journey."

Silence.

"Is anyone going to do anything here, or shall I go and look for him myself?"

Apparently, yes, I shall. Wandering down the road, another stranger approaches me (the whole town seems to know of my tyre saga by now).

"He's coming with your wheel, *monsieur.*"

And so, two and a half hours later than scheduled, I'm back on the road. It's only three more hours' drive from here to Sevaré.

Night has just fallen as I pull into the driveway of Mac's Refuge. It's good to be back. Mac recognizes me straightaway and greets me warmly. I pre-booked a room for 4000 francs a night; a whole lot cheaper than a bashed-up spare tyre.

It's enchiladas on the menu tonight, with chicken, salad, soured cream and homemade guacamole. Around the table this time are three Peace Corps volunteers, two young American backpackers and two middle-aged people: one French, one German. Tonight, we mostly chat about Libya and the situation in the north of Mali, which is hotting up by the minute. I tell Mac my planned journey for tomorrow.

"*That* boat! I hope you're prepared for a long journey. You'll be cold on board: I can lend you a sleeping bag."

Back in Bamako, our children just performed a musical – *my* musical – on the roof of their tiny school. It's about Jonah and the whale, and I was sad not to be there to see it. Thankfully, it was all filmed, so I'll get to enjoy it at a later date.

Lois and the kids have also visited the newly opened *Parc National* in town which, she tells me, has: "open grassy areas where the children can play, an air-conditioned café, a waterfall and a posh restaurant at the far end." The children, she says, were also excited to see a sign by the lake, which read: 'Beware of the crocodiles'.

Following another legendary pancake breakfast with Mac, I'm grateful for the luxury of a restful morning. The boat to Bozo country doesn't leave Mopti until late afternoon and my assistant, Moussa, is coming after lunch. He's bang on time, and we zoom off aboard his white Yamaha off-road bike: 125cc with reassuringly high suspension.

Mopti is a bustling port; a hub on the Niger River between Bamako and Ségou to the south, and Timbuktu and Gao to the north.

"There are two boats to Diafarabé," Moussa tells me, "a good boat and a bad boat."

"What's the difference?"

"The good one has seats."

The port is a natural inlet, where three dusty slopes descend steeply to the water. Around the top of this slipway are market stalls made from rusty corrugated metal and knobbly old branches, selling bread, vegetables, kitchenware, grilled meat and small round doughnuts. Nearer the boats are stalls selling all the necessaries for travel: blankets, coats, peanuts, jeans, water and the ubiquitous tartan plastic-weave 'refugee bags'. There's also a Tamasheq guy selling tagelmust fabric in just about every colour.

"Venez acheter, mossieu. Venez!" he calls when he sees me.

There are huge piles of dry wood for sale, along with a few dozen sacks of charcoal. Carpenters are making bookcases, tables, even beds, all of which perch haphazardly on the sloping edges of the port. Right in the middle sits a huge pile of rubbish: discarded plastic bottles, cardboard packaging, old tyres (don't mention tyres!), crushed tin cans, plastic bags, rotted wicker baskets – even parts of a defunct TV set. I'm not sure what happens to this rubbish; whether anyone ever collects it, or if it just sits there, slowly rotting into the sand.

I forgot to borrow a sleeping bag from Mac this morning, so find a thick ski jacket on one of the stalls. I'm not picky, I just want to stay warm.

The one I choose is red, white and blue and reads 'Ford, Quality Care Service' with the word 'NASCAR' emblazoned across the back.

"It's the bad boat today," Moussa tells me. "No seats. We'll need to get on the roof soon."

"Why?"

"Because that's the only place you can sit down."

Our vessel is a 40-foot *pinasse* with an arched wooden roof covered in taut white tarps. Imagine a very long canoe, seven feet wide. The hull is painted in bright colours, which also incorporate the Malian flag and the year '2002'. The front is open to the elements, and this is where the driver sits. Two long chains run either side of the boat, dangling in the water as they do so; these link the steering wheel with the rudder at the rear – a crude but effective system. Inside the boat it's dark and dingy and, as expected, there are no seats. Heavy wooden struts crossing the boat at regular intervals can be used to sit on, but most of the passengers seem to prefer sprawling over sacks of onions, rice and yams. Many have woven wicker mats they lay out first, not that this makes much difference comfort-wise.

A ten-foot plank bridges the gap between the bank and the boat, and is the only way of boarding the vessel. It bows horribly every time someone walks across, but never quite snaps. From inside the hull, a chap is bailing out water using half a yellow jerrican; every 20 seconds or so, a few more litres are poured out into the river. It's somewhat disconcerting to board a boat you know is slowly sinking. Let's hope the hole doesn't get any larger.

In the centre of the curved roof, a threadbare French flag flies proudly. In front of it, seven motorbikes are laid sideways, and we're about to add ours to the collection. At the rear is a flat piece of roof covered in sheet metal; Moussa and I find our spot here, between a large blackboard (on its way to a school) and three long, white display cabinets. There's enough space to sit or even lie down, but there are already four others up here, so I'm at the very edge with nothing but a four-inch bar to stop me rolling off into the river. It doesn't surprise or bother me that I'm the only white person on board; I'm used to it and feel a warm sense of camaraderie with the other chaps on the roof.

The gang plank is pulled into the boat; a sign we should soon be leaving. But latecomers are still trying to board: one chap rolls up his trousers and wades through the foul-smelling, green water. Others follow suit, and even a couple more motorbikes are raised, dripping and stinking, onto the roof. The engine roars into action, and Moussa and I are cloaked in a cloud of thick, blue smoke. It is only now that I realize that we're sitting directly above the engine. This could be an interesting journey…

Chapter Sixteen – On Pointy Noses

"Without batting an eyelid, he rips off the chicken's head."

WITH A ROAR the boat pulls slowly away from the muddy, rancid slipway and proceeds out of the port, passing several other boats, all colourfully painted. It's 6pm, and if all goes to plan, we'll be in Diafarabé around 5am tomorrow. We soon exchange the bustling, grimy port of Mopti for picturesque scenes of cows grazing peacefully on verdant riverbanks, sparrowhawks hovering in anticipation, pied kingfishers diving adeptly into the cool blue water, and white egrets flying in a V-formation, silhouetted against darkening skies. The riverbank here is formed of a sandy cliff several feet high; sometimes dropping abruptly to the river, sometimes sloping gradually down.

A man with six toes on one foot and a white spot on his left eye clambers past me.

"What is your name?"

"Traoré."

He laughs. "This is my village on the left – it's called Ngomi."

It's a picturesque place, with a small adobe mosque surrounded by date palms and a few donkeys.

Below, I hear a bell ring now and again, and am intrigued.

"That's for changing gear," Moussa explains. "The driver pulls a cord above his head to ring the bell at the back."

"Then what happens?"

"There's a man sitting by the engine; he hears the bell and changes gear. Two rings to go up a gear, one ring to go back down, or to reverse."

As the sun begins to set ahead of us, the pleasant breeze turns cool. I put my Nascar jacket on and huddle down on the sheet metal surface. Lying on my side, I can still see shadows of the riverbank passing by: the occasional village, trees, and livestock.

An hour or so into our journey, the engine begins to jerk and splutter, then everything goes quiet. Loud, frustrated voices bellow beneath us, shouting angrily in Bambara.

"What are they saying?" I ask Moussa.

"They say the engine has no fuel."

"What? We've run out already?"

Moussa listens as the conversation continues. "No, they're saying that the fuel pipe to the engine is disconnected."

Meanwhile, as we were travelling upstream, the boat has now begun to move *backwards*.

"We're on our way back to Mopti!" I proclaim, with a sense of irony which surpasses Moussa. He smiles nevertheless, mimicking my facial expressions out of politeness.

After much fumbling in semi-darkness and lots more shouting, the pipe is reattached and we're off again, passing the very same silhouettes as we did half an hour ago.

"Moussa, I need the toilet! What do I do?" I hadn't even thought about this until now.

"Ah, c'est compliqué!"

He explains, and advises me to take my torch with me. First, I have to squeeze past the end of the blackboard without falling in the river (a gap of roughly eight inches). Then behind this, a narrow, metal step ladder descends to the river. I take this halfway then, grabbing onto the roof (now at head height) swing down onto the deck below. Here the ceiling is only four feet high. I feel something move beneath my feet and am startled. Shining my torch at the floor, I see the chain which controls the rudder; the driver must be slightly changing course. To the front of me, the huge beast of an engine roars away, generating lots of heat. To the rear is a small, square opening, which I squeeze through. Moussa hadn't mentioned the two foot drop at this point, and I nearly fall as I drop down in virtual darkness. I'm now in a large wooden box with an L-shaped hole in the floor, through which the fast-flowing Niger River is clearly visible. This is the toilet. As I relieve myself (torch in mouth), I notice something moving back and forth in the water. Could it be a fish? No, it's the rudder – I'm actually peeing onto the rudder!

Back on the roof, everyone is now huddled down under blankets to keep warm; most have even covered their heads. Not realizing quite how cold it would be – no more than 12 degrees – I came in thin trousers and sandals, but at least I have my new jacket, which I zip up tightly and brace myself for a long, chilly night.

Just then, the boat stops moving again, but this time the engine is still turning over. More shouting down below and, as we're stationary, the exhaust fumes choke everyone on the roof. The boat begins to move backwards once more, then drifts sideways, hits a sandbank and runs aground. We're now stranded on two counts, but nobody attempts to dislodge the boat until the engine problem is solved; at least we're not floating back to Mopti while we're stuck.

After almost an hour, the boat tries to lurch forwards; a good sign from an engine point of view, but we're still lodged on the sandbank. Four men take a pair of long planks to use as levers under the hull. It works, and we're soon continuing our epic journey.

I'm woken by the sun rising behind us. I rub my eyes and sit up. It's not been the best night's sleep ever, but the view makes up for it: the glistening waters of the Niger, untouched by industry or urbanization. Fishermen in small pirogues punt to and fro in search of a morning catch, casting their broad, circular nets into the water like giant frisbees. The golden riverbanks, where long-necked white egrets tentatively strut, contrast starkly with the rippling azure iridescence below them. The villages here are simple affairs: biblical-style square houses with small windows, perched neatly above the water, surrounded by majestic rhun palms – their hand-like leaves waving in the crisp morning breeze. It can't be more than 10 Celsius right now, and my teeth are chattering.

The boat broke down three more times during the night, once for nearly two hours. Each time the voices got louder and more fraught – at one point it sounded as though there were dozens of folk crammed into the engine room.

"This next village is called Nuhun," says Moussa. "It's where all the Bozo boats are built."

Sure enough, there are a couple of dozen long planks of wood laid out on the beach ready to be used, some half-built boats, and a couple of finished articles, their newly acquired coats of varnish sparkling in the morning sunlight.

"Nuhun means 'Noah' in the Bozo language. Have you heard of Noah? He's in the Koran."

"Yes, he's in the Bible too!"

"He was a man who built a boat. This is why we call the village Nuhun."

It's 7am, and we should have arrived at Diafarabé by now. I'm just beginning to feel a tad sorry for myself when the chap on the other side of Moussa – a teacher – pipes up:

"I arrived in Mopti yesterday morning at two o'clock"

"Where from?"

"From Diafarabé."

"So you've spent the last two nights on the river?"

"Yes. I had some important documents to drop off."

"But did you have the *nice boat* coming?"

"I did. It has seats and the driver is more skilled. It didn't break down once."

At 11am, precisely seventeen hours after departing, we dock on the sandy slopes of Diafarabé and carefully unload the motorbike from the roof. Our host, Pasteur Samuel, is waiting by the shore.

"Welcome to Diafarabé! What is your name?"

He clearly hasn't had much information about me. He was simply told 'a white man is coming and he does music'.

"Most of the musicians are in the hamlets fishing, but I'll try and find some for you," he says.

"Thank you."

Diafarabé is a small place, similar to the other villages downstream. Square houses, dusty roads, mango trees. From what I can see, it has precisely two shops: one selling groceries, the other mobile phone credit. Then there's a mosque, a church, and a tiny school. That's about it. The square mud houses are much more spread out than in Dogon Country and number a few hundred at the most.

"You should have been here a few weeks ago, for the *Deegal!*" says Samuel.

"The what?"

Moussa chips in: "The cattle crossing – it's quite famous. When the waters are at just the right level, Fulani herdsmen cross the river here in Diafarabé with thousands of cattle."

"Thousands?"

"Yes. They cross to get to richer pastures. It happens every year, it's interesting to watch."

"And there's a special order for crossing," adds Pasteur Samuel. "First, the chief's cattle, then the religious leaders' cattle."

"...and finally, the *jooro*," adds Moussa, excitedly.

"The what?"

"The head herder who is in charge of the pastures."

"And after that," says Samuel, "everyone else can cross. This has been happening for 200 years. The Fulani men swim beside their cows, hitting the water with a stick to direct them to the opposite bank. And the Bozo fishermen help out too, using their boats to guide the cows across."

"Can the Bozo people swim?" I ask Samuel, knowing many Africans can't or don't.

"They swim. And the children learn, but nobody teaches them."

"Swimming is the only way to get across here," adds Moussa.

"Unless you can walk on water!" I add, smiling.

"There are Bozos who can do that!" says Moussa, nodding fervently.

"Who can walk on water?"

"Yes! And there are others who can come out of the water and still be dry."

"Really?"

"Yes," he says, adamant. "They say there are spirits in the water, and if you become good friends with them, they can help you."

"'To be a co-wife is like a scorpion bite. But you must be patient with the other wife.' That's what this song says. When a husband has two wives, they must get on."

I'm sitting on the sandy riverbank in the tiny village of Barikedaga, playing my Bozo songs to a dozen or so listeners in the afternoon heat. Some are musicians, others are wise old men, who know their culture well. There are also some children who have come to 'watch the curious toubab'. One girl, no older than six, is wearing a knitted Winnie-the-Pooh jumper, and her brother, maybe ten, is sporting a faded blue Barack Obama T-shirt.

I play another song and they all listen avidly.

"Ahh...this one says: 'You must love the children of others, and not just your own,'" croaks an old chap in a brown duffle coat. I play another. The only lady in the group responds:

"This is *Naani Naani*. It's a song for women to rejoice. They sing the names of their parents' brothers in it."

Many Bozo songs seem to be about family and relationships, but the next one bucks this trend:

"This song tells the story of a hippo who is travelling down the river and nobody can stop him. It names the villages he swims past, and then praises the person who finally killed him."

The Bozo don't seem to have many musical instruments, just a few small drums and shakers, (which stands to reason if you spend half your life on the river). One more interesting song catches my attention.

"Ah, yes," says a chap in a pink turban. "This is the genre called *Nungalamawasa*. It's a song for glorifying yourself. In the song, a young woman is saying: 'I'm so beautiful, because I have a pointy nose.' "

"A pointy nose?!"

"Of course."

"Why a pointy nose?"

Moussa explains: "In Bozo culture, the more pointy a woman's nose, the more attractive she is considered."

Before I leave, one older man pipes up: "We've sung you our songs. Now you must sing us a song from your country."

"Okay, let me think a moment..."

I consider 'Old MacDonald', but that's surely American. I also think of 'Ilkley Moor Baht At', but that would be far too complicated to explain. So, I plump for 'Daisy Daisy' – they know what a bicycle is, and they certainly know marriage. Everyone listens intently as to my bold rendition of this folky waltz, applauding enthusiastically at the end.

"We like your song, *monsieur*, but it's difficult to fit two people on a bicycle, especially a woman."

As we bid the villagers farewell, Pooh Bear Girl pipes up: "Goode ba yee!"

"Oh, goodbye to you too!" I reply, shaking her hand in an awfully British way.

"Ank you weree moch."

"You're welcome!"

Tired from an afternoon's work (not to mention the night on the boat), I return to my accommodation: a square adobe hut with a door, a window and a concrete floor. Nothing else, besides my own portable mosquito net and camping mat. I settle down for a much-needed siesta; after last night's sleeping arrangements, this feels like the Ritz.

I wake in need of a refreshing shower. Across the courtyard is the 'bathroom': a square area surrounded by a four-foot mud wall with a hole in the ground to one side (the toilet), and a small drainage hole beneath the wall to the other, for showering. Two stripy plastic jugs sit at the shower end, and as I pour one of these carefully over my head, passing villagers greet my soapy face over the wall; a bizarre and mildly unsettling experience.

When we arrived this morning, I saw an intriguing building just downstream from the village; a kind of mini-chateau perched on the riverbank. I decide to investigate before it gets dark. Upon arrival, I'm instantly struck by the grounds of the place: pristine gardens where pineapples, papayas and mangos grow, as well as lettuces, onions and tomatoes. There's a well in the centre, with two rectangular ponds laid out symmetrically on either side. Surely someone rich lives here.

A well-dressed African chap appears in the doorway: *"Bonsoir monsieur!"*

"Bonsoir. I'm staying in the village and was curious about this building. I saw it from the river."

"You are very welcome. It's going to be a hotel."

"Your gardens are impressive."

"Yes, but the earth is too sandy here, so we had to bring in good soil to put on the top. It's hard to find fruit and vegetables in Diafarabé, so we are growing our own. The villagers can also come and buy it from us here."

"What about the pools?"

"This is where I'm going to breed fish."

"So, are you the owner?"

"No. I'm employed full-time, but the owner is a Frenchman."

I think of the French chaps I met on the Dogon cliff, sizing up the area to build a hotel there, and wonder if this is theirs too. Sadly, given Mali's declining state of security at present (and in the months to come), it seems unlikely either hotel will attract many Western tourists for the foreseeable future.

Inside, there are no furnishings yet, but he points out the two dining rooms, from which four bedrooms are accessible. Each of these is already fitted with its own spiral staircase running up to a roof terrace.

"Would you like to go up and see the view?"

"Yes please."

I step out onto the roof, where one of the finest sunsets of my life awaits, filling the entire vista before me. I stand in awe for at least ten minutes, as my guide patiently admires the sky with me. A thin blanket of mid-level, cotton wool cloud runs towards me from the horizon, reflecting its vibrant orange hues onto the river, where pirogues glide dreamily home. To the left, the orange merges into a deep, soothing purple, and overhead, the clouds break up into tiny particles, creating a mottled effect over a pure, vivid, azure sky. In the foreground are sand dunes and neem trees, silhouetted against this impressive spectacle, unspoiled by pollution, pylons or traffic. Stunning.

Next morning, I awake feeling refreshed and well-slept, which is something of a novelty on a trip like this. In the absence of any curtains, I hung a pair of trousers over the window, which helped keep the light and dust out. And as it's quite chilly at night here, I wore two T-shirts and my Nascar jacket, which helped lull me into a cosy slumber.

It's an early start today, and we're packed up ready by 7am. Our destination is the town of Dia,[50] roughly 20 miles north of here. As there are literally no roads, it could take a while to get there. Moussa kicks the bike into action and we don our helmets, buzzing away across vast furrowed fields. Five minutes out of town, we reach a tributary of the Niger: the Jaka River.

"What happens now?" I ask.

"We cross the river."

"How?"

My answer appears seconds later: a 12-foot fishing pirogue sweeping in from the opposite bank.

"What about the motorbike?" I ask.

"That goes on the boat too! Here, help me lift it."

Slightly wading into the clear, shallow waters, we lift the Yamaha onto the canoe.

---

[50] Pronounced [ja]

"Now sit on it, Robert, to keep it stable. Then I can pay the boatman."

This is certainly a first for me: sitting on a motorbike, standing in a canoe, floating across a river. All goes well, and we're back on the road in no time. The other side of the river is instantly greener than sandy Diafarabé, with grassy meadows, waving rhun palms and mango groves. Riding on almost non-existent paths beside the Jaka, Moussa weaves his way skilfully between bushes and termite mounds. After half an hour or so, the bike begins to splutter and lose speed. I've already endured car and boat breakdowns on this trip – now it's time for my first motorbike malfunction.

"It's okay, I just need to clean the spark plug," says Moussa, pulling over. Using the end of a metal cable, he brushes the contacts clean, then detaches his fuel pipe and drips some petrol onto it. He then gives the plug a shake and screws it back in. The bike starts instantly and we climb back on.

"We're about to enter a Fulani village," says Moussa, a little further on.

A few miles after this, there's a Bozo village, then another Fulani one.

"Do you get mixed villages of Bozo and Fulani?" I ask, curious.

"Never! The Bozo catch fish and grow vegetables; the Fulani herd cattle and are semi-nomadic. When the Fulani cows trample on the Bozos' crops, they are not happy!"

"But do they get on?"

"Yes, but they will not live in the same village, and never intermarry. It's the same with the Bozo and the Dogon."

"Really?"

"Yes, you know the story about the leg, don't you?"

"No."

As legend has it, years and years ago, a Bozo and a Dogon were lost in the bush and had no food. Reaching a point of near starvation, desperate measures were called for: the Bozo man chopped off one of his legs so they could both eat it and live. Since then, the Bozo and Dogon have considered each other brothers, so never intermarry, for fear of spoiling this friendship.

"The Dogon know this legend also," he continues, "but in *their* version, it is the Dogon man who cuts off his leg."

The town of Dia reminds me of a mini-Timbuktu and is full of character: square adobe houses with little staircases onto their flat roofs, narrow streets lined with donkey carts and wood stacks, and men in long blue robes wandering regally to and from the local mosque.

We step from a sandy street into the courtyard of a small house, where a family is sat in the shade of neem trees. In one corner is a sizeable cage containing a couple of dozen Guinea fowl, and in the other, a pale-brown and white puppy is tethered to a post.

A couple in their mid thirties welcome me and my colleague, offering us a seat beneath the trees. Their eight-year-old son, wearing a woolly Manchester United hat, comes running in carrying a recently slaughtered chicken. Without batting an eyelid, he rips off the chicken's head and throws it to the dog, who gobbles it up. He then sits down and begins plucking the bird, his younger sister helping. I turn to the mother:

"Tell me about your musical background."

"I used to sing and act a lot when I was younger. But now I'm a married woman, I seldom sing, apart from at weddings and circumcisions. There have been many deaths in my family in past years, and it is not permitted to sing during a period of mourning."

"How does being Muslim affect your music?"

"We say that music is a thing for children, like football. It's not something a serious adult will do. Once you are over 15 years of age, or married, you will not normally sing or play music."

This makes me quite sad. As I ponder the matter, I realize that the music of Salif Keita is currently playing on the father's mobile phone.

"What about Salif Keita? He's a world-famous singer and songwriter, and also a Muslim."

"He's a *professional* musician."

Salif Keita has produced over 20 albums, and won the 'Best World Music' award in France last year for his song 'La Différence', which sings of his struggles as an albino.

"So, it's okay to do music if you're a professional?"

"Yes! If you're a griot, you can sing. But as a profession, not for fun."

Salif himself said this on the matter:

"Every Arabic country has produced great musicians. But we are faced with a bad interpretation of the Koran in the sub-Saharan Muslim countries. They wrongly believe that playing music means calling Satan."[51]

In the corner, the children have finished plucking the chicken and are playing with the headless bird, pulling its legs and stroking its cold, bumpy skin.

"So, are you a professional musician?" I ask the mother, pointedly.

"I am a *serious* musician."

"And what about people who respond to a griot's song and join in? Is that okay?"

"A professional musician must lead the singing; others can sing the response."

The husband, quiet until now, speaks up: "There was a young woman who sang *Naani Naani.*"

"I know *Naani Naani!*" I say, recalling yesterday's research by the river.

"She was called Nomo Tunkara," he continues, "and sang many *Naani Naani* songs and recorded them. They were broadcast on the radio and were very popular. She was paid 250,000 CFA for her singing."

Just then, a young slender woman enters the compound.

"This is Fatima, my second wife."

"You have *two* wives?"

"Yes. I'm looking for a third one, but they're hard to find in Dia. Four is my maximum."

Wife number one goes off to prepare the chicken, while wife number two greets me.

"She sings *Naani Naani* too!" he adds, proudly.

"Would she be able to give me a rendition?"

He talks to her quietly in Bozo for a moment, then turns to me.

"Yes, she has a song for you."

The tones which resonate from the courtyard are truly beautiful. Passing children peer through the doorway, her step son and daughter drop their dead chicken to the ground and stare in awe and wonder. The

---

neighbours in the next courtyard come through and watch. I get the feeling this is not an everyday occurrence.

"Your wife sings beautifully," I tell him.

"Yes she does!"

"And she has a very pointy nose."

He rises to his feet, shaking my hand warmly as though I were royalty.

"Yes! YES! My wife has a pointy nose! Thank you! Thank you!"

"Robert, would you like to travel back by boat or by motorbike?" asks Moussa, as we leave the house.

"Motorbike would be fun, but I thought the roads were flooded."

"The waters have gone down a little, but we'd still have to go the longer way round. It would take about five hours."

"FIVE HOURS! Let's do it!" Compared with at least eleven on the boat, this is luxury.

"Can you ride a motorbike?" he asks. "I will need some help with the driving."

Well, I rode a mate's moped across a field in Lincolnshire once, and I rented out a single-speed *mobylette* in Mauritius (and crashed it).

"Yes, I can ride a motorbike. Just show me how the gears work."

Should be plain sailing from here…

Chapter Seventeen – Beware The Sacred Tree!

"This feels like a genuine welcome from the heart of the whole village."

"HOW MUCH ARE your two-litre bottles of water?"

"200 francs, *monsieur.*"

"I'll take 32 of them."

"Thirty-two?"

"Yes please."

I open the tailgate and stack them in, one by one. Our next stop is the intriguing little village of *Mafouné,* a stone's throw from the Burkina Faso border, where I'll be carrying out a good old song-writing workshop in the Konabere language.[52] It's June 2011 and I'm accompanied by my old mate Moussa from the Bozo trip, as well as three American interns:

> Anna, the bubbly Californian one, who punctuates every phrase with 'totally'.
> Ursula, a Korean American, who seems to hate almost everything about Africa so far.
> Sam, an African American, keen to explore his own cultural roots.

Their names are easy for me to remember as, put in the right order, they spell USA, which is rather convenient. We made the arduous road journey from Bamako today, stopping for the obligatory breakfast in Ségou. All has gone smoothly thus far, apart from me murdering three unsuspecting chickens beneath my wheels at one point.

Ségou to Bla, Bla to San, and we just turned right off the main road, heading into the bush on a rough laterite track.

"Where are we going?" asks Sam. "This looks like the road to nowhere."

"Oh, it goes somewhere, you'll see!"

"It's very bumpy," moans Ursula. "I don't like the bumps, my back hurts!"

---

[52] Pronounced: [koh-na-beh-ray]

"I'm sorry, it's not far."

"Hey, this is, like, totally awesome. Let me take a selfie of us all!" adds Anna.

The Mitsubishi has been making a curious clicking noise for the past hour or so. I don't suppose it's anything to worry about, but I might get it looked at before we make the journey home. After a few minutes, we pass through what would be an insignificant village, but for one striking feature: a ginormous church – almost cathedral-size – stands proudly and incongruously above the trees and mud huts.

"Now, this is cool," says Sam.

"What is *that* doing here?" asks Ursula.

"This is totally awesome!" says Valley girl.

"Ah, Mandiakuy!" says Moussa, *"C'est magnifique!"*

The building is over a hundred feet long and able to seat 3000 people. Built in a cruciform shape with flying buttresses, ornate brickwork and latticed windows, it's all very impressive. At the front are two imposing square towers, each 100 feet tall. Pillars adorn the entrance porch and a 50-foot cross is built into the facade. Magnificent – Mali's second largest church, after Bamako Cathedral.

I turn to Moussa, fount of endless knowledge: "So, what *is* it doing here?!"

He explains that in 1927, French priest Joseph Scherrer travelled to Senegal by ship, then took the newly opened railway to Bamako. From there, he took boats on the Niger and Bani rivers as far as San, where he hopped on a bicycle and rode out to this village. His church started very small but went from strength to strength under his leadership. He was a kind, warm-hearted man, who would play football with the children in his spare time, and showed a genuine concern for the spiritual and physical needs of his flock. The almost unprecedented success of his work meant that, in 1958, this colossal church was built with the help of Bernard Verspieren, who later went on to create the eco-resort at Terya Bugu.[53]

It's not far from here to Mafouné. The car is still clicking away but drives fine. About a mile from our destination, Moussa says:

---

[53] http://peresblancs.org/Pere_joseph_scherrer.htm

"This is where you used to have to park your car and walk into the village."

"Why was that?"

"The land was too rocky. Now they've cleared the boulders to make way for the road."

"When was that?"

"About five years ago."

The village of Mafouné is unusual, with its houses joined together in rows, a bit like terraces in Britain. But here, they're *all* joined, and in every direction, with narrow corridor-like streets hidden away between tightly packed dwellings. It was originally designed this way to keep out enemies or wild animals, and the houses all had interconnecting doors, so people could move between dwellings undetected. Tall walls bridge any gaps, and there are only two entrances to the village: one to the west and one to the east. These days, crumbled walls provided additional access to the village at various points.

"What kind of wild animals would they need protection from?" I ask.

"Lions, hyenas."

"Wow!" says Anna. "Lions! Any tigers?"

"Don't be stupid," snaps Ursula. "Tigers live in Asia, not Africa."

"She's right, Anna." adds Sam. "Are there still any lions about?"

"No, not for many years. Nor hyenas; they were all killed for meat, or migrated south when the desert began spreading from the north."

News from Bamako and northern Mali remains bleak, and the situation shows little sign of improving. NATO has now got involved in the civil war in Libya, and has been carrying out airstrikes since March. The same month, 4000 Malians took to the streets of Bamako brandishing a huge sign reading:

SUPPORT GADDAFI! DOWN WITH FRANCE!

One protester said: "We consider Gaddafi a Malian."

Local Muslims are seeing the air strikes as a direct attack on Islam and are blaming France.

On April 30th, Gaddafi's son and three of his grandchildren were killed in one of the strikes. I wish there was a peaceful way of resolving this grim situation.

On a brighter note, Lois tells me that the new supermarket, *Shopreate Libre Service,* is now open and has an impressive range of products, as well as its own deli counter. Tins of French lentils, cartons of exotic juice, chocolate bars, ice lollies, newspapers, bottles of fizzy pop, pastries and brioche – you name it. They're even operating a fried chicken and chips takeaway from a small window to the side. Must try it out when I get home…

When arriving at an African village, the first thing to do is greet the chief, or chiefs in this case. Unusually, Mafouné has *two* chiefs: the Chief of the East (who is the most chilled chief I've ever met, wearing shorts and an *FC Barcelona* baseball cap; he didn't even offer us a seat), and the Chief of the West (an aged, skinny, blind chap, who stretches out his hand and waits for one of us to shake it). The latter's house is built on a frame of dark, thick Shakespearian wooden beams and dates back to the 1800s. Historically, there were always two chiefs here; one to guard each of the village's two entrances.

Our accommodation is the most basic yet; slightly embarrassing when I have three visitors fresh to the country, but it'll no doubt do them good. Outside the village, to the east, is a square building with dirt floors and two rooms. No windows, no furniture, and half full of junk and chickens. A mud-brick toilet block a few yards away comprises nothing but a bucket shower area and a pit latrine. The technique with one of these is to crouch over the foot-wide hole, making sure you *aim well*. I've had a few mishaps with them in the past, and they tend to be plagued with cockroaches at night.

I brought four camp beds and folding mosquito nets on the trip, so the plan is for us to camp in the open air. Moussa will stay with a friend in the village. If it rains (and it is June – rainy season), we can all pile into the house.

"What?" says Ursula. "You expect me to sleep *there?*"

"'Fraid so. It'll be okay. It's very safe here."

"And remember," adds Anna, "there are, like, no lions anymore."

"Or tigers!" laughs Sam.

A lady from the village arrives with two bowls of food: one full of rice, the other containing goat and sauce. I take pleasure initiating my Americans into the art of communal bowl eating with the right hand.

"This is, like, totally the coolest way to eat, *ever!*"

"Wow, my great-grandparents would've eaten like this every day!"

"I burnt my hand, I burnt my hand! Can I have a spoon?"

I open the spoon blade on my penknife and hand it to Ursula.

The food is good, and my American guests (mostly) enjoy it. Interestingly, there seem to be zero mosquitoes in this village, which is good news. Of course, our dome-shaped freestanding mozzie nets will also serve to keep any other bugs at bay. After a game or two of Dutch Blitz on the dirt floor (by the dim light of a paraffin lamp) we all climb into our nets and are asleep in no time.

The next morning, I'm woken by the sound of a pig and a dog fighting next to my bed. I knew our mosquito nets would be useful protection from creatures, but wasn't expecting anything quite this large...

After a breakfast of Nescafé and bread, we're off to the marketplace, where a crowd of over 30 is waiting eagerly. The aim is for them to compose alphabet songs to aid literacy, and development songs on topics such as deforestation, child trafficking and malaria. But before that, the customary research into Konabere instruments. They come up with the usual kind of drums: djembe, barrel drum (dun-dun) and the ubiquitous talking drum. There's also a kind of harp, which they don't have, but describe to me, as well as a two-stringed lute. The wind instruments are more interesting: a three-holed vertical flute with a bulbous top I've never seen before, and a simple flute called the *toli yolo,* with three holes and a tiny V shape cut out of the top.

"Do you have a *toli yolo* to show me?"

"Yes, we have many."

They send an old chap off on a bike to get one. He arrives back with two, and a couple of musicians eagerly demonstrate. The sound is pleasant, though quite shrill. I'm wondering why these flutes are so brightly coloured: one green, one blue. Then I realise they're made from plastic bicycle pumps – no wonder they sent the cyclist to get them.

An older lady leans over my shoulder as they play: "They were bamboo in the old days," she explains, "but now it's easier to use a pump. And they last longer."

A younger woman rushes to the front and joins in singing alongside the flutes. This trio slowly walk towards me and the interns in a line, singing and playing the whole time.

"They're coming to welcome you," says Moussa. "This is the purpose of the *toli yolo* song."

Sure enough, they come right up to us, the singer and both flautists crouching down before each of us in a gesture of respect.

"Put your hand on their right shoulder," Moussa tells us. "That's the sign you accept their welcome."

Each of us obliges as they approach us; a bizarrely moving experience for something so straightforward. But somehow, this feels like a genuine welcome from the heart of the whole village, and all our faces are beaming in response.

A guy has turned up who can play five drums at once, not something I've come across before. He has two small barrel drums attached to each upper arm, and two on each thigh. The fifth drum is round his waist. He then sings and plays all five at once with two sticks, as though he were a human drumkit. The rhythms created are very exciting, and we're all amazed at his rare and curious talent.

From instruments, we move onto song genres. There are the usual wedding songs, farming songs, rites of passage, and the all-pervading 'full moon dance' for young women. Other noteworthy genres include a song telling children to care for their parents when they're old, and a wedding song which says 'people have climbed on the roof to see her'. Finally, there's a bizarre dance, which doesn't seem to have any words: *Ma Lido* involves holding the big toe of the right foot with the left hand and hopping, which is more difficult than you might imagine.

Time for lunch, which is spaghetti and some kind of meat.

"Is this pork?" I ask. "I've not eaten pork in months!"

"Yes," says our cook, "this is a Christian village, so we eat pork. That's why we have pigs."

"We might have slept longer if they didn't, eh Rob?" says Sam.

"That was, like, such a cool way to wake up!" enthuses Anna.

"I hate those pigs!" moans Ursula.

After lunch, we're treated to Malian tea – all three cups – and it's exciting to explain this tradition to my interns. These were new, fresh experiences to me a couple of years ago; now I'm suddenly feeling like the expert.

"So, guys, who can remember all three? The first cup is..."

"Bitter as death," says glum Ursula.

"The second..."

Sam has this one: "Pleasant as life."

"Well remembered!"

Anna's turn: "And the third is, like, sweet as...sweet as...candy?"

"No, silly. Sweet as love," says Sam.

"Oh yeah, I remember," she replies, fluttering her eyelids at him. "As sweet as love."

The pigs leave us be the following morning, but the rising sun makes sure we're up bright and early. It's omelettes and Nescafé for breakfast today. As we tuck in, an old man carrying two large axes passes by and greets us.

"Are you going to the fields to work?" I ask.

"No, I'm going to *La Source.*"

"What's that?"

"It's a fertile area a mile away, watered by a natural spring. There are many juicy mangos there, and other fruit trees. What are you eating?"

"Omelettes."

"When I was young, we used to eat porcupine. Hunters would crawl inside their burrows to catch them. You don't see them anymore."

Maybe because they ate them all.

"What does porcupine taste like?" I ask.

"It tastes a bit like hedgehog."

That's helpful.

He's only just left when a young boy from the village turns up.

"These are for you! They're a gift from the chief."

"Which one?"

"West." The blind one.

He's holding two live chickens by their legs, one in each hand. I look at them, and they look back at me, their orange eyes darting wildly in their inverted heads. It would be hugely impolite to refuse such a gift, so I take the birds from him with a nod of gratitude and stand there like a human pair of scales, my newly acquired brace of fowl clucking away furiously. What am I going to do with these? I doubt they'll make it back to Bamako in my car; I'm not even certain *we* will.

"Please tell the chief 'thank you' from us all. It is very kind of him."

"I will do it, *monsieur.*"

Then I have an idea: "One more thing."

"*Oui.*"

"Do you know the woman who prepares our meals for us?"

"Madame Coulibaly, yes!"

"Could you ask her to prepare these two for dinner tonight?"

"Of course!" He takes the chickens back and hurries off to the village. Job done!

Having already created a song each yesterday afternoon, our three groups are composing new ones this morning and have chosen the topics of bushfires, polio and why school is important.

In the afternoon, we can't do any work with them, as they have a rehearsal for the *Fête des Masques*, a traditional event in many African villages. Originally, this would have had a deeply spiritual significance in African traditional religion. However these days (here at least), it's more of a cultural event. As the actual festival is in a week's time, we'll miss it, but they've invited us along to the rehearsal.

In a large open area on the other side of the village, preparations are afoot, and a small crowd has gathered, even for the rehearsal. The costumes are brightly coloured and fluffy looking. To the sound of many drums, the first 'creature' enters the arena, dancing energetically. His orange costume resembles a giant mop head, which begins at the top of his head and runs all the way to the ground. As he spins around, his tassels splay outwards. Another 'beast' joins him with just as much energy. This one is wearing a wooden mask with horns on, and looks like an antelope or buffalo. He approaches children round the edge, who run away in clouds of dust, screaming loudly. Finally, a 'normal' guy comes on ('the hero') and chases the monsters away. The interns watch in fascination, having never seen anything of this kind before. Even gloomy Ursula is smiling now!

Day three, and the songs are ready to record. As always, I need to find a suitable place away from noisy roads or animals and not near concrete buildings, which would cause too much reverberation. First, I check out the village school, which proves to be way too resonant, and the well next to it is in constant use. Behind the school is an open space, with a large tree for shade. This will be perfect.

Back at the market, they're busy rehearsing: talking drums, *toli yolos*, barrel drums, the lot. I tell Moussa of my plan to record behind the school.

"Behind the school? Not near the tree, though!"

"Well, yes, that was my plan."

"You can't go near *that* tree."

"I already did!"

"Did you touch it?"

"No."

"Good! It's a sacred tree, you see. We cannot rehearse there. And if you touch the tree, you will surely die!"

You'd at least think they'd put a sign up, if the risks were that great.

"There are two wooded areas you could try: one beyond your house, and the other down the hill here," he says, pointing.

One of the musicians from the village overhears us: "You can't use either of those places."

"Why's that?" I ask.

"Well the one over there is also a sacred forest, and the one down the hill here is...how do I say...used as the toilet by most of the village."

We finally settle on a large clearing just on the edge of the 'sacred' woods. Not as shady as I might have hoped, but it will do. I drive the Mitsubishi down there to unload and set up the recording equipment. The car takes a while to start, and the clunks are getting louder.

"You ought to get that seen to, Rob," says Sam, concerned.

"Yeah, this could be *bad*," says Ursula.

"That banging noise is like, totally freaking me out!" says Anna.

With their help, we set up quickly: audio recorder, mixing desk and four condenser mics strategically placed in a circular formation. I told the musicians to arrive at 2pm. It's now 2.20 and nobody's here yet. They begin to trickle in by 2.45, but it's 3.30 before we actually start recording.

We're just running through the procedures when a few folk start frantically waving their heads around and swatting their faces. What's going on?

"Bees, *monsieur*, bees!"

"They'll go away soon, I'm sure. Don't worry."

"No *monsieur*, look!"

Up in the tree nearest to us hangs a huge bee hive, with more and more bees coming out by the second. This may not have been a good location after all. We decide to move 50 yards down the clearing, a safe distance from the wee beasties. Everyone helps carry the equipment over.

Before I've said a thing, the first group of women are on their feet, dancing round in circles and joyfully singing their new song:

> *Get a polio jab*
> *Get a polio jab*
> *There was a man in the village*
> *He refused the jab*
> *Then he got polio and died*

Straight and to the point, I suppose. At the end, they all clap, cheer and laugh.

"How was your recording, *monsieur?*" One of them asks.

"I didn't record it."

"Why not? Don't you like it?"

"I *do* like it, but you were all dancing about. You need to stand in front of these microphones." I get up and demonstrate. "Stand roughly this distance away from the mic and don't move," I explain, using both hands to show what 20 centimetres looks like. They start the song again. For many of them, this is the first time they've ever used a microphone.

They'd like to record some existing songs as well as the new ones, bringing the total to 15. I generally reckon on three to four songs per hour, but the sun is setting already. We soldier on and are done by 7.30pm, by which time it's pitch black everywhere.

One of the leaders comes up to me: "*Monsieur,* our group has one more song they'd like to record before we go."

"Sorry, too late. We have to finish now."

I thank them all, even though they're almost entirely invisible by now, and everyone wanders off. The Mitsubishi is still 50 yards away, of course, so I fumble over by the light of my mobile phone. The car starts with difficulty. I drive it over and, keeping the engine running, we all load up quickly and jump on board. I put my foot to the floor: nothing. In desperation, I turn off the engine then start up again. It works. The rocky track home is much trickier in the dark, but I manage to avoid the largest obstacles.

We're planning to leave first thing in the morning, to make the seven-hour journey back to Bamako. So, even though we're all exhausted, I decide we should go and bid farewell to the two chiefs – East and West – before bed tonight. The former offers us each a 'wee dram' of locally brewed palm wine as a parting gesture; the latter tries to give me two more chickens *and* a guinea fowl, which I politely refuse, explaining that our long journey home would not be pleasant for them (or us).

At seven the next morning I'm kneeling under the bonnet of the Mitsubishi examining its engine, with only my bottom visible to passers-by. Several children from the village have stopped to observe this strange phenomenon – what is the toubab up to now? I have no idea which part of the engine to tweak for it to start, but eventually something works and it roars into action. We move off very slowly indeed, gradually gaining speed on the washboard road out of the village. 50 yards down the track, the engine splutters and dies. We sit in silence and bewilderment. After about 20 seconds, I ask Moussa: "Is there a mechanic in the village?"

"Yes, a motorbike mechanic. He lives in this house right here."

How fortuitous, and he's already on his way out. He listens to the engine and says, "There's no problem. Accelerate!"

Somewhat dubious, I do as he asks. My foot is flat to the floor, but there are virtually no revs.

"Turn it off!"

He fiddles around in the engine, pulls out a pipe and bleeds it, then puts it back.

"Now try!"

It starts and – amazingly – the revs are up again.

"Will it get us to San?" I ask tentatively.

"Even as far as Bamako. *Bon voyage!*"

We make it to San, where I decide it's best to just keep going, at a steady 50 miles an hour. At Bla, we hit a humungous thunderstorm with some impressive lightning, forking all the way to the ground. The thunder is so loud it momentarily drowns out the engine noises.

We reach Ségou by 11am and I toy with the idea of continuing non-stop to Bamako. But we're all in need of a comfort break and a coffee. I pull up outside the Auberge, careful the car is facing outwards for our departure.

Ursula disappears the second we stop and is gone for quite some time.

"Rob, let me tell you a secret: it's totally gross."

"What?" I ask Anna, intrigued.

"Ursula hated the pit latrine in the village so much, she hasn't pooped for four days."

"WHAT?!"

Arriving back in Bamako, I hesitate before opening the rear door of the vehicle, which is caked from top to bottom in a black, oily substance, in spite of the earlier rainfall. I call my Chinese mechanic and he tows it in.

"Mobili bù hǎo! Arbre à cam bù hǎo!"

Roughly translated, my overhead cam is broken just before the final piston. So we made the 300-mile return journey home with only three out of four cylinders working!

Chapter Eighteen – Little Donkey

"My trash-filled yard was awash with cockroaches and the occasional rat."

"HI Y'ALL, ah'm Ben and this here's mah beautiful wah'f, Cindy."

"Welcome to Mali. Good to meet you both!"

It's always exciting when new folk arrive, pale-skinned, sweating profusely and with a perpetually lost look on their faces. This couple, from Birmingham, Alabama, landed just last night, and it's not only their first time in Africa but also their first ever time outside the USA. They've been sent by their church to work at an orphanage on the edge of town.

"How many orphans are there?" I ask, as we sip tea beneath wavering neem trees.

"There's about twenny," says blonde Cindy, "but some of them are half orphans."

"Half orphans?"

"Yeah. Only one of their parents is dead."

"Then surely they're not orphans, are they?"

"Oh, but they still need our love. And we're here to spread a bit of Jesus, ain't that right, sweetie?"

"Sure is!" echoes her doting husband, his neat red locks glinting in the bright sunlight.

It sometimes feels like the West creates a new need so it can appear benevolent. Any child with one parent should be living with that parent, not bundled off to an orphanage.

"How long have you two been married?" I enquire.

"Four months," says Ben.

Many organizations would want them to be married at least a year before coming overseas, to establish themselves as a couple.

"And we're shippin' all our belongings out, 'cause we're here for the duration," he continues.

"Have you learned any Bambara?"

"Nope."

"French?"

"Not a word."

"Yes, sweetie," his devoted spouse adds proudly. "Two words: *bone jewer!*"

"Our container should be arrahvin' in Conakry in just a couple o' weeks' tahm."

"Conakry?!"

"Sure!"

Conakry is most people's *last* choice for a shipping port. Dakar – fine. Abidjan (Côte d'Ivoire) – not a bad choice these days. Even Lomé or crazy Cotonou are viable options, but *never* Conakry! Guinea has a reputation for corruption, as well as violent outbursts such as the massacre in a football stadium a couple of years ago. When the former French colonies gained their independence in the Sixties, most opted to remain part of a French community. Guinea, however, went for a *Hard Guexit,* cutting all ties with France in one fell swoop.

"Well…keep us posted," I respond, concerned this may not turn out to be quite as straightforward as they hope.

The much-anticipated *Third Bridge* opened in September, spanning the Niger at the eastern limits of Bamako. A gift from the Chinese, the *Pont de l'Amitié Sino-Malienne*[54] cost forty million pounds to build and was inaugurated by President ATT himself on the day of Mali's 51st anniversary of independence. Thousands flocked to the opening ceremony, then proceeded to cross the river on this mile-long feat of engineering, which took roughly 800 Malians, 200 Chinese and 27 months to build. We drove across it a couple of days later – just because we could – and it was a bizarrely surreal experience. Despite boasting two lanes in each direction, there was almost no traffic and, for some reason, the bridge curves as it crosses the river (intentionally, I assume).

Gaddafi died on 11th October. Murdered in his own country. Dragged from a storm drain by rebels and brutally slaughtered, amidst cries of '*Allahu Akbar*'. Like most heads of state, Muammar Gaddafi had his supporters and his detractors. He committed many unpopular acts as well as some favourable ones, including the development of Mali. He fought

[54] Bridge of Chinese-Malian Friendship

for reconciliation between Jews and Palestinians and openly condemned the terrorist acts of Al Qaeda and Bin Laden. In a rare televised interview last year, Gaddafi said this:

> "I am the leader of a revolution with global ideas and I've actively contributed to liberation movements. And colonial countries didn't want that, of course [...] The West sees liberation movements as terrorist movements. [...] I worked for others, to give service to others. I didn't do anything for myself."[55]

Brutal dictator? Quite possibly. Generous benefactor? Many Malians would say so. Perhaps sometimes, whether a person is considered a terrorist or a freedom fighter only depends upon whose side you're on.

It was Guy Fawkes Night again last month, so we invited every Brit we could find to a bonfire and fireworks fest. This included half a dozen new young Brits I happened to bump into in town recently, here for short-term charity work. With wood from Badala Market and fireworks from the only shop in Bamako which sells them all year round (rather than just at New Year), we were all set for a great evening – or so I thought. The first problem was that nobody could stand remotely close to the bonfire, due to the climate, preferring to retreat to the somewhat cooler distance of twenty feet. Hot baked potatoes were not the best idea either. Then, one of the fireworks exploded violently with a huge BANG, just a second after being lit. I was only just a safe distance away, and my ears took a while to recover. Our evening was rounded off by the Malian children next door throwing used corn cobs at us from the top of the wall. I'm not quite sure why they did this.

I saw Ben and Cindy again yesterday, buying groceries in *Shopreate Libre Service* up the road.

"This place is awesome - they even got mac 'n' cheese here!" says Ben, waving a couple of packets in my general direction.

---

[55] Interview with George Negus:
https://www.youtube.com/watch?annotation_id=annotation_2701508697&feature=iv&src_vid=bUh ZmO6P0NU&v=bUhZmO6P0NU#t=7s

"Nice! You can find pasta and decent cheese in Mali, though. Why not just make your own?"

"Aw no! This is the *real* mac 'n' cheese right here, ain't that raht sweetie?"

"Sure is!"

I ask about his container.

"It's arriving in Conakry at the weekend. I'm planning to hire a truck and go fetch it all."

"You can't do that!"

"Why not?"

"Well, for starters, it's likely to take days or weeks for your container to get clearance. And you'll get a lot of grief if they see your white face at the port. You need a *transitaire.*"

A *transitaire*, or clearing agent, will have a man on the ground in Conakry who can get the container out more easily and arrange its onward transport to Bamako. It may cost more, but it's worth it to avoid major hassles. I hand him the number of Mr Cissé, the chap who got our Mitsubishi to Bamako from Dakar.

"Thanks Rob, I appreciate that!"

"Scary things are happenin' up north Rob and I don't like it!" says Welsh Gary, who's popped round to sample my homemade version of *Baileys Irish Cream*.[56]

"What things, Gary?"

"Kidnappings."

"You mean hostage taking."

"Isn't that the same thing?"

"Not quite, but go on."

"A German, a Swede, a South African and Two Dutchmen."

"All taken? In Bamako?"

"No, in Timbuktu."

There were fifteen or so tourists staying at the Auberge Alafia yesterday (25th November, 2011), a stone's throw from the *Flamme de la Paix monument*. Most were taking a siesta, but the five who stayed up chatting in

---

[56] Condensed milk, *crème fraiche,* cheap whiskey and a spoonful of Nescafé

the courtyard were suddenly and brutally taken. The German refused to get into their vehicle, so was pumped full of bullets, dying instantly.[57] Ironically, the Auberge Alafia means 'Hostel of Peace'.

The day before this, two French geologists were taken in Hombori, where the finger-like mountains mark the eastern extremity of the Dogon cliffs. And to think, I was very close to both these places just a few months ago.

In response to these atrocities, President ATT gave this speech:

> "Let us remain united, whatever our ethnic identity, the colour of our skin or our convictions [...] Whatever happens, we must still close ranks, to definitively stop these evildoers."[58]

Have you ever wondered who collects all the rubbish in West Africa? Sometimes nobody does, and it just lies there on street corners, rotting, reeking and breeding flies. But when the rubbish *is* collected, it's rarely with a hefty truck or plastic wheelie bins. Our rusty-red metal bin sits just inside the garage, next to Monsieur Kouyaté. Twice a week, a rickety old cart, drawn by an aged donkey, calls to empty it. The service costs less than three pounds a month; a very reasonable price for a stink-free, vermin-free life. But last month, for reasons unexplained, the collection simply stopped. As a result, our rubbish heap outgrew its generous container, spewing refuse all over the floor.

Then, a fortnight ago, the doorbell rang, and there was our scraggy bin-man stood on the street. No donkey, no cart. He had a friend with him who, it turns out, speaks some French (as he only speaks Bozo). I invited them into the yard and was handed a folded piece of paper, torn from a French-style exercise book. Clearly written by his companion, the note read:

> *Monsieur,*
> *Mon âne est parti.*
> *Faut me donner 45.000 francs pour acheter un autre.*

---

[57] https://www.afribonemali.net/spip.php?article37666
[58] http://vcafrica2.over-blog.com/article-declaration-solennelle-de-son-excellence-monsieur-le-president-de-la-republique-du-mali-sur-les-even-90276971.html (My translation)

Merci,
Adama

Which, roughly translated, means:

Dear Sir,
I have lost my donkey.
Give me 45,000 francs to buy another one.
Thank you,
Adama

As my trash-filled yard was awash with cockroaches and the occasional rat, I was eager to help, but fifty quid is a lot of money here.

"My friend," I said, speaking through his interpreter, "you collect rubbish from lots of homes in this neighbourhood, don't you?"

"*Oui.*"

"Why don't you ask them first? Then I'll make up whatever shortfall you have."

This sounded like a sensible plan, giving other neighbours a chance to share the cost. And maybe I wouldn't have to pay anything as he'd get all he needed from them. But my offer to pay the shortfall was tantamount to saying: 'don't bother getting any more money; I can clearly afford the full amount.' Sure enough, he called back a couple of days later and I asked him how much he'd collected.

"I have no other money," he replied.

What should I do? My rubbish pile would grow its own legs and walk if left much longer. It's Christmastime – the Season of Goodwill – and we're talking about a donkey here; you can't get much more Christmassy than that.

"Where will you buy the donkey?" I enquired

"From *Faladie* Market.*"

That's a good five miles out of town. Had it been closer, I'd have considered going with him, but it was late afternoon and I had a rehearsal that evening.

"Okay, here's the money. Go straight to Faladie Market and buy your donkey. Today! Now!"

"Yes yes!

"Then come straight back and show me the animal."

"Yes, yes!"

It's almost impossible to 'earmark' donations this way in Africa. Once in the hands of the receiver, the money is generally fair game for any other usage deemed more urgent. Nevertheless, I bade him farewell, naively expecting him to return later that evening with his newly acquired beast of burden. He did not. Nor did he come back the next day, or the next. It was ten days before Adama returned, again with his interpreter.

"Where have you been?" I scolded. "And where is the donkey?"

"*Monsieur,*" his accomplice began, "we heard that the law is changing in Mali: donkey carts will soon be made illegal. So we decided not to buy the donkey."

"Then you made a wise decision, as we wouldn't want you buying a donkey you can't use." Especially not with *my* money.

"Can you buy me a tractor instead?" he asked.

"No! I will not buy you a TRACTOR!!" Do I have dollar signs across my forehead?

"Listen, I'll do some asking around to see if the donkey law you mention is true. In the meantime, can I have my money back?"

To my astonishment, he reached into his pocket and handed me a wad of cash: 23,000 francs.

"Where's the rest?" I asked, frowning.

"I gave it to my friends."

"YOU GAVE IT TO YOUR FRIENDS?!" I'm furious now. "But this was money for the donkey, and it was *my* money!!"

He could tell I wasn't pleased.

"*Monsieur,* I will bring you the rest of the money."

"When?"

"Tomorrow. I will bring you the rest of the money tomorrow."

This seemed impossible as, by his own admission, he had given it to his friends. I turned again to the interpreter:

"Ask him, how is he going to get the money?"

"He says you'll have the rest of the money tomorrow."

"But he's given it away!" I rant, Basil Fawlty-style. "He's given twenty-two thousand francs of mine away. How does he imagine he will get it back by tomorrow? Is he going to magic it out of thin air?!"

"You will have the money tomorrow," he repeats.

"Okay, see you tomorrow."

That was three days ago, and I'm still waiting...

It's almost Christmas, and the Harmattan is thickly cloaking the Malian skies once again. I benefit from this cooler weather and ride my bike to Azar's supermarket, to check out their glittering Christmas goods. On my journey there, I get called 'toubab' 28 times by seven different children. That's a rate of 56 TPM (toubabs per mile). I also had the bizarre (but enjoyable) experience of being challenged to a race by a disabled guy in a hand-cranked tricycle on the river road. It was his idea entirely, but I felt a bit bad when I won.

It's also watermelon season, and these enormous stripy green rugby balls are piled high just outside the supermarket. For me, the taste is never worth the seeds you have to constantly spit out. Instead, I stop by the Star petrol station just next door which – bizarrely – also sells whippy ice creams, right next to the pumps. And there are always three choices: vanilla, something else, or a mixture of two. Today, it's vanilla and/or mango, so I go for a blend of both. Tasty!

On the way home, I stop off at Badala Market to get one of the new Brits' phones unlocked. And any trip to the market is incomplete without a visit to my beturbaned Tamasheq friend.

"*Mon ami!* It's been a long time!" says Youssouf. "Would you like three cups of tea?"

"No, but I'll have two!" I reply, taking my seat, cross-legged, on his colourful rug. "What's happening in the Sahara, Youssouf? Someone said Al Qaeda are there."

"That is correct," he answers, pouring my first cup from two feet up.

"But why here in Mali? And what are they doing?"

"They are violent people who take hostages to finance their mission."

"And what is their mission?"

"To Islamicize the world."

"But, isn't this *your* ideology too?"

"My ideology but not my methods. I do not agree with their violence and terror. They actively seek to attack infidels and their countries."

"Where have these people come from?"

"Some are Malian, some are Algerian; others fought in Afghanistan."

"And are some Tamasheq too?"

He pauses, reluctant to admit the truth: "Yes…many of them are my people. But I do not agree with them."

"I hear they are banning music too."

"Yes, but I do not believe this is right. The Tamasheq sing and make music. Next Cup?"

"Yes please!"

I think back to the *Fesitval au Désert* and the joyous singing and dancing I experienced there. Many of those attending were Muslims too.

"But what's ultimately going to happen? Do they want to Islamicize Bamako further?"

"Maybe."

"Through *violence?*"

"Traoré, I do not know their ways or plans. They are far from Bamako. Do not be afraid."

"Do ya know aboot the Luna Park?" says Canadian Pete, back in town for Christmas. "I'm taking Ben and Cindy there tomorrow. Why don't you come along too?"

"I've heard of the place, but is it any good?"

"It's Bamako's only theme park; you haven't lived till you've been there!" he exclaims, with a healthy dose of irony.

Tonight, I'm conducting the first ever performance of Handel's Messiah in Bamako Cathedral which, in the light of recent events, is both scary and exciting. An American colleague put the oratorio on a couple of times in the past, using Gaddafi's *Hôtel de l'Amitié* as the venue. I felt a bit awkward using it this year, what with him being dead and all, but also felt there must be somewhere more sacred – more appropriate – for such an awesome work. So, back in October, I went to see the padre, who was delighted at the prospect.

"How much would we need to pay?" I asked.

"Oh, just make a donation," he said. Very kind indeed.

We had a full run-through in the Cathedral the night before last. The steps up to the altar worked perfectly as risers, though the men on the back row were slightly squashed between two pillars. We have a somewhat eclectic orchestra, composed of whoever we could find in the expat community: a Swedish harpsichord player (using an electric keyboard), a French trombonist, a clarinet, a violin and two flutes, one of whom is the American Ambassador herself. Not an entirely typical Baroque orchestra, but it'll certainly do.

It's now the morning of the performance and my phone rings.

"Ro-o-o-o-o-b." croaks Dr Dave. "Laryngitis. It's bad. Real bad."

Disaster! Dave – a trained singer as well as saxophonist – was due to sing 'Every Valley' tonight, a key solo in *Messiah*. What to do? I grab the music and head over to our offices to practise the solo myself. I'm not sure what I'll manage, but have little choice.

On my way up the stairs, I notice a small brown parcel in our pigeon hole. It's always exciting to receive packages, especially at this time of year. I rip it open to reveal two packets of *Blutak*. As you may recall, my mother posted this out to us shortly after we arrived in Mali. So, by my reckoning, it has taken a stunning 28 months to arrive. I re-examine the packaging: besides being slightly battered, there's a second circular postmark on the back. It's slightly faded, but what looks like the word 'Bali' is visible.

At the top of the stairs, I meet American Ben, who's been up on the roof admiring the view.

"Rob, you look worried."

I explain my predicament.

"Hey, I can sing that solo!"

"Really?"

"Yeah, I auditioned for it in high school, but another guy got the part."

Ben's already in my choir, along with 40 other expats from roughly a dozen countries. I take him up to my office to run through the song, and he's actually pretty good!

"You've got the part, mate!"

The performance is a huge success, drawing in around 200 spectators (mostly expats), and really sets Christmas in motion for everyone, at a time when we feel the most homesick.

A large multicoloured plastic sign over the entrance gate reads 'PARC'. To the left of this word is an empty space, and lying awkwardly on the ground below is a panel reading "LUNA". There's a small metal ticket office at the gate and it's only 100 francs to get in. In the centre of the park, a further booth sells ride tickets, also 100 francs each. The whole park is no more than an acre in size, and the ground is almost entirely concrete. There's quite a range of colourful rides to enjoy: a rocking pirate ship which looks like it's made from Meccano, a 20-foot Ferris wheel (comprising a total of ten compartments), dodgem cars on a sizeable rink, and one of those spider-like rides which spins around as its 'arms' go up and down. There are also half a dozen carousels for smaller children, including one with teacups to sit in. My kids are loving it! So are Ben and Cindy, I think, though Ben's a little hoarse after his epic solo last night.

"Let's go on the dodgems next, daddy!" says Mads, keen for more fun and excitement. They're not the worst dodgems I've been on in Africa, though only some of them have seatbelts. And there are not the same health and safety rules here about bumping or driving in a certain direction; no age or height restrictions either. We all have a fun time and nobody gets hurt, which is always a bonus. The electricity poles at the back of each car are quite temperamental though, and the assistant has to come out to us roughly six times during our five-minute stint, to realign the metal contact at the top, often narrowly missing having his ankles crushed between two rubber bumpers.

"Let's go on that big roundabout thingy, dad!" says Ruth.

"Okay."

Lois and most of the adults are not keen to try this one, but Ruth and I are game, so is Pete. Small seats, like those on an infant's swing, hang from long chains attached to the top of the carousel. When it spins, the seats swing outwards with the centrifugal force. We get on board, Ruth and I next to each other, Pete just behind.

"Brace yourselves guys; this ride is vicious!"

Back home, rides like this build up gently and gradually; not so at the Luna Park, where the ride only has one speed: very fast! Our seats are now swinging outwards at a 45-degree angle, and the ride continues at this pace for a good five minutes, which feel like thirty. I'm getting terribly nauseous and my vision is blurred. Holding on tightly, I close my eyes. This makes it worse, so I open them again. Round and round and round, as the booming sound system in the centre plays: *Don't stop me now, I'm having such a good time.*

Finally, the ride slows down and we stagger off. I have to lie down on the ground for five minutes, while Ruth violently throws up round the corner.

"Rob, I have to let you into a secret now you're off the ride."

"What, Pete?"

"Last week there was a power cut here, and this ride was in full flow. It stopped so suddenly that everyone's seats collided, chains were tangled together and lots of people were injured. Two were taken to hospital and one of them is still there."

I'm grateful for Pete's honesty, but also astounded he should still think it safe to take us on a ride with such a dubious recent history.

"Beware of the pirate ship too," he adds. "It's safe enough as long as you stay seated, but a couple of years ago, a chap stood up mid-ride and his head…"

"I can guess the rest, Pete. Thanks."

After exhausting all the rides in the park (about 45 minutes later), we head across the road for chwarmas: a Lebanese delicacy, somewhere between a doner kebab and a burrito. Filled with tender meat, crisp salad, spicy sauce and fries, they're a delicious and filling meal rolled into one.

There are only 1000 or so Lebanese living in Mali, but these few run many of the best supermarkets and restaurants here. Powerful in commerce and known for their single-mindedness, perseverance, and business-like manner, these guys have the Midas touch across West Africa. One Lebanese shop manager told me: "It's because we're descended from the Phoenicians. We have many generations of experience in commerce." The largest Lebanese population in West Africa is in Côte d'Ivoire, where they number tens of thousands.

We tuck into our delicious lunch, laughing about the Luna Park and its clear limitations. Pete pipes up:

"Hey, imagine if that place was run by the Lebanese too!"

Adama never came back with my donkey money, by the way, and I've never seen him again to this day. I have no idea what he is doing now, whether he ever bought a donkey or what he, or his friends, used the money for. A new trash man – with a tractor – swung by a few days later, and took over the job, but I'd love to know whatever became of the elusive *Donkey Man*.

Senoufo village, southern Mali

Chapter Nineteen – Saved by the Stick

"The army never came; they had heard about the bees."

THE SETTING MOON projects its aureate light through the dense Harmattan sky, casting a pale, eerie glow on the *Tour de l'Afrique*. I shiver in the early morning air, stooping low to speak through the tiny opening in the CMT[59] ticket office:

"A single to Sikasso, please."

"5000 francs, *monsieur*. What name is it?"

"Baker Robert."

There are half a dozen more people behind me, and the coach – waiting patiently in its allotted bay – will not leave for another 20 minutes. I stand and wait in the cool, dry darkness. People around me are cleaning their teeth with sticks, some have dozed off onto their luggage, while others chat avidly.

"*Ecoutez!*"

The driver appears and reads out every name, one by one. The person called then brings their bags forward and gets on the bus. The driver also crosses them off his list and puts a mark on their ticket – a very efficient and virtually foolproof system.

"BAKER Robert!"

It's my turn. I climb the five steps into this plush coach and find a seat just behind the rear door – one of my favourite places. The cam shaft on my Mitsubishi broke a *second* time last week, hence the need for public transport on this trip.

A sizeable woman with straightened hair and a fake Gucci handbag approaches me:

"You're sitting in my preferred seat!"

"Oh, I can move across and you can sit here," I say, sliding sideways.

"No, I have booked two tickets."

"Two tickets?"

"Yes. Because I am fat, I need two seats!"

---

[59] Compagnie Malienne de Transport

Rather than risk creating a scene at this hour, I vacate my favourite seat and settle for one further down.

At precisely 7am on 2nd February 2012, the engine roars into action and we pull out onto the road. As well as being spotlessly clean, the bus also has air-conditioning and two television screens. I'm amazed at how coach travel has improved since I was first in Africa in the 90s. Then, you'd get a clapped-out jalopy filled with live chickens and children peeing down the aisle. Bald tyres, crazy driving, and full-blast Ivorian pop were the order of the day too. Some coaches even used to put wooden stools down the aisle to fit more passengers in – imagine the chaos Newton's Third Law would create if the vehicle had to brake suddenly!

We're soon out of Bamako, speeding southwards on a straight, smooth road. The TV is showing nauseatingly bad African soap operas, which continue the entire journey.

Lois texts me when I'm halfway there:

Unrest in Bamako. Hopefully you were away before it started.

Then one from our director:

Riots in town. Stay home until further notice.

Apparently, several buildings have been set alight in Bamako, including a pharmacy and a government minister's house. The protesters are mostly young folk, who have erected a dozen barricades (French Revolution style), set fire to cars and, as always, are burning huge stacks of tyres. They're protesting about the situation in the north, where at least 100 Malian soldiers have reportedly been killed in Aguelhok, near the Algerian border. Their army camp was attacked by the Tamasheq-run MNLA[60] group, along with Islamist groups AQIM[61] and the recently formed Ansar Dine.[62] The protestors want more to be done to empower Malian forces and prevent these needless deaths.

---

[60] Mouvement National pour la Libération de l'Azawad (National Movement for the Liberation of Azawad)
[61] Al Qaeda in the Islamic Maghreb (AQMI in French)
[62] Meaning 'defenders of the faith'

"We don't want ATT anymore," said one of the mob. "He has killed our fathers and mothers!"[63]

What they may not realize is that many of the 'bad guys' up north have recently returned from fighting in Libya, bringing with them shed loads of Gaddafi's weaponry. Huge rocket launchers and powerful tanks are no match for the Malian forces.

Just then, there's a huge BANG, and I see a donkey flying through the air at some height, having been hit by the bus. As it crashes onto the road ahead, a *second* donkey is hit by the front corner of the vehicle and wobbles off awkwardly, keeling over beside the road, blood oozing from its skull. What a mess! The driver gets out to inspect his vehicle, while half a dozen brave passengers help drag beast number one off the carriageway. We're given an enforced 10-minute break, where everyone gets out to look. Both donkeys are clearly dead. The bus itself has a nasty dent in its grille, but the engine roars back into action no problem, and the driver orders us back on board.

Texts from Bamako are coming in thick and fast now. A second message from our director reads:

Police have blocked the road somewhere near Medina Koura. Tear gas is being used.

Then another from Lois:

Also unrest in Bougouni. Are you past there yet?

I decide not to reply immediately, as we're about to enter Bougouni. The driver has clearly got wind of events, as he tears through the town, not stopping for the usual comfort break. Scary times. How is this all going to end?

After a comfortable night at the *Hôtel Mamelon* in Sikasso, I'm up and ready to visit some *Senoufo* people in the village of Ngolume, a few miles south of here. I'm particularly interested in their musical instruments, which are very different from the northern ones. Here, they use *balafons* – Africa's answer to the xylophone.

---

[63] https://maliactu.net/emeutes-a-bamako/

Otto Wagner, a colleague who lives and works in Sikasso, has offered to take me on his motorbike and arrives at the hotel as I'm finishing my omelette and Nescafé. Short, round and balding, the German linguistics expert greets me with:

"Von of my cats has disappeared! I sink ze neighbourhood children may have eaten it."

"Hi Otto! I'm sorry to hear that."

"Let's go!"

He's wearing his usual beige shorts; I've never seen him in anything else, even when motorcycling. Within two minutes (the way Otto drives), we're off the tarmac and speeding down a dirt road. A few miles later, we stop.

"Zis is ze river. Ve have to cross it here."

"How will we do that?"

"You take ze stepping stones over zer, I vill ride it."

The river is 30 feet wide and a good two feet deep in the centre, and is flowing quite fast. I guess he's done this before, but it sounds risky.

"Oh, and vatch out for ze crocodiles, ha ha!"

My stepping stones are easy enough but quite far apart, and some are wobbly. Otto revs up and goes for it, making it almost to the middle.

"*Scheiße!*"

"What's wrong?"

"Ze motor has stalled."

Rather than start it again and risk waterlogging the engine, he pushes the 250cc bike – with difficulty – out of the river. It takes a few minutes for him to dry everything out (including the sparkplug), then we're off again.

It's super dusty when we arrive in Ngolume, which is compounded by strong Harmattan winds today. The village is a clean, well-ordered place, where rectangular buildings with tin roofs sit neatly on the side of a gentle hill. Some have triangular windows; something I've never seen before. At the bottom of the hill is a lake with a small creek running into it, and from the top, you can see Côte d'Ivoire, just a couple of miles to the south.

Everywhere you look, cylindrical granaries sit on brick 'feet' with conical straw roofs; some are clustered together like cute little families of huts. And there are more mango trees than anywhere I've been in Mali; hundreds of them, filling vast sections of the village with deep, lush greenery – a clear sign we're in the humid south. There are a few tall, spindly papaya trees too, and up on the hill, huge bare baobabs are silhouetted against dusty skies.

The chief lives in a beamed house dating from 1935, similar to the one in Mafouné but at least three times as big.

"Welcome to Ngolume," he bellows. "May God bless your work here!"

He's an old man with an entourage of seven other chaps of comparable seniority. An oil lamp hangs from the wooden ceiling and there's a large gourd of water in the corner. On the wall is a calendar which, interestingly, features former Ivorian president Laurent Gbagbo.[64]

On the way to our meeting place, an old school by the lake, we pass a large covered porch where an old lady is lighting wood beneath two large cooking pots.

"Rob," says Otto, "zis is our cook for ze workshop. Vee should greet her."

"Okay...*Bonjour madame!*"

Instantly realizing who I am, she shakes my hand warmly, crouching down to the ground in respect. I launch into the customary greetings:

"How is your husband?"

"He's well."

"And your children?"

"They are fine."

"How is work?"

"All fine. There is peace."

She turns to Otto, who speaks Senoufo, and mutters something.

"She says her husband died a month ago."

So he's not well. I turn to her with a sad face. "Sorry. *Désolé.*"

"She'll marry his younger brother soon though," adds Otto. "Senoufo tradition."

The practice of *levirate marriage* is common in these parts; when a woman marries, she is permanently considered part of the husband's family, even if he dies.[65] And so, for her security and well-being, any younger brother or cousin will be obliged to marry her, as is the case here. Next to her kitchen

---

[64] Who was arrested in April 2011 for refusing to stand down after elections.
[65] http://www.academia.edu/4364463/Levirate_thesis_abstract

is a row of curious looking trees: tallish with tiny oval leaves in bunches at the top.

"You know zis tree? Zis is ze miracle tree."

"The miracle tree?"

"*Ja,* ze miracle tree. *Moringa oleifera.*"

"What makes it so miraculous, then?" I'm wondering if, like the balanzans of Ségou, this one also blooms in dry season.

"It is a miracle tree because it will grow almost anywhere, even in hot, dry climates like zis. And its leaves have more nutrients in them than almost any vegetable. And lots of antioxidants too."[66]

Sounds amazing, and a real blessing for Africa.

"Do you make tea from it?"

"Not usually. You dry ze leaves, then you grind zem into a powder. A spoonful of ze powder in your meal, and you have plenty of extra vitamins! You have to dry ze leaves in ze shade though, or zey will lose their potency in ze sunlight."

The first balafon has just arrived in the village, by bicycle! The instrument is almost as large as its carrier, who has it strapped over his shoulder as he freewheels carefully down the hill. As usual, folk filter in slowly, a second balafon arriving almost an hour later.

As I wait, I notice a Chinese guy wandering in the fields across the road.

"He's looking for ze gold here," says Otto. "Everyone's mining Mali's gold, except ze Malians zemselves. South Africa, Australia, Canada..."

"Really? Is there much gold here, then?"

"Much? Zer is loads and loads! Last year, zey mined almost 40 tonnes of ze stuff! 40 tonnes of gold! And you know how much money zat makes?"

"No, pray tell."

"Half a BILLION dollars! And ver is zis money going to? To other countries!"

Mali is Africa's third largest producer of gold, after Ghana (formerly known as 'The Gold Coast') and South Africa. But, sadly, it is being mined by foreign companies, and Mali remains the world's fifth poorest country. A spokesperson from Oxfam America said:

---

[66] https://aduna.com/blogs/learn/moringa-oleifera-the-moringa-tree

"Mali's gold exports have more than tripled in the last decade yet its citizens have so far seen little benefit from mining revenues."[67]

The balafon has 19 wooden keys of varying sizes from large to small. These are attached to the top of a rectangular wooden frame. Underneath each key, a gourd of corresponding size is hung in just the right position to act as a resonator. Without these, there would be almost no audible sound from the instrument. A small round hole is bored into each gourd, which is then covered with white spider's web material (or these days, pieces of black plastic bag). This creates a kazoo-like buzzing effect on each note as the tiny membrane resonates.

"I see you have *two* balafons – is this the norm?"

"Yes, they are always played in pairs," replies one of the musicians.

"Why is that?"

"It's what we do."

"And do both balafons play the same tune?"

"No. One plays the big, low notes, and the other plays higher pitches. We will show you."

And with that, they begin playing. Sure enough, one of them is playing a repeated bass ostinato, while the other plays a fast, undulating melody in octaves – also very repetitive but with some variety. The buzzing effect is very clear, especially in the lower pitches. When I first recorded balafons, I would listen back and think there was distortion on the track, but it was just the buzz of these notes which, to the African ear, is considered a beautiful sound.

Two other instruments join in: a large gourd drum, called the *gbogi*, and the ever-present talking drum. A tall, middle-aged guy wearing a weathered fedora and smoking a hand-rolled cigarette is our gbogi player. Once the music is up and running, he whips the cigarette out of his mouth, continuing to play the drum with it held between two fingers. He then takes a deep breath and launches into a strident, high-pitched vocal solo, with long held notes at the start of each phrase followed by faster,

---

[67] https://eurodad.org/4157/

descending melodies. Although somewhat resembling the *griot* style, this guy's singing is less ornamented or lyrical. Very powerful stuff, though.

I turn and look at Otto, who has just donned a peach-coloured Tamasheq turban.

"To keep ze sun and ze dust off. Very effective!" he announces proudly.

"It suits you, Otto. *Sehr schön!*"

"*Danke!* You know, I was wearing this turban in the Hôtel Mamelon last week and someone told me off!"

"Why?"

"Zay said: 'Take zat off! It's not good to wear that at ze moment!' But I disagree."

"Me too."

The song ends, and we all clap and cheer. Such a great sound! More people have arrived and are gathering round. I can't help but notice that colourful African fabrics – known as *pagnes* – are the order of the day, much more so than in the north. This is partly due to the Ivorian influence, as this kind of fabric is plentiful and commonplace in Côte d'Ivoire. And, like the ones on Badala market, they come in a wide range of garish colour combinations and somewhat incongruous motifs. Today's designs include paint brushes, chickens, keyholes, leaves, double-decker buses, butterflies and boiled eggs in eggcups. It doesn't seem to matter which way up the design is placed; it's more about the colours and the overall effect. So the eggcups today are sideways on, and the buses are upside-down.

"The balafon notes have different names too, *monsieur*," one of the musicians tells me. "The first and largest key is called *jenu*, which means 'mother', and the one next to it is called *jebo*, or 'father'."

I'm intrigued to discover that the father is smaller than the mother on balafons. And many of the other keys have names too: the third one along is called *konkon*, which means 'buzzy', as this one buzzes the loudest; key number four is *jejon*, which means 'respond', as this is the key which often responds melodically to key number two, the father. Key number 11 is associated with death and, for decades, prevented the instrument from being played in churches in the region.

At lunchtime, I try to call Lois to see how things are in Bamako. No signal. I even try climbing the hill: nothing. An elderly villager sees me waving my phone about and intervenes:

"Go further along the hill, *monsieur*. There you will see a stick in the ground. This is where you will have a signal."

I follow his instructions and find the stick protruding from a small crevasse in the rocky hillside. As I approach it – hey presto! I have two bars on my phone. I step a couple of feet away in any direction and there is nothing. Apparently, the signal travels through a narrow stream valley to reach this point, but surrounding hills prevent any other route. The stick itself has only one purpose: to mark the spot which someone – somehow – once discovered.

All is well at home, but the protests in Bamako city centre have not died down yet. Unable to leave the house, our children have been filming their own pop videos in the garden to pass the time.

On my way back down, the old man sees me again: "Did you get your signal?"

"I did, thank you!"

"How are the people at home?"

"All is well, thank you."

He asks me what I'm doing here and I explain.

"You see that hill up there?" he continues, pointing at a much larger hill on the far side of the lake. "Every time a child is born in this village, a stone is taken to the top of the hill by the village chief. This is so that the spirits who dwell there will protect our children."

"How so?"

"You see, there are bees on the hill, and one sting from them will kill you! If anyone harms one of our children, the gods on the mountain will know about it."

"How will they know?"

"Because of the stones, of course!"

"Okay," I respond, feigning comprehension.

"And when the gods of the mountain find out, they send the bees down to sting that person."

"That sounds serious."

"It is! Once, many years ago, an army was approaching the village from afar, and already the bees had descended the mountain in a huge swarm and were waiting at the entrance to the village. The army never came; they had heard about the bees."

As I return to the school, I sense panic. Folk are running out to the fields. What's happening?

"Quick!" says one villager. "Find a branch and follow me!"

I oblige, no idea where I'm going, or why I need a branch. It soon becomes clear: in a field just beyond the chief's house, a bush fire is rapidly approaching, consuming the short, yellow grass at a rate of a couple of feet per minute.

"Get close to the fire, toubab, and beat it hard but low down, so you don't make a draft." Others are doing the same across the whole width of the fire, a distance of almost 100 metres. As the grass is very short, it is quite easy to put out. Some folk with sandals on are even using their feet. Within 10 minutes, the panic is over. Had it been allowed to spread further, it could have wrought havoc in the village.

It's almost the end of the final day, and I think back over my trip. As usual, there has been some amazing music and plenty of wonderful people. But – also as usual – there have been numerous setbacks: the donkeys, the riots in Bamako, the bush fire, the lack of phone signal when I most needed it. Every trip is the same: some good, some bad, but they're all worth it.

We're done now, and I've just finished packing away my recording equipment. 17 songs recorded in one day!

"Come and see ze grey plantain eaters, Rob!"

"The what?"

Apparently, he's talking about birds.

"Come!"

I follow him down to the lake.

"Look! Zer zay are," he says, pointing out two large grey birds in a tree.

He steps further into the long grass by the water.

"Ouch! Ouch! *Scheiße!* Vat vas dat?!"

I spot a streak of green slithering quickly away from him and am struck with terror.

"Otto! We need to get help, fast. I think that was a green mamba!"

The green mamba is one of Africa's most venomous snakes. If he has been bitten, he could be dead in half an hour! Before I can say anything else, Otto is hobbling the 30 yards back to the school where he collapses on the floor just inside the building.

"Pierre noire! Pierre noire!" he shouts. "Tell them to bring a *pierre noire!"*

Folk are gathering as the word spreads: a deadly snake has bitten the older white man.

"Pierre noire, quick!" I say to the crowd, my heart pounding.

The black stone, used across Africa to treat snakebites, looks like a tiny piece of coal. It's so porous and dry that it will stick to the leg and, theoretically at least, suck out the venom.

"And, get someone to bring a car here, fast."

Otto knows Africa. He also knows that this bite could be fatal. Halfway up his calf are two tiny red dots less than an inch apart. It's amazing to think something as small as this could cost him his life.

"One more thing," he says, trying to relax his breathing to maximize his chance of survival. "Grab that floor fan and rip the electric cables out."

"What?!"

"Go on! Do it!" he says, pointing furiously towards the wall.

It takes some serious tugging to detach the wires.

"Now, put the plug in the wall and give me those cables! I'm serious!"

"But Otto, hasn't the electric shock theory been debunked?"

"Anything is worth a try – it has sometimes worked!"[68] With that, he takes the live cables and electrocutes his leg, just above the bite.[69] I look on aghast as he shrieks violently with each shock.

The theory is that the current causes muscle spasms which constrict blood vessels, slowing down the spread of the venom. But it has never been proven, or particularly recognized by medical professionals.

"Now, call the clinic in Sikasso. Take my phone for ze number."

Amid further voltage-induced shrieks, I race out of the building, scaling the steep hill at a rate of knots. I make it to the stick in under two minutes

---

[68] http://scribol.com/science/medicine/can-electric-shock-therapy-be-used-to-treat-snake-bites/
[69] Please don't try this at home!

and call the number, still gasping. No reply. I try again and get through, explaining the situation as quickly and clearly as I can.

"Come at once. We'll have the anti-venom ready." No ambulances here, of course. We have to go to *them*.

Back at the school, I fight my way through ever-growing crowds, which include a bunch of folk praying fervently outside the building. Otto's leg is starting to swell, but he now has a black stone stuck to his leg at the point of the bite. No more than a couple of inches in size, it beats me how the stone works, but many Africans swear by it.

A taxi – just about the only one in Ngolume – turns up, and several of our musicians help Otto onto the back seat, while I get in the front.

Down the dirt road, over the river, more dirt road, then onto the tarmac. Otto is feeling understandably rough. I look at my watch: 26 minutes since the bite. The taxi rushes to the entrance of the clinic, parking as close as possible to the doors. People in white coats are waiting just outside.

"Snakebite?"

"Yes!"

They have a stretcher ready too; I feel this may not be the first time they've done this. They whisk him off down the corridor and, precisely 29 minutes after the bite, he receives the anti-venom.

What an adventure that was! Otto lived, by the way, and his leg is fine now. The next day, one of the villagers rode his motorbike back to Sikasso for him. Upon being discharged, this crazy German even rode home on it. Since this event, though, I can't help but notice that Otto wears long trousers a tad more often than he used to.

Chapter Twenty – Fireworks!

"This isn't just a few crazy gunshots in the city – something bigger is happening."

WHAT A DIFFERENCE a day makes. It's a strange and disturbing experience to have your entire world turned upside-down within less than twenty-four hours. It's a huge and unexpected shock, with far-reaching effects upon every part of one's being, and upon the whole of society. If we're honest, we all saw it coming in recent months; we just didn't want to believe something like this would actually happen, preferring to naively hope things would settle back down to normal. Now, there *is* no normal. These are the events as they happened, beginning on that fateful day.

Wednesday, 21st March 2012

I'm in a meeting a few miles out of town when, at 1.20pm, I receive a text from Lois:

News of unrest in Kati. Could spread to Bamako.

This is nothing new, and Kati is a small town half an hour from here, home to one of Mali's main military bases. It is also on the same side of the city – and river – as the Presidential Palace (and me at the moment). A couple of minutes later, an almost identical text arrives from my boss, addressed to all members of our organization. I decide to cut my meeting short and head straight home. My drive back across the bridge is entirely uneventful. The traffic is definitely busier in this direction than into town, but I think nothing of it.

By 2.15pm, I'm home and working at my laptop when I hear news that my kids' school is closing a couple of hours early, just in case. As I have the car, Lois is taking a taxi home, and our kids are getting an earlier lift with Patricia, their Brazilian French teacher, who lives on our street.

At 3.07pm, this more substantial message arrives from work:

US embassy reports of gunfire in Kati. Recommend limit unnecessary movement in Bamako due to possible civil unrest. STAY HOME. Our offices will be closed tomorrow, as the embassies are expecting protests in the city all day.

Lois just got home, but our kids are still somewhere en route. I call Patricia: no response. It's only a short drive from the school, so we're beginning to worry, especially since Lois left *after* they did. A nail-biting half hour passes with no news. We've sent Abdoulaye home early, though he insisted on preparing dinner before leaving (not that I'm feeling remotely hungry right now).

"Try calling Patricia again," I say to Lois, as I pace nervously round the lounge. Still no reply. In desperation, I text other friends who teach at the school, but to no avail.

At 4pm, a further text from our boss reads:

Unrest in Bamako city centre. Go straight home.

This is followed by one from Doctor Dave, reporting *gunfire* across the river. What's going on? If we were worried before this, we're now chewed up with anguish; our three children are somewhere in Bamako, and there are bullets flying through the air!

I call Patricia's number, for roughly the twentieth time in as many minutes. Nothing. The thought of driving into town briefly crosses my mind, but I quickly dismiss the idea as much too risky; and it would be like searching for a needle in a haystack.

Two minutes later the doorbell rings: I rush to open it and find Patricia – but only Patricia – standing there.

"WHERE ARE OUR KIDS?!" I frantically blurt. "What has happened to Mads, Ruth and Micah?"

Patricia, laid back and Brazilian as ever, calmly replies: "They're in my car."

"Where have you been? Lois has been home for an hour!"

"Oh, I needed to do some shopping," she replies calmly, "so I took them to Azar's with me. They enjoyed it!"

Well, we certainly didn't.

"They'd like to go for an ice cream at the Star Station now – would that be okay?"

"No! Have you not heard the news?"

"What news?"

Blissfully oblivious of anything untoward, Patricia is shocked when I explain this afternoon's events. She apologises for worrying us and returns our children, who have no idea why we're giving them such big hugs after a normal day at school.

My phone rings: it's Welsh Gary, who lives at the far end of our neighbourhood.

"Rob, is everything okay over there?"

"Yes. All quiet here. How are things with you?"

"Well, you know when everything is alright, then suddenly everything is not alright?"

"Yes."

"Well, I was walkin' back over the Old Bridge from the *Grand Marché*, when a huge crowd started rushin' towards me from town. I had to run for it!"

"What happened in town?"

"I don't know, but I hyurd gunshots, and there was thick black smoke rising from the market area. I think they're burnin' tyres."

Why do they always burn tyres to protest in Africa? I suppose it creates an instant signal and wards people off, but the resultant smoke – and smell – are far from pleasant, not to mention the environmental effects.

"Right now it's chaos," he continues. "Everyone is headin' across this side to get away from whatever's going on in town."

Bamako's narrow *Old Bridge* is currently chock-a-block with droves of motorbikes, cars and worried-looking pedestrians, all hurrying like frightened sheep towards Badalabougou. Some are walking calmly; others are running in panic. School children in beige uniforms are dashing between vehicles, desperately trying to survive this incessant mêlée. And taxis headed for town are hurriedly doing three-point turns on the bridge, adding to the mayhem. Like hoards of refugees, they keep on coming, with no idea of where they are going; just where they don't want to be. Almost silently they move, like holocaust Jews; a tacit parade of fear and panic, held together only by a common hope of somehow surviving this mess.

"Are you home now Gary?"

"Almost. I'm at the corner of my street, by the German Embassy. There are lots of others standing around watching too. The main street is gridlocked, but there's been no gunfire this side of the river."

"Thanks for calling, Gary. Now get yourself home and safe mate."

As I hang up, another text comes in from work:

> *16:16 Gunfire in city centre. Go straight home.*
> *Non-confirmed rumour that they have taken control of ORTM.*

ORTM is Mali's national television and radio station.[70] Why would anyone want to take over these studios at a time like this? And who are 'they'? Almost instinctively, I turn our TV on and select the ORTM channel. The screen is blank. I try the one other Malian channel. Dead too.

Meanwhile, my kids are getting changed and ready for their usual post-school swim in the pool, pretty much unaware anything out of the ordinary is happening. Under Lois' watchful eye, they each jump into the cool, blue water with a huge SPLASH.

Just then, we hear a noise:

BANG!

What was that?

BANG…BANG…BANG!

It sounds like fireworks, but we both instantly know it is not.

"Inside now, children. It's almost time for dinner," says Lois, in the calm way she always does.

"Why are they letting off fireworks, mummy?" asks Micah.

"I don't know, darling. Inside now."

Just then, another text comes in from Doctor Dave:

> *17:23 Gunfire heard in Badalabougou, also at Presidential Palace.*

I sense panic welling up inside me, as the reality of what's going on around us begins to sink in. There are guns being fired on my own street!

---

[70] Office de Radiodiffusion-Télévision du Mali

Once the kids are dried and changed, we sit down to our dinner of beef with peanut sauce and rice, punctuated with further bangs from the 'fireworks' outside.

After dinner, Ruth asks:

"Daddy, can we play in the garden now?"

"NO!!" I reply, a little too vehemently. I check myself and continue as calmly as possible. "No, darling. Not tonight. It'll be bedtime soon anyway."

It's been a warm day, so we turn on the air conditioning in the children's rooms; as well as keeping them cool, the constant whirring of the unit will also help drown out any further bangs, especially as their windows will be shut. Sure enough, a few moments later, the gunfire restarts, some clearly right outside our front gate. And whereas it began with isolated rifle shots, this is now the fast, repeated fire of machine guns.

TAK-A-TAK-A-TAK-A-TAK-A-TAK!

What to do? What *can* we do but sit tight and pray hard? Leaving the house right now is out of the question. Mr Kouyaté has understandably not turned up for his night duty, which puts our security even more at risk. I decide to try and receive e-mails, in case there's any further advice there. It takes a while as we only have internet via a desperately slow USB dongle, which works intermittently. One message of interest comes in from Steve, a science teacher at the American School, who lives round the corner. He writes:

> *At around 5.30pm, I saw a white pickup full of soldiers at the end of my street. They were wearing camouflage and green berets. One of them stood up and fired half a dozen shots into the air in quick succession. Then they got out and seemed to be looking for something – or someone. A few minutes later, they all got back on board and sped off towards the river.*

Who are these people? What are they looking for and why? My only two consolations in this bit of news are that they have driven away from here, and that the gunshots were only fired into the air, not at people. The reality of what is happening outside our four walls has still not fully sunk in for either of us, and we're both numb with confusion.

We've left the television on for the past few hours, but it's still completely blank and silent. Then, at 11pm, we both jump out of our skins as a loud Malian pop video suddenly blasts out. A female artist is singing in the traditional *griot* style, surrounded by joyful dancers in matching costumes on the banks of the Niger – the very same river that thousands were crossing in terror earlier this evening. The song is interrupted by another black screen, but this time with a message in large letters across the middle:

Dans un instant une
Déclaration des
MILITAIRES

'In a moment, a declaration from the army'. I can't help but notice that 'militaires' is in capital letters, as though to give them greater status and gravity than perhaps they deserve. I suddenly feel a wave of cold terror sweep through my entire being as the reality of these words slowly sinks in: this isn't just a few crazy gunshots in the city – something bigger is happening. The army are about to make an announcement on national television.

We wait eagerly for the announcement, but nothing comes. Instead, more pop videos. The joy and exuberance of these skilful Mandé musicians could hardly be further removed from how we – and most of the country – are feeling right now. Between each song, the text about the army returns for a couple of minutes. After watching roughly eight of these in a row, we decide to turn in. It's almost midnight and the announcement has still not been made. Their definition of 'in a moment' is clearly a very African one. Right now, sleep is more important.

Thursday, 22nd March

It's still dark when I wake, exhausted and confused. It was a predictably restless night, in which I was woken at least a dozen times by continuing gunfire. I turn to my clock: 5.37am. Outside, all is quiet. I crawl out of bed and make my way, bleary-eyed, to the lounge, turning on the television. A group of twenty Malian soldiers is standing in a small studio, looking menacingly at the camera. Dressed in at least four different shades of military fatigues, some are wearing green berets, others baseball caps. On the screen, the following words appear:

LIEUTENANT AMADOU KONARE
SPOKESPERSON FOR THE NATIONAL COMMITTEE FOR THE
REINSTATEMENT OF DEMOCRACY AND THE RESTORATION
OF THE STATE[71]

I've never heard of this committee before and rightly assume it's only just been created. Lieutenant Konaré speaks into the small table-top microphone in front of him. Stood directly behind him is a tall soldier with stripes on his shoulders, looking intently at Konaré's sheet of A4, as though to check he's reading it correctly.

"Dear compatriots, considering the inability of our regime to manage the crisis in the north of Mali, given the failure of the government to provide adequate finances, armed forces or security to accomplish their mission of defending the integrity of the nation, [...] the republican force of the state and democracy, the CNRDRE, is taking control of the entire Malian armed forces, in order to put an end to the incompetent regime of Mr Amadou Toumani Touré." [72]

The Malian army has long complained of a lack of support in the fight against the Tuareg Rebels in this, their fourth uprising. So they've now taken drastic measures which, they believe, are for the good of the country. He rounds off his speech in almost Napoleonic fashion:

"Vive le Mali! Vive le CNRDR!"

Lois joins me midway through and I summarize the gist to her. The speech is followed by a clip of more Malian musicians, after which the same speech repeats. This loop – though not always with the same musicians – continues all morning. Meanwhile, text messages are coming

---

[71] Le Comité National Pour Le Redressement de la Democratie et la Restauration de l'Etat (or CNRDRE)

[72] http://malijet.com/actualite-politique-au-mali/40599-communiqué-du-comité-national-pour-le-redressement,-la-démocrati.html (My translation).

in at a ridiculous rate, mostly from expats across the city – some reporting further gunfire in their neighbourhoods, others saying all is calm. A text from our boss confirms that a military coup happened around 5am today and that a 24/7 curfew is now in place until further notice.

A coup d'état is bad news for any country's stability, and this is Mali's third. The first was in November 1968, when Moussa Traoré ousted President Modibo Keita. Then, in March 1991, ATT overthrew Traoré and became president. And now, ATT is being overthrown by…well…we don't actually know who yet, or even if the president has definitively been removed from power.

The news has quickly spread to the UK too, and over the next few hours messages flood in from friends back home, offering prayers, support, consolation and inspirational words to encourage us. There's even one from a friend in New Zealand, who's texting just before he goes to bed. I'm in the middle of reading these when the phone rings. It's American Ben:

"Rob, we're gonna leave. Leave Mali. Today."

"Ben, you can't. There's a 24-7 curfew."

"But we don't like it. There are men with guns and it's gonna get worse. We wanna take a taxi to the airport and get on any plane outta here."

"Don't do that, Ben. Too soon. This'll probably all blow over soon. Sit it out, mate…"

As I'm talking to him, Lois appears, waving the screen of her phone in front of my eyes. The message reads:

All Malian borders are closed, so is airport.

"Ben, the airport is shut."

"Then we'll get a taxi to Burkina and fly out from there." Insane idea, and a 12-hour journey at best.

"All the land borders are all shut too, Ben."

"WHAT?! So, you mean we're *imprisoned* in Mali?"

"Technically, yes. Have you got enough food at home?"

"Man, we got so much mac 'n' cheese, we could keep goin' for months."

Good news, though not the most nutritious of diets.

After the next pop video, a different army message appears on the screen. Although clearly filmed in the same room, the camera angle is closer, showing only the necks and chins of the standing soldiers. A sign on the screen, similar to the first one, reads:

PRESIDENT AMADOU HAYA SANOGO
PRESIDENT OF THE NATIONAL COMMITTEE FOR THE
REINSTATEMENT OF DEMOCRACY AND THE RESTORATION
OF THE STATE

Dressed in khaki fatigues, 'President' Sanogo has no hat on his shaven head and speaks quickly with a very hoarse voice, asking the Malian people to remain calm and condemning all acts of vandalism and pillaging. He says he's taking the necessary steps to ensure everyone is safe, and asks the armed forces not to disturb or worry the population.

We've not seen any pillaging over here, but a couple of sources say the military pickup on our street last night was actually raiding a Togolese bar for its beer.

Sanogo finishes off by confirming a curfew until further notice. There has nonetheless been further gunfire in our neighbourhood this morning, though much less than last night. There's still no mention of what's happened to ATT, though everyone's saying he's no longer at his palace, and most say he fled before the coup happened. But is he still alive? If so, where? Some rumours suggest he's at the American Embassy, but Doctor Dave doesn't think so.

Reports are coming in of the death toll which, given the amount of shooting, is incredibly low: roughly three people are said to have died, and forty injured. One message tells the tragic tale of an elderly African man sitting in his house, when a bullet fired into the air returned to earth at great speed, breaking through his flimsy tin roof and penetrating his skull in a split second. Needless to say, he died instantly.

Our offices are closed and will remain so until further notice, the same for the kids' school. Government services plan to reopen again in five days' time, though it's still unclear who the government will actually be.

Our children are enjoying their day off school, more or less oblivious to what is going on, apart from Mum and Dad being glued to the television whenever anything new comes on. They've dragged a mattress into the lounge and are taking mid-air photos of each other diving onto it, as Shiloh the dog pees excitedly everywhere. We've got enough food to last us several days and actually enjoy the novelty of cooking our own meals in Abdoulaye's absence.

Thankfully, I put 5000 francs of Orange credit onto my mobile phone yesterday morning, so manage to transfer some of this to our USB dongle, allowing me some internet access.

An article on *Radio France Internationale*'s website, posted at 14.08 today, says that the Tuareg rebels in the north plan to exploit the confusion borne out of the coup to make new territorial gains. It goes on to explain that Moussa Ag Achara-Toumane, spokesman for the MNLA,[73] says they are preparing to take control of further towns in northern Mali."[74]

In a report later today, another spokesman for MNLA denies they're exploiting the situation, stating that the Tuaregs had already made the decision to reclaim their land back in January this year.[75]

On TV, the ORTM channel is now showing scenes from the Presidential Palace on the hill. There's no commentary, just an eerie silence as the camera roves around outside the now derelict building. The first scene shows multiple bullet holes in the otherwise plush white palace walls, then pans over to an arched balcony upstairs. Behind this opening, the walls are jet black – clearly evidence of fire. Back downstairs, the camera zooms in on the palace floor, which is strewn with debris: mostly pieces of paper and card, but plenty of it. Outside, a grey Toyota four-by-four stands on what would have been a pleasant terraced garden at the front of the property. The car's boot and bonnet are wide open and, zooming in further, we are shown bullet holes – more than twenty – in the windscreen, side pillar and wing of the vehicle.

Next, we see the first bit of human activity, as khaki-clad soldiers leave the building, passing beneath further bullet holes in the ceiling. On the

---

[73] Mouvement National pour la Libération de l'Azawad (Tuareg rebel movement).
[74] From http://www.rfi.fr/afrique/5min/20120322-mali-mutins-bamako-toure-konare-kone-diarra-sanogo (My translation)
[75] https://www.youtube.com/watch?v=USMkzKlGY0U

ground in front of them lie a dozen or so dark-green cylinders, each a foot long: discarded shells from a tank (although there seems no evidence they've actually been used). More soldiers are then seen walking confidently around the grounds, while others stand proudly and resolutely, posing for the camera as if to say: 'Look what *we've* done!'

To round off this spooky collage of destruction, the camera zooms in on a man wearing a black turban and holding an armed machine gun: a clear message to viewers that the site is still protected. The clip, lasting no more than two minutes, continues to loop for the next few hours, to show everyone that the government has indeed fallen and that Captain Sanogo and his men now rule the roost.

Reports on the radio this evening say that soldiers have been looting the homes of government officials and have arrested several of these.[76] Other texts mention the looting of civilian homes, though across the other side of town. The gunfire seems to have stopped for the time being, which is consoling.

Before bed, I receive a text from my good friend Ed Phillips back in England:

> *Hi mate r u up 4 a Skype call tomorrow morning?*
> *Got e mail 2nite will pray 4 u all of course! Ed*

A chat with Ed would really cheer me up right now. But what he doesn't realize is how slow our internet is here, so Skype will be impossible without going to the office, which is closed. Sorry Ed: no Skyping tonight mate.

---

[76] https://bridgesfrombamako.com/2012/03/22/coup-update-thurs-march-22/

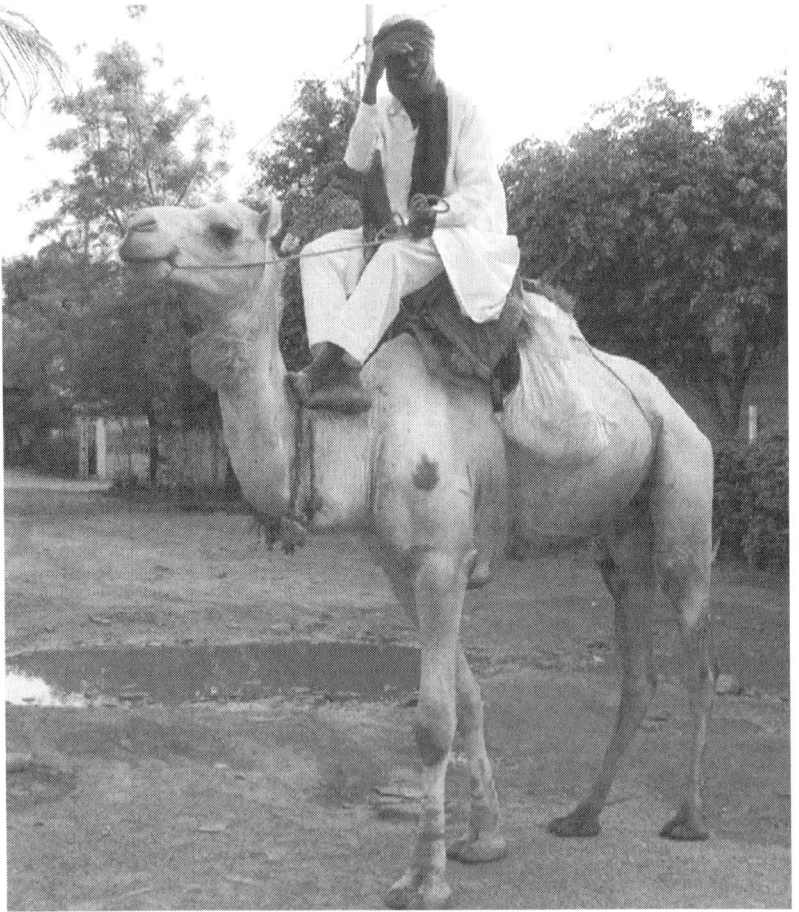

A Tamasheq on his camel

Chapter Twenty-One – Limbo

"For now, we're preparing for the worst and hoping for the best."

<u>Friday, 23ʳᵈ March</u>

MORE GUNFIRE LAST night – so much for Sanogo's curfew. It was less than the night before though, and seemed to fizzle out shortly after midnight. The electricity was out for a couple of hours too, which did little to improve my already poor quality of sleep. Exhausted from the past two days, we're all still in bed at 10am, when I'm woken by a text from our director:

> *Please text Dieter if everyone in your location is accounted for.*

Dieter, an Austrian colleague, is our charity's security manager. I quickly text him, saying: 'All Bakers are here and fine'. This will be a daily formality for the foreseeable future. As I reply, I notice another text in my inbox:

> *24/7 curfew now lifted. Still in place 6pm-6am.*
> *Advise caution when venturing out.*
> *DO NOT GO INTO TOWN*

I crawl out of bed and, in what has become routine these days, turn on the television. A large red banner across the bottom of the screen confirms that the daytime curfew has been lifted. I suppose you could call that progress. On the screen, Captain Sanogo is being interviewed:

"Where is the president?" the reporter asks.

"That, I will not tell you. But he is in a safe place."

"Is he okay?"

"He's fine. But I will not tell you where we are keeping him."[77]

The doorbell rings – it's Ray the pilot.

---

[77] https://www.youtube.com/watch?v=I4r-HUHtXtE (My translation)

"Hey Rob. My flights are all grounded at the moment, so I thought I'd pop by."

With him is a young, timid-looking woman.

"This is Carly. She just arrived to work in our admin office."

Carly, I find out, arrived on the last flight in before the coup; the following flight was turned around midway and sent back to Paris. And so Carly's first ever visit to Africa was heralded by gunfire and a coup, minutes after touchdown. To leave the comfortable, predictable West and be dropped into this mess must be a huge shock to the system. I shake the limp, quivering hand of this young, skinny American girl.

"Sorry about all this. How have you been?" She looks at me with a forlorn gaze, which says: *I wish I'd never come here.*

Another text arrives, this time from Patricia, the laid-back Brazilian:

Bored? Chocolate Factory on ORTM

Sure enough, the new Willy Wonka film is showing on Malian TV, in stark contrast to the recent scenes of smug soldiers and dereliction. What on earth the average Malian child will make of everlasting gob-stoppers, chocolate waterfalls and *Oompa Loompas*, I do not know, but our three are loving it, even though it's dubbed into French.

At around 4pm, I rise from my siesta and decide to explore the neighbourhood. I've not stepped out of the house for almost 48 hours. Our front yard looks untarnished by recent events – I was half expecting to find it littered with used bullets.

Out on the street there's an eerie silence. Where there would normally be children playing, tailors busily sewing costumes, African ladies chatting on the way to the market and motorbikes buzzing past at regular intervals, there is nothing. Just silence. All shops are still shut and, in spite of the curfew lift, virtually nobody has ventured out yet. It feels like there's been some dreadful apocalypse and I'm the only survivor. Turning the first corner, I see a middle-aged Malian man coming towards me on his bike. He sees me and slams his brakes on, skidding to a halt.

"Toubab! What are you doing out? Go home!" And with that, he rides off.

Turning a second corner towards the Niger River, there is nothing of any consequence, although some pretty deep tyre marks run almost the full length of this dirt road. Round the third corner I see the Togolese bar, rumoured to have been looted two nights ago. The boundary wall has been completely knocked over in one corner, as though ram-raided. Somewhat foolhardily, I decide to step over the wall into the bar's garden, calling out: "*Il y a quelqu'un?*"[78] as I do so, to check if there's anyone about. No reply. Inside, the place is chaos: overturned tables, smashed bottles, an open, empty fridge and a severely damaged cash register. No sign of any injury (or, heaven forbid, death) having occurred though.

Rounding the final corner, I'm grateful to see my front door again and run the last few metres, quickly unlocking the door. As I step in, my phone rings again:

"Hello boyo! I just went into town but didn't stay long."

"You did *what?*"

"It's still pretty chaotic. There are tanks on the streets and quite a few soldiers about – some on foot, some on the back of pickups. There are heaps of burning tyres everywhere and the shops are all shut. There weren't many people about; a few motorbikes but hardly any sotramas. Then I hyurd a big BANG, like an explosion going off and people were panicking. It didn't feel very safe, so I came 'ome fast."

That evening, the ORTM television channel cuts out again, shortly followed by a text from our director, which reads:

> *The president's forces* (Les Berets Rouges) *trying to take back ORTM.*
> *Military barrage at Lumumba Square. Finance offices set on fire by military.*
> *STAY AT HOME.*

Lumumba Square is on the main road from the Old Bridge, at the junction to the TV studios. This news fills us with a momentary – yet sadly unfounded – optimism, that maybe ATT's men will overpower Sanogo's and take back power.

Just then, the electricity cuts out altogether. Lois and I fetch all the buckets and receptacles we can find and fill them with water. Experience tells us that a water cut often follows a power cut. We also fill the bathtub

---

[78] Anyone there?

as high as we can. Thankfully, after a few minutes the electricity returns, and the doorbell rings. I call out over the wall:

"*C'est qui?*"

"*C'est Kouyaté, ton guardien!*"

I recognize the voice immediately and welcome Bourama in at once. It's been a traumatic couple of days for him and his family too, but they are all safe and well. It's already 6.20pm, so I ask him if he knew about the curfew.

"Yes, it's fine, I was on the bridge at 6pm and nobody stopped me." Brave, if a tad foolish. "Our food is running out, though," he continues. "We don't have *le frigo* like you white people, so there is not enough to eat. They say the shops will reopen soon."

I make a note to leave him some rice, meat and tinned tomatoes before going to bed. Kouyaté settles down into his egg-slicer chair for a night's work.

Now the power is back, we decide to watch something non coup-based with our children. Some friends recently sent us out a DVD of 'Blue Planet', a documentary about life in the North Pole and other cold places. Roughly halfway through watching a seal being eaten alive by a polar bear, a text comes in from Dieter, our security guy:

19:39 Got info that military is looting houses in Badalabougou West.

No text has ever filled me with such panic so quickly. This is exactly where we live! Rather than alarm the kids, I beckon Lois out of the lounge and show her the message. Our hearts pound with panic as we try to think coherently; they could be on our doorstep any second! Lois says we should get more information: is the looting right now, or is the info older? Who is the source? What does Dieter think we should do? I text these questions back to him. He replies immediately, saying an old lady in our neighbourhood was his source. He advises us to inform our guard, lock all doors and think about spending the night at our offices. I rush outside and tell Kouyaté to turn out all of the lights and lock the doors firmly.

"But if someone knocks, I will let them in, yes?"

"NO! Keep the lights out and do not open the door to ANYONE!" I reply, a little too forcefully. I'm in utter panic now, with a million thoughts and possibilities – many too unsavoury to mention – whizzing through my mind. Staying the night at the office is not feasible as it's too far to easily walk, especially with looting soldiers about. It would also be unsafe to drive there, as the chances of having our vehicle hijacked are very high at the moment. If they do come for us – and I'm hoping and praying they don't – then my plan is this: Lois and the kids will lock themselves in our en-suite bathroom, having already locked the bedroom door behind them. I will then let the soldiers in to take whatever they want. If they try our bedroom door, I'll fob them off that it's just a cupboard full of junk. Beyond that, I have no plan, except to hope and pray they don't come down our street. I text Brazilian Patricia, round the corner, who replies:

Thanks for telling us. Actually I'm a bit scared.

She's not the only one. A few minutes later, restless, I pop my head outside the house: all is quiet. I stealthily make my way over to Kouyaté and whisper: "Have you heard anything?"

"Nothing at all," he replies.

Back in the lounge, as a huge polar bear drifts away on an ice floe, a further text comes in from Dieter. I hardly dare open the message:

20:37 Hi, I just double checked. The looting happened in Jelibugu and Korofina! Sorry. Looting of rich people's houses.

Jelibugu and Korofina are over the other side of the bridge, roughly four miles away. Still bad news, but the likelihood of them coming to us is pretty slim. I pass my phone to Lois, as the credits roll for Blue Planet, and she and I both breathe a huge sigh of relief. We decide, nevertheless, to leave the outside lights off all night, just in case.

Sanogo is on telly again tonight:

"These acts of vandalism are not from my soldiers [...] You can buy army uniforms from any market. What proof do you have that it's not others dressed as soldiers, trying to tarnish the image of our cause?"[79]

---

[79] https://www.youtube.com/watch?v=kcHBWbQkIuo (My translation).

We hit the sack, exhausted yet relieved, wondering what horrors are taking place over the bridge at this very moment. We have friends living near Korofina, but their texts are not reporting anything untoward for now.

I doze off thinking about the night before the coup. That was only three nights ago, but it feels like a lifetime. I'd organized a beer-tasting session at my house, and what would have been a pleasurable yet mundane evening, I will now always remember as my 'last normal night' in Mali. Doctor Dave was there, Welsh Gary, Ray the pilot, Henk from Holland, and American Ben, as well as Otto Wagner, now recovered from his green mamba bite (and, I notice, wearing long trousers). And there was a newish chap from the American Embassy: Duncan, who I met at a recent yard sale.

Before the evening, we'd all scoured Bamako's half a dozen supermarkets and, between us, came up with nine different beers: French, Dutch, Lebanese, even a rare Russian specimen called 'Baltika'. These we combined with tasty kebabs from the *Petit Gril* up the road and Vietnamese nems wrapped in lettuce. Roughly half-way through the evening, Duncan received a text, made his excuses and left suddenly. I thought nothing of it at the time, but in the light of the past 48 hours I'm pretty sure he knew something we didn't.

Saturday, 24th March

That was an eerily quiet night: not a single gunshot. It's strange to think that, until two nights ago, this was the norm and I'd never even heard a machine gun. But following the recent turmoil, it feels like a luxury to have a night punctuated only by chirping insects. I wake around 9am and send Dieter the daily message saying: "The Bakers are all accounted for." He replies, saying: "So sorry for the misinfo last night." Well, we certainly burned off way more calories than we would have watching polar bears on TV.

At 9.50am, a text from Dr Dave says:

*Shopreate are opening this morning in order to serve their best customers!
We're going to head over in about 20 minutes. Give Jacob a call when you get
there and they'll let you in.*

When I reach our local supermarket, it's teeming with a couple of dozen
edgy expats; many out for the first time since the coup. I recognize most
of them, including a few friends and colleagues. Although some shopping
is going on, most aisles are partially blocked by folk standing and chatting,
sharing their experiences of the past 72 hours. Nothing quite replaces the
therapy of face-to-face interaction at times like this.

"Mr Baker – 'ow nice to see you again!"

"You too, mate!"

We give each other a warm hug, like old friends, and I ask Welsh Gary
how things have been for him and the family.

"Bloomin' awful, really. I'm bored out of my mind. My wife's been run
off 'er feet with crisis management, and I'm left at 'ome with nothing but
bad telly and knock-off DVDs for entertainment. Believe me, even
Merthyr Tydfil had more to offer than this!"

"I feel your pain, Gary."

"Lighting cockroaches has helped pass the time, though…"

"What?!"

"'Ave you never tried it, Rob?"

"I can't say I have."

"You put a spot of nail varnish on 'is back, see, then get the lighter and,
woof! Off he goes!"

"Isn't that a bit cruel?"

"It's only cockroaches, innit? And they don't half whizz off round the
room when they're alight. Then after a few seconds they just keel over.
It's more satisfying in the dark and with a few at once, though."

The cockroach, they say, can live for an entire week without its head
and survive a nuclear blast. Yet they're clearly powerless when faced with
Sally's nail varnish remover and a naked flame.

I fill two shopping baskets with powdered milk, chicken, onions, tinned
vegetables, cheese, and an extra-large sack of rice (just in case), and head to
the checkout.

"What's going to happen to Mali now?" I ask Jacob at the till.

"*Le bon Dieu seul le sait,*" he replies – the good Lord only knows.

Wandering back home down the still semi-desolate dirt road, I see that one or two African shacks are open today: the tailor with his foot-operated sewing machine, and the metal welders, blow torches at the ready. I also pick up a couple of recharge cards for our phones, both of which are running low on credit.

Back at home, a text comes in from our Brazilian friends, Patricia and Raul, inviting themselves round for lunch. Under normal circumstances, this would be unusual to say the least, but we're delighted to accept their 'invitation' and enjoy catching up.

There's an air of relative positivity amongst Bamako's expatriate population today; although things are still far from normal, the absence of gunfire and the reopening of some shops is certainly an improvement. Sanogo has told petrol stations to reopen too, saying that 'safety measures are now in place'. Many had not done so, for fear of being plundered. No fuel yet though, and Mali's borders are still firmly shut on every side.

Sunday, 25th March

On most Sundays, I'd be grateful for a day of rest, but today is just more sitting around, pondering recent events and wondering what will happen next. Everyone's going a bit stir-crazy with the lack of *anything* meaningful to do. The usual weekend activities are out of the question: eating at a restaurant, going to the pool or – heaven forbid – visiting the Luna Park. But meals together with other expat families are a real source of consolation. It's funny how a crisis brings people closer together and how, united in our common adversity, barriers are broken down.

Today, many members of the country's leading political parties met to establish a united front against the military junta, demanding they give them back their democracy. No change as yet though, as Sanogo continues to hold power, such as it is. There's still no sign of ATT, and nobody seems to know where he's hiding. And several government ministers imprisoned following the coup are said to have begun a hunger strike, demanding their release and a return to civilian rule.[80]

Monday, 26th March

Like sitting motionless in the eye of a storm, our lives hang in a bizarre limbo between the normality that was and the normality we hope will return. The military say everything *has* returned to normal today, but it's not the same normal we knew a week ago, and nobody knows what the new normal should look like. There have been more and more power and water cuts, some several hours long; another sign normality is still far off.

The situation in the Sahara remains volatile. In the wake of the Tuareg advance are the militia groups AQIM and Ansar Dine, both intent on implementing a strict Islamic regime in Mali. And they're all working their way southwards in our direction. Canadian Pete is still up in Gao with his long white Toyota. Although a seasoned Africanite, I imagine he'll be heading our way pretty soon.

At 9.02am, this text comes in from our director:

> *US embassy & twitter say demonstrations today (10am at the old bridge?) Stay at home.*

These anti-coup protests are unlikely to achieve much besides creating further unrest in the city. I turn on the TV. A large map of Mali fills the screen and the National Anthem is playing loudly. Its lyrics speak of Mali's banner of freedom and of its fight for unity. The first verse closes saying that fields are blooming with hope and that hearts are resonating with confidence. These words could scarcely be more ironic in the light of recent events; there's very little hope, unity or confidence right now, and nobody knows what the Mali of tomorrow will look like.

As soon as this finishes, Captain Sanogo comes on screen to address the nation, saying that: "The CNRDRE promises to reintegrate the entire population, as well as the international community," and that he has

---

[80] http://africasacountry.com/2012/03/malis-coup-second-thoughts-politics-is-bad/

"ordered all units to ensure peace and safety are restored in our country."[81] He goes on to speak of the unstable situation in the north and why he believes the coup *had* to happen, asking the international community to support him in his quest to restore peace and unity. It feels like an attempt to convince the world that he is, in fact, 'the good guy' and that his intentions were honourable.

This afternoon, Mali's borders reopen and international flights are recommencing. I can't imagine flights in this direction being very popular, though. Our kids' school is still closed and it's uncertain whether they will go back tomorrow, later this week, or ever.

Tuesday, 27th March

There's an air of cautious optimism on the streets of Bamako today. The fact the country still has no constitution or official president is, nevertheless, something of an obstacle. And my positive feelings are soon shattered by this text from our director:

> *Rumours that banks will all shut at 13:00 today, maybe long-term.*
> *Go to an ATM as soon as possible.*

It appears that ECOWAS,[82] who control the CFA franc, could cut off the supply of cash in an attempt to 'starve out' the military junta. Apparently the USA, the EU and France have already stopped their aid to Mali, as a sign of their disapproval.[83]

Our most reliable cashpoint is almost a mile away, but it wouldn't be wise to walk it in the current climate (political or meteorological). A taxi would be difficult to find, and those which are in service are charging at least double due to the scarcity of fuel. I opt for the Mitsubishi, but take the quieter dirt tracks through our neighbourhood instead of the main road, to stay under the radar as much as possible. As I bound along the bumpy lanes, a young girl steps out from nowhere, directly into my path. I

---

[81] https://www.youtube.com/watch?v=xmpkwqFeTvs (My translation from French)
[82] The Economic Community for West African States
[83] http://www.newsday.com/news/world/african-leaders-send-strong-signal-to-mali-coup-1.3625786

slam the brakes on and the car skids in the sand, stopping literally inches from her nose, my heart pounding in terror. The girl's mother rushes out.

"Oh merci, merci, monsieur!"

She's thanking me for not killing her daughter, shaking my hand repeatedly, as though I've just committed a heroic act. She takes her daughter back inside, and I just sit there, stunned, for several minutes, before driving slowly on.

It's pretty much business as usual in Badalabougou this Tuesday lunchtime: rusty, green sotramas chugging by, a smattering of two-wheelers, and a few yellow taxis near the shops. About half the roadside stalls are open again, selling the usual mangos, flip flops, sacks of rice, French bread and pirated DVDs. There doesn't even seem to be a higher presence of police – or military – in this part of town. Within five minutes I'm at the cashpoint next to the Amandine, a large Lebanese restaurant on the road to the old bridge (where, less than a week ago, there was utter chaos as Welsh Gary legged it home). It's all pretty quiet now, though I notice the German embassy has a visible presence of armed guards at its gates.

There are two cashpoints closer to home than this one: the first is in a small air-conditioned cubicle not far from my Chinese mechanic. This machine tends to keep your card for roughly eight minutes before spitting it out and saying: 'card not recognized'. I once had a card swallowed entirely by a machine like this; a risk I'm not prepared to take right now. The second cashpoint is reliable but located right next to a police checkpoint on the main road; the last thing I want today is to be charged for a traffic offence I didn't commit.

The Amandine is quieter than normal, but a few hardy expats are still sat on the terrace, tucking into their chwarmas and fries, several imbibing tall, cold beers, even at this hour. The cashpoint works like a dream, and I draw out the daily limit of 200,000 CFA (roughly £250), then do the same with Lois' card, giving us a total of around £500, which should keep us going a while.

My next job is to fill the car with diesel from the Star petrol station (the one which usually sells whippy ice creams, but has none today). Much of Mali's fuel comes via the Ivory Coast, whose president, Alassane Ouattara, has already spoken of 'giving a strong signal' to Mali's military junta.[84] So it makes sense to fill up now; at a push, this tankful could get us to the Burkina Faso border, if it comes to that.

On the way home, I stop off at our Vietnamese nem stall for a delicious takeaway lunch. The children are delighted to have this treat – the first since the coup, but hopefully not the last.

Sanogo appeared on Al Jazeera today. The interview took place in the captain's office, where a large framed photo of him now hangs on the wall, labelled:

LE CAPITAINE AMADOU SANOGO, CHEF DE L'ETAT

In the picture, he's smartly dressed in a dark uniform, the Malian flag draped patriotically behind him – like every other photo of an African president I've seen. Except that he's not *really* the president.

Sanogo states that he wants his junta to become more widely known and that he plans to elect a Prime Minister very soon. He also told Al Jazeera several times that the coup was the 'only way to save Mali'.[85]

We're all still praying this mess will just blow over, but with each further day of limbo, that's looking more and more like a whimsical pipedream, as our beloved Mali spirals slowly into chaos. For now, we're preparing for the worst and hoping for the best.

---

[84] http://www.newsday.com/news/world/african-leaders-send-strong-signal-to-mali-coup-1.3625786
[85] https://www.youtube.com/watch?v=VklmSFOkiCM&list=PLIKUYGTzSvUqSGPYLvZEvkhHluGa5lyfq

Chapter Twenty-Two – Exodus

"Friends, I have some important information to share with you."

<u>Wednesday, 28th March</u>

NEWS IS COMING in that Mali now has a new constitution, put in place by Sanogo and his cronies. Apparently, all of its 69 articles[86] were read out on Malian TV late last night; a tonic for insomniacs if nothing else. Amongst other things, it puts in place a 'transitional committee composed of 26 members of the security forces and 15 civilians', and rather craftily also states that 'those who serve on the committee will be given immunity from prosecution'.[87]

There's another huge protest going on in the city today, this time by those *in favour* of Sanogo and the coup, and against 'foreign interference' in Mali's affairs.[88] The ORTM news tonight[89] shows thousands of people protesting on Bamako's streets, waving home-made placards, one of which visibly reads:

BIENVENUE
C.N.R.D.R.E.
BYE BYE
A.T.T.

Though largely peaceful, there are reports of some casualties from youths throwing stones, and of cars being burnt.[90]

Talking of ATT, we've finally had news of him today: he's free and still in Mali. In an exclusive phone interview with French radio station RFI, he states: "I'm very well. The only thing I'm lacking is a bit of exercise."[91]

---

[86] Some sources say 70
[87] http://www.bbc.co.uk/news/world-africa-17557926
[88] http://www.bbc.co.uk/news/world-africa-17543387
[89] http://www.maliweb.net/video/ortm-journal-tv-du-28-mars-2012-68932.html
[90] http://content.time.com/time/world/article/0,8599,2110545,00.html
[91] http://www.rfi.fr/afrique/5min/20120328-amadou-toumani-toure-mali-coup-etat-entretien-exclusif-libre-cedeao (My translation)

It's also clear from the interview that he no longer sees himself as president.[92] One key question he's asked is how on earth he managed to escape from his palace on that fateful night.

"I spent the entire day under gunfire from practically 4pm onwards," he says. "All kinds of shots were aimed at my office, my home and my family." He goes on to say, somewhat vaguely, that: "as an ex-commando, there's always a way to get out of a tricky situation, and that's what I did."[93] What we don't realize at this point is that ATT is currently hiding out at the Senegalese embassy, less than half a mile from our doorstep…

Thursday, 29th March

Today the first messages began coming in from friends and colleagues fleeing this 'sinking ship' now the borders have reopened. American Ben and Cindy fly out tonight, leaving all their treasured belongings behind. Welsh Gary is itching to leave, but for now his wife has too many embassy duties to fulfil. Most diplomatic staff are hanging on in there, as are the missionaries/charities, as they might be needed for support or relief. Chinese Ray is still about and has begun flying again, but his quivering colleague Carly has decided Africa isn't her cup of tea and is off tonight too.

The only positive thing today was having a kora lesson, my first since the coup. I've been managing to practise my 21-stringed Mandé harp during the troubles, but my lessons – at Toumani's house – have been on hold. Boubakar phoned this morning, offering to travel over and give me a lesson at my house. I'm guessing he needs my £10 hourly fee to feed his family. He teaches me a new kora tune called *Alla L'a Ke* – tricky as ever, but a nice diversion from an otherwise barren existence.

"How is Toumani?" I ask Bouba.

"Toumani's in Europe on tour, in your country, I think."

---

[92] https://bridgesfrombamako.com/2012/03/28/the-devil-they-dont-know/

[93] http://www.rfi.fr/afrique/5min/20120328-amadou-toumani-toure-mali-coup-etat-entretien-exclusif-libre-cedeao

<u>Friday, 30th March</u>

We've all been summoned to a meeting at the office at 10 o'clock this morning. The reason has not been given, but we all fear the worst. Our boss calls the meeting to order:

"Friends, I have some important information to share with you, and it would really help me if you can all cooperate with what I say. Our international office has ordered that, for security reasons, we make a strategic withdrawal from Mali. With international sanctions tightening, we have no guarantee of fuel, finance or food being available in the coming days or weeks. The military junta show no sign of standing down, and jihadist groups from the desert are advancing further south each day. Given all of these uncertainties, it was felt this was the best decision for everyone. And so, by Sunday at the latest, we want all expatriate colleagues to have left Mali. Those with vehicles will drive to the Burkina Faso border in convoy. We have arranged accommodation for you at our headquarters in Ouagadougou, where you will live and work until such a time as it is both safe and feasible for you to return to Mali."

As he finishes, the entire room of around fifty is overcome by a palpable sense of despair, disarray and mourning. Perplexed faces, many in tears, folk comforting one another, others just sitting and staring, too nonplussed to even speak. Until now, we'd all hoped for some kind of resolution to the coup. That normality would return. That we'd get our lives back. Instead, we are to become refugees in a neighbouring country.

There then follows a tirade of questions, all of which our director does his best to answer.

"Are the roads safe in that direction?"

"What about our houses?"

"How long is this likely to last?"

"What about our Malian colleagues and employees? Who will keep *them* safe?"

"Can we stay at our own risk?"

The answer to this final question is clearly 'no', but I have a third option for the Bakers:

"We've already agreed to let our house go at the end of this month and were due to leave indefinitely in July. If we can clear out our belongings quickly enough, would we be able to fly straight out to the UK instead?"

Our director agrees to this option, granting us a maximum of *five* days in which to do so. Evacuating to Burkina would be tricky for us: if the situation doesn't clear up by July, we'd end up flying home and leaving a houseful of belongings in Bamako. And so, making a swift departure now is the most logical and economical thing to do.

Following an hour of chatting with (and consoling) colleagues, it's time for action: somehow, we need to change our plane tickets. I try to do this online, but the internet connection is virtually non-existent, at work or home. So I make the bold decision to travel into town. This means crossing the river for the first time since the coup – away from the airport and my family. I take a taxi with Monsieur Diarra but am in no mood for bean-eating jokes today; I just want to get the job done. The travel agent is located in a newer neighbourhood immediately the other side of our bridge, behind the 'Malibya' government buildings. The moment I step into their spacious air-conditioned office, one of the three agents looks up:

"Have you come to book a flight out?"

I'm guessing I'm not the first. It's all done within minutes: we fly out at 19:30 on Wednesday 4th April with Air Brussels. Bamako airport is closed again at the moment, so I'm buying the tickets in faith that it will reopen by then. I haven't thought of a plan B if not.

Saturday, 31st March

Today we're holding an impromptu yard sale to get rid of all our stuff. I e-mailed every contact I could think of last night, and folk will be arriving from 10am. We already sold half our furniture to some incoming missionaries a few weeks ago. Whether they'll now come or not remains to be seen.

By 9.55am our entire front veranda is filled with kitchenware, clothing, toys, fans, tennis rackets, curtains, picture frames, table lamps, towels, bed linen, DVDs, books (how did we accumulate so many books in three years?) and, of course, lots of clothes. I sadly have to sacrifice some of my favourite brightly coloured African shirts, all draped over railings in front of the house. Then there are the musical instruments: Micah's drum kit, a guitar, a violin, a djembe drum, a broken electric piano, even a didgeridoo. We're also hoping to give away Shiloh the dog, as well as our two cats, Delcie and Nyah. Much of the above we'd rather keep but have no choice but to sell.

There's a constant flow of expats and Malians all day, and our yard is looking much emptier by late afternoon. We're totally worn out now, and the next four days look like being just as frantic. This, combined with the heat, power cuts and daily farewells, is making our lives completely exhausting right now.

A local lady from our office has agreed to take Shiloh the dachshund. Nobody wants our cats; they may have to just fend for themselves in the neighbourhood, as they did before we took them in.

The airport has opened again today. More folk are flying out tonight, and most of our work colleagues are driving to Burkina tomorrow. Only a hardy few will stay beyond next week. This includes Doctor Dave, who pops round this morning for our leftover supplies of beer and wine.

On the news today, we hear that thousands of Muslims and Christians are meeting to pray for peace at the Modibo Keita Stadium. Key leaders of both faiths will also exhort the rebel groups in the north to put their weapons down and to engage in dialogue.[94] Meanwhile, the UK Foreign Office has issued this statement:

> *Given ongoing instability in the country*
> *you should leave if you have no pressing need to remain.*[95]

We're working on it.

The doorbell rings around 10pm tonight. I'm taken aback, but it's unlikely to be looters at this stage in the game. Opening the door, I'm surprised to see Monsieur Kouyaté bringing in a hot, sweaty and exhausted Canadian Pete.

---

[94] https://www.youtube.com/watch?v=XcBWeCF9fZg
[95] http://www.reuters.com/article/us-mali-britain-idUSBRE82U07M20120331

"Hi Pete! Are you okay?"

"Not really," he replies, far from his usual bubbly self. "I left Gao in the early hours of this morning." His face – usually ruddy and full of life – looks pale, anxious and weathered.

"What was it like up there?"

"Mayhem buddy," he replies, collapsing into our armchair as Lois brings him a glass of water and some banana bread. "I thought I could stick it out there until things calmed down. I know all the local folk in Gao, so felt completely safe. But last night some Songhai colleagues came to my door just before three saying: 'Monsieur Pete, you *must* leave! The rebels are coming!'"

"Ansar Dine?"

"No, the Tamasheq. The MNLA. They were on the edge of the city, about to attack."

"What did you do?"

"I packed a small bag, locked up my house and left immediately. I live right behind the bus station, so went straight there. They told me the last bus had just left, at 3am, and there were no more to follow."

"So, did you come in your Toyota?"

"No," he replies, between sips of water. "A white guy in a four-by-four would be an instant target, especially at night. A taxi driver friend offered to try and catch up with the bus; a crazy idea but my only chance of getting out. Nice cake!"

"Thanks. Lois made it."

"I jumped aboard and we raced southwards out of town, faster than I've ever travelled on those roads, skimming the potholes at almost 100 miles an hour. After a few minutes, we could see the red taillights of the bus ahead, and finally managed to overtake it and force it to stop. There were two other white people on board – Norwegians – but we were the last three *toubabs* to leave Gao. The bus driver agreed to take me on board and sat me at the very back with Knut and Ingrid. There were loads of checkpoints on the road south, manned by Tuaregs, or perhaps jihadists; I don't know. At each stop, the people on the bus threw blankets over the three of us as we crouched down beneath the back seat. The driver did all he could to stop the officers from entering the bus. One of them did come on board near Sevaré. He came two thirds of the way down the bus, then turned around."

"Wow, Pete. That was a seriously close shave!"

"I've had plenty of 'em in Africa, but that was definitely the closest."

He pauses for a couple of minutes, just staring at my blank walls. Then he looks up and continues:

"They're coming for us, Rob! The jihadists are heading south, and their goal is to take Bamako. If they get here, we're done for."

The MNLA attacked Gao minutes after Pete's departure and are now gaining control of the entire city. Behind them are the jihadist groups Ansar Dine and AQIM, all working their way slowly southwards in our direction, bringing with them Sharia Law.

Sunday, 1st April

Nobody's in the mood for practical jokes this April Fool's Day. It's Sunday, and we're resting as best we can, in between sorting out the remains of our belongings. There's been no electricity since last night, and it's 40 Celsius outside. The kids manage to strip their bedroom walls of posters as Lois and I do more packing and clearing. After an all-important cup of tea (boiled on the gas hob), a small silver lining pops into my head. I turn to Lois:

"We should eat the Easter eggs!"

"Yes, we should," she replies, without hesitation.

A month ago, my good friend Mike Webb came to visit for my birthday and brought chocolate eggs for all the family. You can't buy them anywhere in Mali and they've been sitting in our fridge ever since, ready for Easter. Today is only Palm Sunday, but as we plan to leave on Wednesday there's no point taking them back home with us. So we enjoy a premature but very welcome choc-fest, which brightens up our Sunday immensely.

A text from the UK tells me that the Tuareg Rebels have now taken Timbuktu, a few hours closer to us than Gao. We've been too busy and had too little electricity to hear much news today. Another source tells us that Captain Sanogo has pledged to 'return power to civilian hands'. We'll see.

<u>Monday, 2nd April</u>

Two days to go, and we're dismantling water beds and have booked into our charity's guesthouse for the next two nights; the very place we first stayed after our bumpy landing in Mali almost three years ago. Today we paid off our two employees, Mr Kouyaté and Abdoulaye, and said our tearful farewells. Our car – also sold to the incoming missionaries who may never arrive – will be left at the office, along with all the furniture they've paid for. This means lots of carrying and transporting in blistering heat, amid almost constant power cuts.

That evening we tuck into our last ever chicken kebabs from *Le Petit Gril* feeling like Death Row convicts. We've just finished eating when there's a *'ko ko ko'* at the door. Who can this be? The guesthouse guard opens the door to reveal a familiar, wrinkly turban-clad face.

"Bonsoir Traoré."

"Bonsoir. How did you know I was here?"

"Ah, the Tamasheq know everything. I even know that you're leaving soon."

I welcome Youssouf in, as Lois puts the children to bed, and offer him a seat. Suddenly, a thought occurs to me: "Youssouf, can I make you a cup of tea?"

"Your tea?"

"Yes!"

Rummaging amongst the heap of *Lipton's Yellow* teabags in the kitchen, I find one genuine bag of *PG Tips* and make him a strong cup with plenty of sugar.

"Milk?"

"Aggh, no! That is for the Fulani, not the Tamasheq!"

The mug of tea looks huge in his hands, compared to the tiny glasses he usually drinks from.

"We've been ordered to leave," I explain. "Because of the coup. Because of the violence in the north. These are *your* people carrying out the rebellion!"

"The Tamasheq are reclaiming what is rightfully ours. When Mali was colonized, we lost Azawad. This was *our* land – nobody else's – and they stole it from us." He tentatively takes his first sip of tea, then glares into his mug, frowning.

"Youssouf, is it true they are introducing Sharia Law in Gao and Timbuktu?"

"Yes, but in an extreme way. It is Ansar Dine, not the MNLA, doing this."

"But isn't Sharia a *bad* thing?"

"Sharia brings peace and harmony to society," he says, grimacing at his next mouthful of tea. "Are the streets safe in your country? Do you have secure family units with a married father and mother? No! You have locks on your doors and much adultery and divorce. Why is this? Because they have turned from the ways of Allah."

"But is there peace and harmony in Mali right now?"

He pauses, gazing pensively at the tiled floor for quite some time. "What about *your* religion, Traoré? Does it ensure peace?" He takes another hefty sip of tea and coughs, almost spluttering it all back into his mug.

"We call Isa the Prince of Peace," I explain, "and he said we should love our enemies and pray for those who persecute us."

"How can you love your enemies? This is not possible!"

"Yes, it is! He also told us to treat others how we would have them treat us, and to turn the other cheek; these are all ways of maintaining peace and order. My country has turned away from Isa; that's why it's in a mess."

He downs his last gulp of PG Tips, his brow furrowed with revulsion. "You are a good man, Traoré. Maybe Christians are not as corrupt or immoral as I imagined. I give thanks that we met. *Alhamdulillah*."

"We come from completely different worlds, my friend," I reply. "But it has been an enriching experience to know you. Would you like a second cup?"

He pauses, glancing woefully into the dregs of his first.

"Thank you, but one will be enough."

<u>Tuesday, 3rd April</u>

Tomorrow we leave Mali. We don't want to leave Mali, and we love Mali. But all is not well in Mali right now. The chaos in the north is worsening by the day, Sanogo continues to act as president, aid has been stopped from numerous countries (just when we need it most), there's no electricity to speak of, fuel is short and banks are threatening to close. The city centre is still a no-go area and many charities and missions are evacuating as we speak. We've been forced to sell and give away belongings we'd rather have kept and have made two Malians redundant. I had work planned for the next three months; it will all have to be shelved now. Mali is one of the world's poorest countries, yet also one of the richest in so many ways. It has now been deprived of the security, leadership and international support it needs to move forward.

This crisis has forced us into action out of sheer survival instinct, but our feelings are numb and our emotions roller-coastering. The looting threats, the violent demonstrations in town, the tearful farewells, the stench of burning tyres, the sleepless nights, the angry voices shouting and the waving of placards. The realization that soldiers have taken over our beloved Mali, have raped it of its longstanding democratic stability and tainted its worldwide reputation for generations to come.

And the guns! The guns! I still hear those ghastly guns! Their incessant rat-a-tat resounding metres from my window will haunt me indefinitely. And every firework display I attend – however pleasant – will instantly take me back to this horror for many years to come. Ten days ago, I'd never heard a machine gun in my life; now they are indelibly carved into my very being – oh, that I could erase the past ten days and just return to normal.

Ségou, Timbuktu and Dogon Country will now become ghost-town shadows of their former selves, as tourism is annihilated by violence, terror and fear. The Bandiagara Cliffs with their iconic Tellem houses, onion plantations and unique Dogon culture; Timbuktu's world-famous Sankoro Mosque, salt market, music festival and now somewhat ironic *Flame of Peace* monument; and the dreamy riverside streets of Sévaré with its 4444 balanzan trees, welcoming hotels and Tamasheq artisans. All of these wonders will now be off limits to the tourists for many years to come.

When we return to England, I don't even know what I'll do, or how on earth I'll readapt. We'll be greeted by the usual, predictably British small talk; well-meaning but utterly nauseating:

'You must be cold!', 'You're not as brown as I expected!' or, 'You must be pleased to be back…'

I won't be pleased to be back. I want to stay in Mali, but the *old* Mali. The good Mali. The peaceful, friendly, unthreatening Mali, where folk randomly make jokes about bean eating, and drink tea three cups in a row. My normal Malian life of two weeks ago.

And when we get home, we will not receive the 'hero's welcome' we are expecting, as well-meaning Brits opt to 'give them space – they've been through a lot'. We'll feel lonely and isolated for many of our first days back; like aliens in our own country, scarcely interacting with other humans outside our family, and regularly confused, exhausted and angry.

And there will be almost no opportunity for us to share our rich and exciting adventures from Africa. As usual, any meaningful questions on the subject will quickly dry up, as Western society forces us to fit in and conform to *its* norms, rather than celebrating the richness and diversity of our experiences. And the much-needed questions about the coup will be entirely taboo in British etiquette, as 'it might upset them, and we don't want that, do we?' Instead, I'll be singled out for the way I eat, the way I dress, my accent, my vocabulary and my outlook on life, all of which have been moulded and honed by a total of eight years in Africa. But most Brits won't understand this, opting instead to jauntily mock my non-conformity.

Transitioning back to one's home culture is never easy; reverse culture shock is an unexpected, unseen adversary. Very real indeed, but often undetected, unrecognized, ignored or denied. It will take me months – probably years – before I cease to mourn Africa and see England as 'home' again. I may never fully reach this point, remaining in a tolerable limbo where I am neither fully at home in Britain or Africa but can function in either. And this will be compounded by ongoing bad news from Mali – of political instability, hostage taking, music being banned, and Sharia police amputating limbs; even executing those infringing their draconian laws.

And months after returning, we will still have moments of tears and mourning, resentment and disillusionment. Some long-term friends I will no longer be able to connect with, having moved in such different directions over the past years. Others, unable to relate to us any more, will simply 'give up trying' and leave us be. Where is my life going now? What will I become? How will I ever reconcile these two vastly different worlds?

Our final evening in Mali is spent with our dear Brazilian friends, Patricia and Raul and their children, whose flights are booked for a couple days after us. A simple meal together, some laughter, some tears, and an emotional farewell, Latino-style.

Wednesday, 4th April

I'm woken on our final day by some kind of disturbance outside my window. The intense morning sun is streaming through gaps between my flimsy patterned curtains, just like it did on that first morning three years ago. Bleary-eyed, I squint at my bedside clock. 10.27am. That was a longer sleep than expected, but just what we needed after such an exhausting couple of weeks.

I dizzily drag myself out of bed and pull back the curtains: there are people protesting on the dirt road below: a couple of hundred of them – mostly young folk – all chanting "MALI! MALI! MALI!" as they march by, driving their angry fists resolutely into the air.

A thousand and one fearful thoughts fill my mind:

What if this is happening all over the city? Will we even be able to get to the airport this afternoon? Will they close it again?

It's reached that point where the end is so palpably in sight that the thought of anything hindering it is just too much to handle. The protest passes quickly, with no further news of violence in town.

We've booked two taxis to the airport: with five of us plus luggage, we'd never fit into just one. It's a typically hot and sunny afternoon as we drag our cases down the tiled stairway to the stony car park below, where two ancient Mercedes-Benz D190s are waiting for us: one with splayed rear wheels and no seatbelts, the other with a cracked windscreen and the words 'Air Mali' painted across the side. The drivers do all the lifting and carrying as usual, and the hot afternoon sun beats on my head and neck as the bags are being loaded. Normally, I'd step into the shade or put a hat on at this point. But today I don't mind a spot of intense heat, knowing I'll be experiencing a damp, drab British April within a matter of hours.

The two yellow taxis pull away in convoy, crossing the filthy open sewer and turning onto the street, where children play in the dirt, goats forage for scraps, tailors busily sew away, and women in bright costumes balance goods skilfully on their heads. Across the dusty football pitch and past the mosque and market, where Fulani weavers are busy at their looms.

We turn onto our street – our *old* street. I glance at the nine-foot walls of our garden as we drive past, the blooming bougainvillea flooding over the top in flamboyant pink and white glory. *It could do with a prune*, I think to myself, knowing this isn't going to happen for a while. There's nobody home, of course; no smiley welcome from Mr Kouyaté, eager to wash our car, or Abdoulaye back from the market on his trusty moped. Just the empty shell of a white, single storey building we called 'home' for three years.

Leaving the neighbourhood, our taxis filter onto the main dual carriageway out of town, climbing steeply from the Niger valley onto the parched plains above. At the city limits, we pass through a large decorative archway which mimics the adobe architecture of the troubled north, and which reads:

'Au Revoir, à bientôt'.[96]

I certainly hope so.

A new checkpoint, manned by soldiers brandishing AK47s, lies a hundred yards on. I gulp at the sight – will they let us through? I'm in the first car with Mads. We pull over in front of the makeshift oil-drum barrier, Lois and the others closely on our heels.

"Where are you going?" the austere soldier asks, glancing into the back of the taxi. My response is rather predictable, as the road only leads to one place.

"No, where are you *flying*?" he clarifies, with hard stare that could burn through lead.

"*Angleterre*. The car behind is the same," I add, hoping to spare Lois a similar inquisition.

"Passports!" he says, sternly.

---

[96] Goodbye, see you soon.

We hand them out and he scrutinizes each one for what seems like hours.

"Open the boot!" he commands, gesturing towards the rear of the vehicle with the end of his rifle. At the same time, his colleague is checking the second taxi. What they lack in customer service, they certainly make up for in thoroughness, opening every bag and rummaging indiscriminately through our belongings. Finally, we hear the words we've been waiting for:

"Drive on!"

Sitting in departures, I'm greeted by a familiar voice:

"'Ello boyo!"

"Gary! I didn't know you were flying out today!"

"Well, neither did we till yesterday, but they told us we 'ad to leave, see?"

"I thought I'd need to stay longer," adds his wife Sally, "but the embassy decided to evacuate all staff besides the ambassador himself."

"Are there any other Brits still in Mali?"

"Pretty much just the seven of us here. There's one guy way over in Kayes, and a couple down south near the Côte d'Ivoire border. As it's calm there, they plan to sit it out."

Just then, the tannoy bursts into life, distorted as ever:

"Ladies and gentlemen, would all passengers for Brussels please begin boarding now."

We join the queue and are soon aboard the Airbus 310, conveniently all in the same row about halfway down the cabin. As we sit waiting, Gary and Sally pass by.

"'Ave a good flight boyo."

"You too, Gary."

"I'm glad to be out of that bloomin' mess!"

"Ditto."

The plane taxis down to the runway, then roars into action. As the wheels leave the tarmac, I gaze out the window at Bamako city and the meandering Niger River, the Hills of Knowledge and Power rising on either side of this majestic waterway. Suddenly, and unexpectedly, tears begin to roll down my cheeks. Tears of sadness, regret, relief and gratitude all mingle as Bamako shrinks into the distance.

I thank God for these three incredible years and all they have taught me about Africa, life, faith, hope and relationships. This is not the way we had planned to leave the country, nor the timing. But even considering all the hardships: sickness, adverse climate, car trouble, harsh police, power cuts, and the traumas of the coup – even taking all of these into account, I wouldn't have missed my time in Mali for all the tea in the world.

Other books by Rob Baker:

Adventures in Music and Culture

(Ambassador International, 2012)

And

Fifty Things You Should Know About Music

(QED Publishing, 2016)

Printed in Great Britain
by Amazon

44178239R00163